'With startling originality, George Hagman's *Psychoanalysis of Aesthetic Experience: Self, Relationship and Culture* radically expands psychoanalytic aesthetic theory beyond the great early seminal contributions on art and idealization.'

Malcolm Owen Slavin, Ph.D., Co-Founder, Massachusetts Institute for Psychoanalysis; Author of *The Story of Original Loss: Grieving Existential Trauma in the Arts and the Art of Psychoanalysis* (Routledge)

'*Psychoanalysis of Aesthetic Experience: Self, Relationship and Culture* opens clinical insights into intersubjective and transitional realms, showing how sensitivities to aesthetic meanings and the relation of artists to their artwork can transform the ways we practice psychoanalysis.'

Maria D-S. Dobson, Ph.D., Professor of Classics at Colorado College; Private practice in psychoanalytic psychotherapy in Colorado Springs, Colorado; Author of *Metamorphoses of Psych in Psychoanalysis and Ancient Greek Thought* (Routledge, 2023)

'Now in its 2nd edition, George Hagman expands on his definition of art, extends further the application to psychoanalytic treatment, and explores new perspectives on literary and historical investigations. Those who love the arts, or work with artists in their practice, will find this book invaluable.'

Carol M. Press, EdD, Emeritus of the Department of Theatre and Dance, University of California, Santa Barbara

The Psychoanalysis of Aesthetic Experience

In *The Psychoanalysis of Aesthetic Experience: Self, Relationship and Culture*, George Hagman eloquently provides an overview of ideas regarding the aesthetic foundation of human experience and the way in which this aesthetic perspective can shed light on human development, culture, and analytic clinical process.

The book discusses the relationship between the psychology of art and the aesthetics of psychoanalytic treatment. Hagman presents a comprehensive psychoanalytic model of the psychology of aesthetics, creativity, beauty, ugliness, and the sublime, as well as a theory of aesthetics across the dimensions of subjectivity, self, intersubjectivity, and culture. Starting from the point of early childhood development, he argues for the importance of exploring the implications of this important psychological phenomenon for clinical practice, highlighting how aesthetics can shed light on a dimension of the psychotherapeutic process that has thus been neglected.

This book is an illuminating and informative read for all psychoanalysts, and anyone interested in the intersection of psychoanalytic practice, aesthetics, creativity, and culture.

George Hagman is a clinical social worker and psychoanalyst in private practice in Stamford, USA. He is on the faculty of the Training and Research in Intersubjective Self Psychology Foundation (TRISP) and the Westchester Center for the Study of Psychoanalysis and Psychotherapy. He is the author of *Art, Creativity, and Psychoanalysis: Perspectives from Analyst-Artists* (2016), *Creative Analysis: Art, Creativity and Clinical Process* (2014), and *The Artist's Mind: A Psychoanalytic Perspective on Creativity, Modern Art and Modern Artists* (2010).

Art, Creativity, and Psychoanalysis Book Series
Series Editor
George Hagman, LCSW

The *Art, Creativity, and Psychoanalysis* book series seeks to highlight original, cutting-edge studies of the relationship between psychoanalysis and the world of art and the psychology of artists, with subject matter including the psychobiography of artists, the creative process, the psychology of aesthetic experience, as well as the aesthetic, creative and artistic aspects of psychoanalysis and psychoanalytic psychotherapy. *Art, Creativity, and Psychoanalysis* promotes a vision of psychoanalysis as a creative art, the clinical effectiveness of which can be enhanced when we better understand and utilize artistic and creative processes at its core.

The series welcomes proposals from psychoanalytic therapists from all professional groups and theoretical models, as well as artists, art historians and art critics informed by a psychoanalytic perspective. For a full list of all titles in the series, please visit the Routledge website at: https://www.routledge.com/ACAPBS.

Poetry and Psychoanalysis
The Opening of the Field
David Shaddock

Affect in Artistic Creativity
Painting to Feel
Jussi Saarinen

Scansion in Psychoanalysis and Art
The Cut in Creation
Vanessa Sinclair

The Story of Original Loss
Existential Trauma in the Arts and Psychoanalysis
Malcolm Owen Slavin, Ph.D.

The Psychoanalysis of Aesthetic Experience
Self, Relationship and Culture
George Hagman

For information about the series: www.routledge.com

The Psychoanalysis of Aesthetic Experience

Self, Relationship and Culture

George Hagman

Routledge
Taylor & Francis Group

LONDON AND NEW YORK

Designed cover image: Scrambled Eggs (2015) by Karen Schwartz

First published 2026
by Routledge
4 Park Square, Milton Park, Abingdon, Oxon OX14 4RN

and by Routledge
605 Third Avenue, New York, NY 10158

Routledge is an imprint of the Taylor & Francis Group, an informa business

British Library Cataloguing-in-Publication Data
A catalogue record for this book is available from the British Library

ISBN: 978-1-032-87397-8 (hbk)
ISBN: 978-1-032-83622-5 (pbk)
ISBN: 978-1-003-53248-4 (ebk)

DOI: 10.4324/9781003532484

Typeset in Times New Roman
by Apex CoVantage, LLC

To Moira – still, beautiful

Contents

Foreword to the First Edition

by Carl Rotenberg

In Puccini's opera *La Boheme*, the background of which is Bohemian Paris in 1830 – an environment that highlights life's hardships – the two main characters upon meeting introduce themselves to each other and fuel their eventual love by describing who they are. Rudolph, the poet, declares that, though poor, he is nevertheless "rich in the rhymes and hymns of love." His *amour*, Mimi, ailing and equally poor, embroiders silks and satins with lilies and roses that speak to her of dreams and fancies and "all things called poetry." One of the truths of this great and passionate opera is that human life is made meaningful in large degree to the extent that it is coextensive and commingled with aesthetic experience. It is this unique intermingling of self-experience, self-structure, and aesthetic feeling that has led one social observer to call our species *Homo aestheticus*. In fact, aesthetic experience is so necessary to human nature that cultural and artistic expression has continued to be asserted, at times with risk to life, even in such places as concentration camps and the Soviet Gulag of Siberia. Indeed, even as the Nazis decimated its population, cultural life flourished in the Polish town of Vilna, the Jerusalem of the East. Thus, even in the face of trauma and death, aesthetic experience can persist like a spiritual oxygen for the survival of meaning.

George Hagman, in this landmark work, has undertaken to explore how cultural and aesthetic experience is "as important to human life as sex, hunger, aggression, love, and hate" (p. 1). George's approach is a psychoanalytic one in that he views all experience as having an aesthetic dimension, and his examination probes the depths of human psychology. Influenced as many of us have been by the British Object Relations analyst D. W. Winnicott, George deepens Winnicott's concepts with his detailed conceptual elaboration. He seeks the root of aesthetic experience in the earliest somatic, perceptual, and kinesthetic experiences of infant and mother, that intersubjective domain that he refers to as the maternal aesthetic. His psychoanalytic exploration conflates present experience with a developmental perspective that plumbs the multiple strata of mature self-experience to illuminate the hidden influence of early childhood development. This approach informs his overall perspective and each of the individual chapters.

As with many other creative endeavors, George's work has evolved in a context of collaboration and dialogue. I am proud to write this foreword because I hear the echoes of many discussions between George and myself in his book, as well as those we have had with coworkers. For several years, George and I have organized psychoanalytic workshops at the Annual International Self Psychology Conferences, where many of these ideas have germinated and matured. We have explored the significance of aesthetic experience to the self and tried to demonstrate its relevance for understanding and appreciating some of the great artwork of Western culture. For example, we have examined the lives and works of Pierre Bonnard, Paul Gauguin, Edgar Degas, and Pierre Auguste Renoir. With other collaborators, Carol Press, David Shaddock, and Anna Ornstein, we have explored the psychological interaction of self and talent, the dynamics of the dancing self, and the fate of creativity, art, and culture during the Holocaust. George's contribution to this project is in the way he takes the concrete experience of artwork, creative processes, and specific aspects of aesthetic experience and explores these issues on a higher psychological, philosophical, and conceptual plane. Soon we will be widening our investigation in a forthcoming issue of *Psychoanalytic Inquiry*, coedited by George and me, which brings together a host of contributors to further enrich and deepen our understanding of the depth psychology of aesthetic experience.

For now, in the following pages, I know that readers will find their understanding of the humanity of aesthetics illuminated and expanded, as they travel with George down the conceptual path that is *Aesthetic Experience: Beauty, Creativity and the Search for the Ideal.*

Carl Rotenberg, M.D.

Author's note: My friend and colleague Carl Rotenberg, M.D., died soon after the publication of the first edition of this book. Carl was a well-respected psychiatrist in Wilton, Connecticut, for many years. A psychoanalyst and lover of art, he published several wonderful papers often from the perspective of self psychology, inspired by the work of Heinz Kohut, and his insights into the mind of the artist and the psychology of art appreciation. Carl and I met frequently and engaged in extended and entertaining discussions, which led to additional writings and workshops that we conducted over the course of several years. I had the honor to coedit a special edition of *Psychoanalytic Inquiry* devoted to art, creativity and psychoanalysis in 2006. Carl's companionship and inspiration were important to the publication of this book and my subsequent writings. Our relationship was cut short all too soon. I have missed him.

George Hagman, August 2024

Preface

In my twenties, I was an artist. Primarily, I was a painter; but for years, my interests shifted widely between various types of art – cinema, literature, and music. I ended my artistic life as a poet. Success was elusive, and the joy of creativity was replaced by the recognition that the career of an artist was not what I wanted. I turned to another, earlier ambition: I became a social worker, psychotherapist, and later a psychoanalyst.

I have never lost my love of art and artists. For many years as a student and then as a practicing therapist, I was interested in the psychological exploration of creativity and the meaning of art. I found that D. W. Winnicott and Heinz Kohut captured the dynamics of the creative personality in a way that retained the mystery and uncontrollable nature of the artist's mind. I realized that there was more than interpretation of image and symbol in analytic art appreciation.

But for a time, another subject captured my attention: the problem of death and mourning. This resulted in several papers, the writing of which seemed to be an important part of my own self-healing. In the end, the burden of thinking so much about loss proved too much for me, so I was happy to turn to a more positive topic, one representing an old interest.

However, I did not decide to sit down and write a book about aesthetic experience. The ideas emerged slowly and in a different order from that found in this book. It was written as a series of papers over a five-year period. It began with "The Creative Process," which was an attempt to formulate a model of creativity using concepts from Heinz Kohut's self psychology, Susanne Langer's aesthetic philosophy, and Winnicott's concept of the use of the object. The most important idea in that paper was the notion of dialectic between internal subjectivity and externalized subjectivity, the goal being the increasing elaboration (idealization) of the created object. This process I hoped would explain both the tendency for refinement in art, the source of personal expression, and the creation of something new.

As a result of my work on that paper, I began to think about aesthetic experience in general, apart from the arts. This led me in two directions: (1) the notion of aesthetic experience as a relational phenomenon that emerges from the psychological elaboration of our experience of first relationships and the dynamics of aesthetic experience as a developmental line, and (2) the specific nature of the sense of beauty. These two subjects began to be connected in my mind with the vicissitudes of archaic idealization, and, specifically, the experience of the mother, whose beauty is the first compelling aesthetic organization.

The problem was that idealization plays a part in many human endeavors and areas of creativity and aesthetics, so a separate paper on idealization seemed indicated in order to try to understand that process not as a symptom of pathology, but as a fundamental means of engaging with the world and articulating ourselves. Along the way, I thought, "I have tried to explain beauty, what about its opposite – ugliness?" So I developed a concept of aesthetic trauma to capture the disruption of our aesthetic sensibility. This was followed by an attempt to formulate the unique form of the father's contribution – the paternal aesthetic – the sublime. Finally, I tried to pull the whole thing together with a chapter on what Gadamer calls *festival*, where I integrate the important work of Ellen Dissanayake and Heinz Holtzkamp's three levels of subjectivity into a model of multi-subjective dynamics of aesthetic experience across history and societies.

These are big, complex topics, and the investigation into them has led me well beyond my own areas of expertise – for example, to a discussion of the philosophies of Kant and Hegel. I have tried to limit my discussion of philosophy; however, the psychoanalytic approach cannot be fully appreciated without some discussion of the influential ideas generated by Western thinkers over the past few hundred years. I apologize to any experts who find my philosophy a bit thin and perhaps distorted.

Although I write alone, keeping my ideas to myself until the paper is well through the chaotic, uncertain business of writing and close to completion, nonetheless I must thank several people for helping me during the writing of this book.

First, I wish to thank the late Carl Rotenberg, M.D., whose intellectual companionship during the initial five years of this project was a source of continuous inspiration and support. Carl's writings on creativity and aesthetics compose an important part of the foundation of many of the ideas in this book. I have also valued the enthusiastic support and friendship of Carol Press, Ph.D., whose book *The Dancing Self* showed me how contemporary psychoanalytic thinking, when rigorously applied, can clarify broad areas of creativity and aesthetic experience. Carol's encouragement has been of great value to me and to the production of this book. More recently I have valued the interest and collaboration of Anna Ornstein, M.D. Encouragement also came from the members of the Connecticut Self Psychology Study Group: Nancy Boksenbaum, Nancy Bronson, Allison Brownlow, Lois Fox, Alexis Johnson, Grete Lane, Larry Ludwig, Carl Rotenberg, and Susanne Weil. Over the years, important help was obtained from Alan Roland, Ph.D., Peter Zimmerman, Ph.D., and Ted McCrorie Ph.D., as well as Dr. Steven Axelrod's simple encouragement that I should write about "what I want" was invaluable in clarifying what should have been obvious to me all along. I especially want to thank Ellen Dissanayake, whose work I stumbled upon during my writing. Ellen's brilliant synthesis of cultural, anthropological, and developmental research on art has been enlightening and inspirational. Finally, I wish to thank my family, Peter and Elena (who never could understand why I was writing about ugliness), and my wife,

Moira (whose love has been the foundation that has supported my professional life and intellectual interests for twenty years). I hope this volume provides some assurance to her that I wasn't just throwing away money on all those books that have appeared in Amazon.com boxes on the doorstep of our home over the years.

As I said, several of the chapters were previously published, and I wish to thank the editors of *The International Journal of Psychoanalysis*, *The Psychoanalytic Quarterly*, and *Progress in Self Psychology* for permission to reprint the papers here. These journals and their editorial readers made very practical and important contributions to the project, and I appreciate their support and criticisms.

A version of chapter five was previously published in 2000 in *How Responsive Should We Be? Progress in Self Psychology*, Volume 16, A. Goldberg (Ed.), Hillsdale, NJ, The Analytic Press, 277–297. A version of chapter six was previously published in 2002 in *The International Journal of Psychoanalysis*, Volume 83, 661–674. And a version of chapter seven was previously published in 2003 in *The Psychoanalytic Quarterly*, Volume 72, Number 4, 959–985.

Addendum

The first edition of this book, *Aesthetic Experience: Beauty, Creativity, and the Search for the Ideal*, was published in 2006 by Rodopi Press. Since that time, I have published three additional volumes, which have extended the ideas from that first book to various aspects of art, the psychology of artists, and clinical practice for Routledge Press (Hagman, 2010, 2015). In addition, I have written several other articles, which have not been included in book form. More recently, I have wanted to publish a second edition of *Aesthetic Experience* for Routledge to complete the four-book series which I originally intended to write but ended up with different publishers. Complicating the matter was the sale of Rodopi to Brill Publications, which led me to fear that the book would be lost in the transition. This did not come to pass, and I am grateful to the editors at Brill for making it possible to obtain the rights to the original book, which allowed me to approach Routledge regarding a new edition. In this light, I feel additional gratitude to Routledge (most important Kate Hawes and Zoe Meyer) for the opportunity to publish this second edition of *Aesthetic Experience*. Although I continue to find much of the original book sound and agreeable to me, I have also been able to add some important material, for example the importance of aesthetic gesture and the problem of the therapeutic function of art. I have also been able to include several papers as additional chapters. One of these, "Art and Self," now chapter nine, presents a definition of art that I had not yet developed during the writing of *Aesthetic Experience*, but that subsequently became a central part of my model and the cornerstone of the later publications. Another paper, *Creative Analysis*, now chapter ten, concerns the application of my ideas to psychoanalytic treatment. These additional chapters explore the application of my ideas in several areas: the psychology of musicians (chapter twelve), the function of beauty in erotic obsession (chapter thirteen), and the abuse of beauty in Hitler's fascist aesthetics (chapter fourteen). Some readers may find these an odd choice of subjects. All I can say is that they were each written under unique circumstances with no plan to include them in any book. It is just that, with the opportunity for the new edition' I have seen their value in demonstrating the application of my ideas to diverse areas. Despite my concern that I have complicated the original simplicity of the original edition with the addition of these chapters, I hope that the reader finds this expanded volume a more informative and perhaps entertaining book because of their inclusion. Given the expanded range and focus of this edition, we have also retitled the book to reflect these changes.

In closing this preface, I want to thank the various reviewers of my book and the many colleagues to whom I have presented my ideas at conferences and workshops, who have shared their attention, questions, and comments. Lastly, I want to thank John Riker and Marcia Dobson, my coeditors-in-chief at the journal *Psychoanalysis, Self and Context*, for reading parts of this book and offering valuable advice.

Several of these added chapters have been previously published. They are:

Hagman, G. (2009). "Art and Self. Self and Systems: Explorations in Contemporary Self Psychology," *Annals of the New York Academy of Sciences,* edited by Vanderhide, N., & Coburn, W., Volume 1159, New York.

Hagman, G. (2005). "The Musician and the Creative Process," *Journal of the American Academy of Psychoanalysis*, 33, 97–118.

Hagman, G. (2005). Hitler's Aesthetics: A Psychoanalytic Perspective on Art and Fascism. *Psychoanalytic Review*, 92, 963–981.

Chapter 1

Introduction

Aesthetic experience is as important to human life as sex, hunger, aggression, love, and hate. Although we may rarely be conscious of it, aesthetic experience gives form, meaning, and, most importantly, value to everything we are and everything we do. Theoretically, without it, life would be a shapeless, meaningless, and colorless series of sensations, events, and reactions.

Although aesthetic experience achieves its most refined form in art, all that we sense, imagine, and dream is shaped by it, for better or for worse. When I say *shaped,* I mean that aesthetic experience is not a quality of objects or sensations; it is an emergent phenomenon that arises in the transitional psychological zone in which our creative engagement with the world is lived. We see its most archaic manifestation in the curve of the mother's shoulder during nursing, her heartbeat and breath, the melody of her voice, the balance of her eyes and smile – all embedded in the warmth, nourishment, and security of the mother/infant interaction. In its mature forms, we find aesthetic experience in the works of, among many others, Michelangelo, Titian, Degas, and Picasso. Although the nursing situation and the viewing of Picasso's *Guernica* are radically different experiences, I will argue in this book that the fundamental nature of the aesthetic experience is the same, having a common source – the human drive to give form and value to the experiences of self and self-in-relation.

I will offer a definition of aesthetic experience in the next chapter, but let me say here that I am extending its meaning beyond the limits of its traditional one. During the eighteenth century, a new approach to aesthetics emerged that emphasized individual experience and a specific type of emotional response to aesthetic objects. Most importantly, Western thinkers were concerned with the internal source of the sense of beauty. Later areas of aesthetic experience, such as the sublime, ugliness, and the picturesque, were also studied, but aesthetic experience continued to be approached as a delimited psychological process, mostly involving responses to artwork or special natural phenomena. Although in this book I highlight these types of special aesthetic responses, the heart of my argument lies in the belief that every aspect of our experience has an aesthetic dimension (or perhaps dimensions), and that this dimension is optimally elaborated and refined throughout life. Examples of this are endless: from the way we dress, the cars we drive, the gardens we tend,

DOI: 10.4324/9781003532484-1

the hair we comb, the sunsets we admire, the tone of voice we appreciate, the gestures that entrance us. We each have our aesthetic that is directly linked to our sense of well-being. As we will see, the source of this aesthetic dimension is the internalization of the experience of the formal elements of human relationships, to be investigated in depth in chapter three.

The psychology of aesthetic experience has always been of interest to psycho-analysts. Early on, Freud viewed creativity and art as defensively motivated, sub-limatory channels for forbidden sexuality (Freud, 1908, 1910, 1925a, 1925b). His was an interpretive approach in which the symbolic forms of artistic expression revealed hidden wishes. This classical view of creativity as a type of dreamwork has been the center of psychoanalytic aesthetics for generations. Later analysts, such as Ernst Kris (1952), viewed art more progressively, with the ego harnessing the resources of the unconscious for the purpose of self-expression. This approach retained Freud's emphasis on symbolism, but now we see regression as existing at the service of the ego rather than the other way around.

Eventually, psychoanalysts such as Gilbert Rose (1992) and Jerome Oremland (1997) would elevate creativity to the status of a complex developmental accomplishment – almost a meta-ego function resulting in a higher level of human experience. Consistent with the classical psychoanalytic perspective on the mind as a self-regulating system, most of the more recent analysts have approached the psychology of art and the artist from a primarily intrapsychic viewpoint, only tangentially related to other people (for example, the potential audience). This has been echoed by our culture's myth of the artist as a solitary rebel who defies convention and critical judgment. However, some recent thinkers have argued that the artist is a far more social being than has generally been realized (Dissanayake, 2000; Press, 2002; Rotenberg, 1988).

I believe that the major limitation of the traditional psychoanalytic approach has been its focus on a closed-system model of the artist's mind. This has become increasingly obvious, given the recent revolution in psychoanalytic thinking, which views human psychology as more relational and intersubjective than previously thought (Beebe and Lachmann, 2002; Mitchell, 1988).

This book emphasizes the central role of relatedness and intersubjectivity in the aesthetic experience and the creative process. From this perspective, I develop a model of aesthetic experience that involves the gradual emergence of a sense of idealized form out of the matrix of the mother/infant interaction. I then apply this model to several problems that I consider important to our understanding of aesthetic experience. In this introductory chapter, I will highlight seven of the most important points of this developmental/relational perspective, in the sequence that they will be discussed in the remainder of the book.

The Developmental Matrix of Aesthetic Experience

In the next two chapters, I will introduce the problem of aesthetic experience through a close examination of its developmental and relational sources. Since Freud saw art as a compromise formation between conflicting parts of the mental apparatus, the relational and developmental sources of art were not relevant to him. For Freud, art was just one of many manifestations of the defense mechanism of sublimation, and. while taking on the trappings of culture, it was at heart an intrapsychic phenomenon (Freud, 1908). Later, Ernst Kris viewed art as resulting from regression in the service of the ego, whereby earlier forms of mentation and instinctual life would be temporarily allowed access to consciousness in order to permit aesthetic expression for the purpose of mastery (Kris, 1952). However, once again, the source of art lay in the functions of the ego – which made use of early mental life – but these infantile experiences in no way constituted aesthetic experience itself. Ultimately, the notion of elaboration of the products of regression during the later phase of the creative process placed the heart of successful creativity in the mature capacities of the artist (Rose, 1980; Rotenberg, 1988).

The core of aesthetic experience contains an intensely interactive component in which the mutual engagement of artist with both artwork and audience results in the emergence of an archaic state of self-experience, associated with the early bond with the mother. Mature creativity involves the activation of archaic affective states and cross-modal perception. This is the adult elaboration of the emergent organization of the infant's subjective world as a template for aesthetic experience.

Early regressive ego states and experiences play a part in creativity, but, additionally, the progressive organizational capacities of the infant – not just regression – underlie aesthetic processes in later life. These organizational capacities emerge and are elaborated within an interpersonal context. Mature forms of aesthetic experience and creativity involve a type of "rematriation" (Rose, 1992, p. 64), but, in addition, they involve the self-experience-in-relation-to-other that infant research has highlighted.

Art is linked to the re-creation of early experiences of relationships with important caregivers and is related to the expression and embodiment of psychological processes of idealization. Thus, the psychological function of art and creativity is powerfully linked to the intensely relational core of infantile experience. Considering recent insights gained in infant research and in the intersubjective nature of human psychological experience, some authors have begun to consider how the fundamental drive for and experience of mutuality and intimacy play a part in aesthetic experience and the creative process.

Recent developments in infant research have elucidated the complex interpersonal relatedness of the human infant and the affective interplay that characterizes the parent–infant dyad. The internalization of these rhythms and modes becomes the bedrock of the aesthetic forms, values, and experiences that eventually develop among members of a given culture. In fact, one can find the intimate aesthetics of mother and child in the rituals and art forms of larger cultures, which seek to increase connection and mutuality among members through the evocation of developmentally early experiences of attunement.

Idealization

In chapter four, I focus more closely on the place of idealization in human psychological life and aesthetic experience. Though traditionally viewed as a defense, a displacement, or a protection from one's own or the other's aggressive wishes, idealization is fundamental to our valuation of self, our relationships, and our experience of the world. Its source lies in the early affective connection between infant and caregiver, during which the communication of mutual idealization arises and is elaborated – this, I argue, is a crucial though unacknowledged motive for attachment. Ultimately, it is the extension of idealization beyond the dyad that gives life value, forming the basis of mature levels of self-esteem, love, and moral judgment.

Chapter four also explores the role of value affects in idealization and suggests how idealization is elaborated into adult relationships and self-experience. Finally, I argue that idealization is the link between the ideal nature of the parent–child bond and mature forms of aesthetic experience. Specifically, it is the idealization of the formal organization of interaction that grants high value to the gestures, shapes, sounds, colors, and rhythms that characterize the interaction of parent and child.

The Creative Process

Chapter five concerns the psychological processes in creative work. The normal boundaries between self and other are fluid as the artist engages reality. He or she is not introspectively ruminating in his or her own private world; to the contrary, the artist's self-experience is powerfully linked to the world of objects and others who are also, paradoxically, creations of the artist. In fact, I would argue that creativity is fundamentally intersubjective in this sense. Once an action is taken to alter the object in some way, it can be said that subjectivity is externalized, and the artist enters a relationship with an object that is now invested with qualities of the artist's own subjective experience. This is a non-solipsistic model of aesthetics in which the qualities of the external object are essential (as in the maternal–infant dialogue). In fact, the action taken upon the object *must* include the qualities of the object (its color, plasticity, and so on), as well as the changing relationship between internal and external aspects of subjectivity.

However, once an action is taken and an aspect of subjectivity is expressed in the work, this externalized subjectivity becomes, to a greater or lesser degree, disjunctive with self-experience (either because of the object or the form of self-expression or because of the rapid unfolding of the artist's self-experience). The artist then acts upon the subjective objects as both internal and external to self-experience. There is a unique dialectic established between internal and external aspects of subjectivity (impacted also by the nature of the medium and dynamics of the art world). Because of this dialectic, further actions are taken, and the artwork develops toward perfection. The artist engages with an "other," which was in fact once part of the self but is now external, possessing through concretization in media or language a separate subjectivity. That which has been made external, in other words, has been "expressed"; it is the objectification of the artist's self-experience.

Self-expression in aesthetic experience is not limited to emotion, affect, or even ideas or impressions (although it may contain all of these). The form of self-expression contained in artistic creation is best captured in the idea of *being*, of conveying in the work aspects of how it feels to *be* the living person who one is.

However, art is not simply a mirror, a representation of us; it is a new creation that evokes self-experience and embodies the self-in-relation through aesthetic perfection. This allows us to include within the rubric of art the ornate majesty of Chartres Cathedral alongside the cool simplicity of a Rothko painting. As different as these two may be, both can be said to contain within them some perfect expression of human experience.

The unfolding dialectic between artist and artwork is accompanied by the fluctuation of states of emotional tension and self-experience. The sense of resonance between the external and internal aspects of subjectivity is self-confirming and pleasurable. Dissonance leads to varying levels of self-crisis. *Aesthetic resonance* is the degree to which internal aspects of subjectivity, and its external aspects – both concretized in the artwork – are conjunctive, one to the other. In other words, aesthetic resonance is the way in which the relationships between the colors and forms of a painting express the organization of the artist's internal world.

Fundamental to this idea is that the artwork and the artist's subjectivity form a single intersubjective field, in which *inner* and *outer* are irrelevant. As a result of the experience of aesthetic resonance, the artist feels vitalized, more cohesive, directed, and alive. If he or she is successful in developing the work toward greater perfection, this inner state can be quite powerful, and the artist's self-experience is idealized. However, this resonance can also be fragile and easily lost – thus fueling the desire to create.

Self psychologists use the term *selfobject experience* to capture this psychological state. It is a psychological experience in which the individual enters a relationship with an object that is felt to have ideal qualities (an idealized selfobject) and/or when one experiences the object as reflecting ideal qualities of oneself (the grandiose self). In most cases, successful creativity involves both an idealized and a grandiose selfobject experience. The artist feels the self to be in the presence of an ideal object that reflects an experience of the ideal self.

However, selfobject experience tends to be precarious or fragile. The individual inevitably experiences a sense of failure, in which the object, for whatever reason, is no longer experienced as ideal or reflective of one's grandiose self. Such a disjunction occurs, for example, when an artist begins work in the morning and finds that the piece under creation is only a confusing jumble, when the night before he or she had left a "masterpiece." In such a case, externalized aspects of subjectivity are no longer in conjunction with self-experience, and they are experienced as something *other* – at times, as something far removed from what is imagined or desired.

This situation leads to a state of self-crisis that can result in a permanent rupture of the relation to the artwork – or, optimally, to further efforts to restore the tie through work. It is important to remember that it is not solely the qualities of the object that determine resonance and dissonance, but rather the relation between the internal subjective world and its externalization in the object. From the point of view of a third party, the object may be beautiful, but the artist may nonetheless experience a sense of disappointment or even failure.

Successful art involves the artist's creation of an opportunity for selfobject experience. He or she does this by externalizing some aspect of subjectivity by means of an action upon of the external world. The artist then enters a dialectical relationship with these externalized aspects of his or her own subjectivity. The intent of this dialectic is to take further action to alter the artwork toward the goal of greater expressive perfection. On the other hand, the artist is affected by the artwork, by his or her inner working model of the work and the emotional state in response to the object being created. Optimally, the artwork not only resonates with inner experience, but also externalizes subjectivity in an increasingly ideal form. The relationship with the ideal artwork that reflects the perfection of the artist lies at the heart of the successful creative process.

The Sense of Beauty

Chapter six focuses on beauty. The developmental source of the sense of beauty is the longed-for experience of perfection found in the early mother/infant bond. Beauty is an invariant formal aspect of anything that is experienced as ideal. We all value and seek beauty as an opportunity for selfobject experience. When we are in the presence of something beautiful, we are enlivened; we feel whole and happy. Beauty is a special element in the aesthetic experience in which the investment of reality with subjectivity creates an experience of that reality as both ideal and harmonious with our inner life (see also Hagman, 2001; Lee, 1947, 1948, 1950).

This chapter discusses the nature and function of the sense of beauty in psychological life. Noting the reemergence of interest in beauty by philosophers and art critics, I offer a definition of beauty as *an aspect of idealization in which (an) object(s), sound(s), or concept(s) is (or are) believed to possess qualities of formal perfection.* Eleven points are discussed: (1) the sense of beauty is a transitional psychological process in which the world is invested with subjectivity – specifically, idealization; (2) beauty is a primary characteristic of idealization; (3) the archaic sources of beauty lie in early relational experiences – most important, in the recognition of the mother's face; (4) the sense of beauty is interactive, not disinterested or passive; (5) beauty involves aesthetic and non-aesthetic emotions; (6) the sense of beauty is a normal process, with no necessary relation to psychopathology, although beauty can function in the following processes: (7) it may play an integrative role in self-disorders; (8) it can assume a reparative role when internal objects are at risk or felt to be damaged; (9) it may fulfill a defensive role to protect against conflict or shore up self-deficits; and, in addition, (10) identification with the beautiful object results in the experience in the enjoyer of being "loveworthy," thus enhancing well-being and self-esteem; and (11) beauty can protect against the fear of mortality and vulnerability in general. The chapter closes with a discussion of Freud's until-now unexplained reverence for beauty as a primary trait of civilized life.

Ugliness

On the other hand, our aesthetic sensibility may also suffer disruption, and it is this traumatic disruption of our aesthetic experience that we call *ugliness*. In chapter seven, I will discuss how ugliness is *the provocation and projection of unconscious fantasies that alter the sense of aesthetic experience in such a way that the formal qualities of the experience – its shape, texture, and color – become what we experience as sources of the most disturbing and repulsive feelings*.

This chapter reviews the psychoanalytic writings concerning ugliness. It offers a psychoanalytic model that addresses several key points: ugliness as a failure of sublimation, the collapse of idealization, ugliness and interaction, the affective dimension of ugliness, and ugliness as a symptom in psychopathology. Clinical vignettes and reminiscences are used to illustrate various points. I close the chapter with a discussion of how ugliness can provide an opportunity for the psychoanalyst and the artist: he or she confronts ugliness, and, through the creative and/or the psychoanalytic process, brings form and perfection to disintegration and disorder. In this way, ugliness ultimately succumbs to beauty.

The Sublime

Beauty is the aesthetic of maternal preoccupation. It is the organization of the ideal elements that composed the formal sense of the interaction between mother and infant. Balance, integration, and clear meaning characterize beauty. On the other hand, power, formlessness, obscurity, and immensity play important roles in the paternal aesthetic, the aesthetic of the sublime.

Chapter eight focuses on the aesthetics of the childhood experience of the father. Several decades ago, Phyllis Greenacre (1953) argued that awe before the sublime was derivative of the child's first encounters with the father's phallus. Its strangeness, size, and power (all inseparable from fantasy) became the prototype of all experiences in which we perceive the sublime and extraordinary. Building on Greenacre's view, I discuss how the infant moves outward from the enclosed and managed aesthetic space of the mother, into an open, dynamic, and uncontrolled engagement with the world as introduced by the father. The father's relative size; the child's fantasies of the father's power, aggressiveness, and perhaps even omnipotence; the perception of immense and obscure reality beyond and outside dyadic experience – all these combine in the first aesthetics of awe and astonishment.

This chapter concludes with a discussion of the functions of the sublime and consequently the reasons why we are drawn to seek out and cultivate such experiences. The sublime functions to bring several different terrors within a containable, ordered universe. It is the powerful discharge of desire and aggression without catastrophe; it can portray the results of discharge without the destruction of self or a loved one. Death, sexuality, aggression, loss of self, vulnerability, and isolation are embraced and overcome, although not by being negated or denied. Paradoxically, the experience of these terrors in the sublime is vitalizing and self-confirming, not disorganizing. There is an emotional state of arousal/tranquility. What is internally threatening is safely put outside the self. There is an externalization of fantasy, desire, and fear.

The sublime is thus the experience of vulnerability from a position of safety. It begins with the father as observed from the arms of the mother and continues with the world surveyed from within his firm grasp. It is the rawness of affect, the passion of fantasy, and the shock of the new, contained and expressed within a formal structure that is experienced as astonishing and ultimately transcendent.

Festival

In the final chapter, I offer an integration of the multiple levels of subjectivity that make up the aesthetic life of mankind. I will show that art and creativity serve different functions when you approach them from the vantage point of one's culture, relationships, and individual subjective life. The social function of art in the preservation and enhancement of group relations within a particular society is quite different from the psychological function of art in the affirmation and enhancement of the self-experience of the individual working artist. Yet a complete psychoanalytic aesthetic theory must acknowledge the relationship between these different domains.

In this chapter, I emphasize that creative acts are intelligible only from within the culture and social milieu out of which they emerge. Culture provides the language of art. Art cannot be conceived of outside of a cultural milieu in which not only the forms and methods of art are promulgated, but the general standards that define quality are developed as well (at the level of metasubjectivity, as will be elaborated further). This is true of even the most personal aspects of art. The artist who climbs up to the privacy of her garret to create finds there the tools, maps, and measuring instruments of an outside culture, and although she might challenge that culture, she cannot escape it. We take our artistic language from culture, which becomes the horizon within which aesthetic experience is possible and intelligible.

Artists are embedded in a network of relationships, within which their aesthetics develop and are perfected (at the level of intersubjectivity). Many have noted the frequent occurrence of artistic dyads in which an artist or artists rely on dialogue with a valued other person who functions for them as a muse. It is out of this intersubjective matrix that many revolutionary aesthetic movements are spawned and sustained. These groupings of artists take from the metasubjective horizon of culture those themes, styles, values, and art forms that are best suited to express their special intersubjective vision. Then, through dialogue, these artists together create the unique aesthetic of their generation. It is these cultural and relational contexts that compose the working ground of individual artistic effort.

In the end, neither culture nor relationships have the adaptability and resourcefulness of the individual artist's creative process (at the level of the subjective). This is why, although art spawns grand cultures and great movements, it is nevertheless the individual struggle of the single artist that gives life to these larger processes. The artist working on his or her own, taking from and acting against the culture and relationships within which she lives, creates something new. It is this domain of aesthetics that is the primary concern of chapter nine.

I will emphasize the way in which self-experience (which includes the experience of self-in-relationship) is expressed in the formal structure of the artwork. However, I must be clear that the individual intrapsychic experience of the artist crystallizes out of and is constituted by relational and cultural meanings that are also the artist's motive, form, and subject. In fact, artists may be more profoundly engaged with their environment and social milieu than are many others.

This book provides an approach to psychoanalytic aesthetics that emphasizes the central role of early childhood experience in the emergence and structuralization of the sense of aesthetic form. It argues that because of developmentally based processes of idealization, the child's formal aesthetic sense takes on a profound and lifelong concern with form and quality. Thus, the creative artist is concerned not just with articulation of subjective states of feeling, but also with the most refined and perfect expression possible of her internal vision.

The most exquisite embodiment of ideal aesthetic form is beauty, and it is the multiple functions that the sense of beauty fulfills in our psychological lives that motivate us to pursue creation and to get nearer to it. On the other hand, ugliness represents the failure of our aesthetic sensibility, in which fantasy and desire disrupt the formal structure of our experience. Conversely, the sublime offers us a means through the paternal aesthetic to contain fear, and even horror, which we can then integrate into a powerful and astonishing aesthetic form. Finally, I propose that aesthetic experience is elaborated by means of multiple levels of subjectivity: the metasubjective (social), the intersubjective (relational), and the personal (subjective). It is the rich interrelationship between these levels that composes the complexity and profound depth of human aesthetic life.

This is a book for persons interested in the psychoanalytic approach to art and aesthetic experience. I have tried to make clear that, even though I focus mainly on art and artists, many of these ideas are applicable to psychological life in general. We all organize our lives aesthetically, whether or not we are aware of it. Of course, it is in our experience of art that the aesthetic experience is most intensely felt, most clearly illustrated and explicated. It is my hope, then, that the book may have a broader audience and find some application to areas of psychological life beyond art. (In fact, a psychoanalyst colleague who read the chapter on beauty felt that the capacity to experience beauty might constitute a sign of psychological health.)

Although this book is not primarily clinical, I have included clinical process to illustrate some of the ideas presented. In this respect, I hope that there may be a way to elaborate on some of my thoughts to inform psychotherapeutic treatment. However, I should also note here that I consistently emphasize a nonpathological orientation toward my topics. I will discuss how aesthetic experience develops and is elaborated, with less attention to pathological variants. For example, it is acknowledged that idealization can be used as a defense and that, at times, this can result in significant internal and social distress. Much has been written about this topic, but it is not my focus in chapter four.

In addition, the sense of beauty can also be misused, and I make a brief comment regarding this in my discussion of anorexia and depression – but this is a brief and very incomplete discussion. I do not want to suggest that psychopathological conflicts, deficits, and distortions are not important in understanding aesthetic experience, but a thorough consideration of such areas will have to be carried out elsewhere. In the present project, I will begin by establishing some agreement about normal processes – an important first step.

Art and Self

This chapter presents a contemporary self psychological perspective on aesthetic experience, art, and creativity. I argue that aesthetics is as important to human life as sex, hunger, aggression, love, and hate. Although we may rarely be conscious of it, aesthetic experience gives form, meaning, and, most importantly, value to everything we are, all we experience, and everything we do. Theoretically without it, life would be a shapeless, meaningless, and colorless series of sensations, events, and reactions. Aesthetic experience achieves its most refined form in the fine arts. However, we can also see its most archaic manifestation in the curve of the mother's shoulder during nursing, her heartbeat and breath, the melody of her voice, the balance of her eyes and smile–all embedded in the warmth, nourishment, and security of the mother/infant interaction. This chapter reviews recent analytic writings on psychoanalytic aesthetics that emphasize the central role of early childhood relational experiences in the emergence and structuralization of the sense of aesthetic form. I argue that because of developmentally based processes of idealization, the child's aesthetic sense takes on a profound and lifelong concern with form and quality. I extend this model and propose a new definition of creativity and the nature of art, arguing that the creative artist is concerned not just with articulation of subjective states of feeling but also with the most refined and perfect expression possible of his or her internal vision. Although a major application of this model is to art and creativity, it is argued that aesthetic experience is a pervasive human trait that impacts on our entire experience of life, self, and relationships.

Creative Analysis

In this chapter I extend our discussion of the aesthetic foundation of human experience and show how an aesthetic perspective can shed light on the psychoanalytic process (Hagman, 2010, 2015, 2016). I begin with a review of the aesthetic dimension of early childhood experience, the emergence of aesthetic form and value from the child's experience of the relational field, and its elaboration into a mature, fully developed aesthetic sense. I then show how aesthetics can inform our understanding of psychotherapeutic process in terms yet neglected. Finally, I discuss creativity as it is manifest in psychotherapy through the construction of the cotransference

(Orange, 1993), an aesthetically organized subjective object, which becomes the focus of analysis and creative change (Winnicott, 1971). The chapter closes with a case example as an illustration of the structure and dynamics of a creative analysis (Hagman, 2015)

The Aesthetics of Music, the Musician and the Creative Process

Music is the embodiment through sound of lived experience. Conscious and unconscious modes of subjectivity are woven together in a tapestry of tone and sound, which is less about the world and more about the symbolic equivalent of human subjectivity itself. Musicians through their interpretation of a composition invest their performance with self-experience, and they come to experience themselves as vibrantly mirrored in the ideal form of the music. In other words, the musical performance is an opportunity for selfobject experience. Musical performance involves a two-phase process. The first is the practice phase, during which the musician seeks to achieve the experience of aesthetic resonance in which self-experience and music are brought into sync through the perfection of the performance. The dynamic role of selfobject failure and restoration in the musician's motivation to perfect the performance is stressed. The second phase is the public performance, during which the musician exhibits his or her ideal creation and experiences the mirroring of the audience. During these phases, there is a creative dialectic between internal and externalized aspects of self-experience. An examination of case material from analytic work with a musician shows how an inhibition in the creative process may be based on the expectation of selfobject failure and how musical creativity can be facilitated through new opportunities for selfobject experience in the transference.

The Erotics of Beauty

This chapter is a study of *Death in Venice* by Thomas Mann, a 1911 novella that dramatizes the function of the experience of beauty in the main character's struggle to ward off impending self-disintegration. Interestingly, it was Heinz Kohut who published the first full psychoanalytic interpretation of the work considering the psychology of its author (Kohut, 1957). There Kohut argued that the breakdown of the sublimating function of art resulted in the main character's decent into previously forbidden drive fantasies and disruptive desires. Written in 1948 and published in 1957 after Mann's death, Kohut's analysis understandably reflected his theoretical background at the time. In this paper, I would like to reinterpret Von Achenbach's erotic infatuation, the dramatic focus of the work, as his effort to maintain self-cohesion through the experience of an archaic, sexualized idealization of the beautiful boy Tadzio. I will argue that Aschenbach's obsession, rather than being a symptom of self-disintegration, is in fact a restorative effort, the boy's beauty offering Aschenbach an experience of perfection, in other words an opportunity for a transcendent selfobject experience.

Hitler's Aesthetics

Beauty, the formal aspect of idealization, can embody the finest and most trans-cendent values in human aesthetic experience, but beauty can also be perverse and in some instances it can serve the needs of evil. This paper will examine the dark side of beauty. We will see how beauty can become grotesque and ultimately be destroyed when it is forced to fulfill the needs of the most terrible of self-disorders. In his book *Hitler and the Power of Aesthetics*, Frederic Spotts (2003) argued that our image of Hitler as a monster is incomplete. He asserted that historians have failed to appreciate the place of Hitler's aesthetics in our understanding of his motives and aims. Spotts pointed out that the young Hitler pursued a career as an artist for several years, until professional failure and the opportunity for political success offered him the narcissistic gratification through demagoguery that he so longed for from the arts. Once in power, it was Hitler's obsession with aesthetic matters that dominated his passion for culture and disguised his hatred and aggres-sion. Monomaniacal, he pursued the destruction of Western culture in his quest to remake and mold the aesthetic landscape according to his own idealized and grandiose self-image.

Chapter 2

Understanding Aesthetic Experience

The Philosophy of Aesthetic Experience

Western philosophers and psychologists have always been interested in art, the appreciation of art, and the psychology of artists. Plato argued that aesthetic experience involved the apprehension of the good in nature. The nonsensuous pleasure, perhaps awe, of aesthetic feeling resulted from the reflection of an ideal form in the object (a flower, a mountain glade, a beautiful face, a painting) that only hinted at the profound perfection and beauty of its higher model. For Plato, it was the apperception of this hint, the glimpse of the ideal, which was the source of aesthetic experience.

Later, religious thinkers believed that aesthetic experience was linked to the revelation of divinity in the world, the sense of worldly beauty reflecting the eternal beauty of God. Like Plato's views was the belief that some objects, most especially art, expressed God's love and perfection more than others – or at least, the divinity was more easily glimpsed in some objects than in others. It was not until the eighteenth century that a true psychology of aesthetic experience began to emerge. Starting with David Hume and Immanuel Kant, these modern thinkers tried to explain aesthetic experience in psychological terms. The objective nature of "the good" and "the beauty of God" came to be replaced by psychological processes by which our experience of the world is given aesthetic qualities and values.

Hume (1775) argued that aesthetic experience was associated with sensitivity to the association between a perception and a feeling. The aesthetic feelings were those of refined pleasure, delight, awe, admiration, joy, and so on – in other words, affects and passions considered to be of special, positive value. Hume believed that certain types of experiences, those possessing beauty, attained higher qualities in the formal expression of these feelings. Thus, for Hume, human sensibility and emotion replaced divinity and ideal form as the basis for aesthetic experience.

Art, as opposed to natural sources of beauty, expressed certain associated feelings in refined and highly valued ways. Hume argued that a person could develop his or her critical judgment in aesthetic matters by means of experience and study. He also stressed the need for the audience member to keep "his mind free from all prejudice and allow nothing to enter into consideration but the very object that is

DOI: 10.4324/9781003532484-2

submitted to his examination" (1775, pp. 114–115). Hume claimed that the audience must be comfortable and without other intentions when viewing something aesthetically. This was one of the initial arguments for the role of "disinterest" in aesthetic experience (this would become important to later aesthetic theory, especially for Kant).

What Hume was describing was a type of empathy, an ability to put aside one's normal position and needs and to "place oneself in that point of view that the artwork supposes" (p. 114). Thus, aesthetic experience assumed a special form of relationship with the object in which the audience members would approach the experience with benign neutrality and a willingness to give themselves over to the experience without prejudice. This relationship would then ideally result in a pleasant emotional state evoked by the specialness and refinement of the object.

Immanuel Kant (1790) postulated that aesthetic experience was a type of subjective judgment distinct from other human emotions, referring to this as *taste*. Essentially, taste was a type of universal and natural human capability like other modes of perception. As one experiences something aesthetically, there are sensations of pleasure within an attitude of disinterest. In fact, for Kant, *taste* was closer to reason than to emotion or sensation; it constituted recognition of a priori truths (such as beauty) in the concrete, "objective purposiveness" (1790, p. 187) of objects.

This was Kant's attempt to separate out aesthetic taste from other emotions or sensations and to claim it as a primary form of mental experience. Thus, the source of aesthetic experience lay not in the enjoyment of the beautiful object, but in the recognition of the subjective knowledge of universal ideals. These ideals do not exist in some abstract realm (as with Plato) or in divinity (as with Augustine, for example); rather, they are a priori universal conceptualizations that form the basis of our rational judgments. For example, though we have all had innumerable experiences of individual men of various statures, sizes, and shapes, we also possess a mental model of *man*, the perfect, formal concept of the beautiful man. Aesthetic experience is based on this understanding of inner ideals. Thus, Kant attempted to develop a theory of aesthetic experience that was both human and rational, a form of perception that formed the very ground of rationality and judgment.

Hume and Kant were the most important contributors to the modern approach to aesthetics and the psychology of art. For our purposes, the key elements of their models can be summarized as follows: (1) the source of aesthetic experience is within the mind of the artist and audience, not inherent in the object, (2) the formal characteristics of the object are important to the extent that they evoke an inner knowledge or feeling associated with an idea or emotion, and (3) aesthetic experience involves an attitude of "disinterest," or distance, that is characterized by suspension of prejudice, psychological security, and the willingness to give oneself over to the experience of the object.

These elements presupposed several assumptions that psychoanalysis would challenge. First, Kant believed that the educated and sensitive man can know his own mind and be fully aware of his feelings. Second, he saw an association between the representation and the concept that is open rather than defensively motivated. Third, he believed that disinterest is simply a suspension of prejudice rather than a complex process involving specific psychical mechanisms (e.g., sublimation).

The history of psychoanalytic aesthetics must be seen in the context of the theories promulgated by Hume and Kant and elaborated by their followers. Most importantly, psychoanalysis developed the notion of art and aesthetics as expression, as derivative of psychic concepts and specifically of unconscious fantasies. Freud saw aesthetic experience as equivalent in function to a neurotic symptom or the manifest content of a dream. The psychoanalytic approach to aesthetics was concerned with the symbolic nature of art and its instinctual sources rather than with the aesthetic experience itself.

This symbolic/interpretive approach to aesthetics has dominated the psychoanalytic literature. However, recent authors have been interested in the primary function of aesthetic experience in addition to its defensive role. They argue that its true meaning and purpose are not merely determined by unconscious conflict; rather, there is a primary function of aesthetic experience, and one can trace its source to the earliest phases of human development.

This chapter will explore and elaborate on this developmental approach. But first, considering our discussion of the development of the modern approach to psychological aesthetics, let me offer a brief definition of aesthetic experience that will be helpful in the discussion we will engage in over the next two chapters.

Aesthetic experience involves a phenomenon (an object, event, sound, or other perception) or a set of phenomena (a group of objects, a sequence of events, a melody, or a complex structure of perceptions) that is/are felt to possess perfection or ideal form. Aesthetic experience is fundamentally subjective, but also grounded in the objective qualities of the object. It may include affects such as joy, sadness, wonder, and awe, or a calm sense of quiescence. The quality of self-experience is also part of it; the individual feels whole, vitalized, more positive, and closely engaged with the world.

Furthermore, aesthetic experience varies in intensity. The tragic drama of *King Lear* is an unsurpassed aesthetic experience, an example of perfection and idealization. However, aesthetic experience also characterizes the enjoyment of a sunny day or the more mundane beauty of an oily puddle in a city street. While aesthetic experience may be passionate, it must also evoke feelings of safety for the observer. Consistent with Kant's viewpoint, aesthetic experience involves a balance between personal investment and emotional disinterest.

In a broad sense, a person's aesthetic is the formal dimension of the unique way in which he or she experiences, responds to, and engages the world. It is that aspect of experience in which the *quality* of the formal organization of a person's relationship to an object, activity, or sensation is manifest. Aesthetic experience can occur in either the foreground or the background of subjectivity. In the background, it is the source of our sense of the world as having value and perhaps beauty. Otto Rank (1932) discussed how this ongoing, low level of aesthetic experiences helps us endure life's problems. When in the foreground, aesthetic experience is compelling; we experience ourselves as being in the presence of great truths and vivid realities. H. B. Lee (1948) described this level of aesthetic experience as "spiritual," noting that the object is felt to be "divinely perfect and ideal" (p. 511). Alternation between foreground and background reflects the ongoing struggle to reconcile fantasy and reality, the ideal and the real, the archaic and the mature (Kainer, 1999).

Freud viewed aesthetic experience as the sublimation of forbidden sexual desires, a displacement and transformation (desexualization or neutralization) of libido that, denied direct expression, is allowed discharge in alternative, culturally valued ways. Aesthetic pleasure is the result. The close link between art (a highly idealized cultural institution) and regressive processes and fantasies seems to support the sublimation approach. From this viewpoint, symbolism, a fundamental component of most forms of aesthetic expression, is the same process as that occurring in dreamwork, and thus it opens art to psychoanalytic interpretation.

For example, in several references, Sandor Ferenczi (1952) viewed aesthetic experience as arising from defenses against anal eroticism, the preoccupation with messy feces being transformed into structural elegance and formal beauty. Limiting themselves to the investigation of the symbolic nature of art, Ferenczi and Freud felt that the relation of analysis to art was interpretive, uncovering the unconscious meanings of imagery or the covert instinctual motivations of the artist. Freud did not identify any specific, defining process in aesthetic experience, focusing instead on the functions and mechanisms that it shared with other psychic processes. This approach, while illuminating the hidden meanings of art, also limited the explanatory use of drive psychology in understanding aesthetic experience – a point Freud (1914b) freely admitted. In fact, he remarked on several occasions that he could not appreciate art unless he could interpret its meaning. In his paper on the *Moses* of Michelangelo, he wrote:

> I have often observed that the subject matter of works of art has a stronger attraction for me than their formal and technical qualities, though to the artist their value lies first and foremost in these latter. I am unable rightly to appreciate many of the methods used and the effects obtained in art.
>
> (p. 89)

Freud further noted that he was deeply moved by some art (the *Moses* is one example), but only when he could explain its impact on him. On the other hand, music gave him no pleasure whatsoever. He noted that "some rationalistic, or perhaps analytic, turn of mind in me rebels against being moved by a thing without knowing why I am thus affected and what it is that affects me" (Freud, 1914b, p. 89).

This raises a question: why is it that Freud could not appreciate either the formal quality of art or its content unless he could analyze it? I believe the answer is that aesthetic experience has its roots in early childhood experience (something that Freud did not emphasize) and that it involves a form of knowing that is nonrational and irreducible, at least according to the metapsychology of classical psychoanalysis. (See also Bollas [1978], for his discussion of aesthetic experience as part of the *unthought known*.)

The classical approach to the psychology of aesthetic experience was primarily content oriented. That is, it considered the interpretation of the unconscious message as it is encoded in the imagery and expressed meanings of the artwork. The drive psychology model of aesthetic experience as sublimation also highlighted one of the primary functions of art – and certainly there is an affective, even passionate, aspect of most forms of artistic expression. But Freud's viewpoint failed to explore the crucial role of quality and form in aesthetic experience.

In other words, Freud argued that the sublimating person channels instinctual drive energies through valued cultural channels, but he did not investigate the formal nature or quality of value that characterized those channels, the cultural forms themselves. If we believe that aesthetic experiences possess special qualities that make them distinct from other psychological phenomena (dreams, work, or play), I think that the most important area to consider is the nature of aesthetic form and the sources of the experience of quality or value that the forms seem to possess. When an artist expresses meaning through perfected cultural forms, or a person experiences a sunrise as extraordinarily beautiful, he or she is tapping into archaic aspects of human experience by which the formal aspects of our relationship to the world are felt to be both special and valuable.

From Sublimation to Regression

In 1961, Robert Fleiss published an interesting elaboration of Freud's sublimation model of aesthetic experience. Fleiss believed that in aesthetic experience, especially in the sense of beauty, there is a normal regression to an "early perceptory relation" involving the "modality of primary perception," which he conceived of (after Rene Spitz) as the combined perceptions of the labyrinth – outer skin, hands, and mouth unified into a single, nondistinguishable experience.

According to Fleiss, in aesthetic enjoyment, there is a muscular discharge of neutral energy. Rather than aggressively cannibalizing the object, the person experiences an empathic introjection of it. Fleiss located the developmental level of aesthetic experience in the first oral phase prior to the mobilization of aggression that results in incorporative actions and fantasies. He argued that the sublimation of this neutral oral libido is "inseparable from aesthetic enjoyment" and includes muscular discharges involved in the "modality of primary perception" – "a modality that continues to function throughout life" (1961, p. 283). Thus, for Fleiss, sublimation is not simply a defense, but a normal aspect of the vicissitudes of libido that are essentially neutral during the first oral phase.

It is the activity of this neutralized libido throughout life that accounts for the ubiquity of aesthetic experience. In an interesting series of case reports, Fleiss illustrated the relationship between sex and aesthetic enjoyment, and even argued for the simultaneous experience of both in mature, healthy sexual relations.

Space does not permit an in-depth discussion of Fliess's wonderful contribution. However, given that he did elaborate on Freud's model of aesthetic experience in several important ways, I will briefly touch on some of his points. Unlike Freud, whose reaction to art was by his own admission lukewarm at best, Fleiss viewed aesthetic experience as a passionate sublimation. For him, neutralization does not take the physicality or drive out of the libido; it merely changes its aim. This helps to explain something that Freud's sublimation model failed to address: the frequently passionate nature of many aesthetic experiences.

Although art is never equivalent to actual coital discharge, some successful and aesthetically perfect forms of beauty are frankly erotic and/or aggressive. Therefore, Fleiss proposes that art as sublimation allows for a form of discharge regulation in which drive is channeled rather than simply disguised. This suggests that aesthetic experience may be linked to early vicissitudes of sexuality and aggression that are contained and expressed through ego mechanisms having more to do with containment, regulation, and expression than defense. In this light, Fleiss viewed aesthetic experience not as a defense but rather as a normal regressive process having developmental sources in the early (nonaggressive) oral phase of the libido. He argued that aesthetic experience involves the multiple sensory modalities of interaction with the nursing mother – hand, eye, mouth, skin, and ear – all linked together in a sensory mosaic. In these ways, Fleiss gave the drive perspective on aesthetic experience a developmental bent, but he continued to see it as essentially a regression and therefore did not elaborate a truly developmental approach to aesthetic experience.

As discussed later in this chapter, I strongly support the notion that aesthetic experience has its source in early infantile experience. One of the problems with regression models such as Fliess's is that they do not go far enough to explain the developmental elaboration of aesthetic experiences from the archaic processes to mature forms of artistic appreciation and other sophisticated aesthetic judgments. As with any other culturally sanctioned and articulated form of behavior, the refinement and elaboration of early forms of aesthetic experience into the complex and refined forms found in adult life need to be explained.

From Regression to Reparation

Unlike Freud and Fleiss, who stressed the derivative nature of aesthetic experience, object relations theorists posited a progressive function for it. Melanie Klein (1929, 1930) and Hanna Segal (1952) both argued that aesthetic experience assists in the resolution of internal psychological distress arising from the feared consequences of aggression felt toward good objects. However, this resolution is not accomplished by means of denial or other defensive mechanisms; rather, the aesthetic experience can contain both the aggressive fantasy (the bad object) and the libidinal fantasy (the good object) in a single experience.

According to object relations theory, in some cases, there is an amalgam in which beauty and ugliness are expressed with simultaneous vividness, with neither canceling out the other. In others, there is a balanced but separate depiction of evil and goodness within a single aesthetic field. In either case, instead of suppressing, neutralizing, or eliminating aggression, the aesthetic experience allows for the safe, even reparative, recognition that aggression and libido can exist within the same psychological realm without annihilation of the good. Thus, object relations theory was the first psychoanalytic theory to offer the possibility of a developmental aesthetic. Specifically, the idea that aesthetic experience is an aspect of the depressive position supports the notion that it has early developmental roots.

Lee (1948, 1950) was also critical of Freud's model of sublimation and developed an approach to aesthetic experience like the object relations one. Lee believed that aesthetic experience arises from efforts to achieve atonement for guilt associated with destructive fantasy. He summarized the aesthetic experience of the artist:

> In redeeming himself with conscience, the artist achieves not only a rare sense of unification among the institutions of his mind and with the alienated world; but more than this, for the restoration of love and approval from conscience is felt as a lyrical kind of at-one-ness, and as an exhilarating rapture called spiritual pleasure. A marked alleviation of self-esteem results from recapturing the flavor of the moments in early life when, guilty to his mother over destructive rage, the child regained her love, approval and gratitude in the reconciliation that occurred when appropriate action demonstrated his renewed allegiance to her teachings of pity. He experiences not only a moving sense of order, peace and wholeness, but is flooded with his most passionate experience of spiritual pleasure with his most intense experience of vitality and of becoming.
>
> (1950, p. 240)

What Lee described was a psychologically confirming experience that followed the restored sense of connection with the attuned, loving, empathic parental object. Thus, Lee also supported the notion that aesthetic experience was linked to early infantile experiences of connection to parental objects or imagoes.

Developmental Aesthetics

In the last twenty years, psychoanalytic developmental theory has also been used to explore aesthetic experience. From this perspective, aesthetic experience is a type of regressive state in which early developmental phases (such as symbiotic fusion with caregivers) are revived. Gilbert Rose (1992) was the first to address the bridging of contemporary and archaic developmental states in *The Power of Form* (1992). He wrote that aesthetic experience is rooted in phylogenetic adaptations to internal and external reality. The way in which aesthetic experience organizes affect and perception and transforms occasions for anxiety into transcendent pleasure and insight compels us to speculate on its biological function. In this regard, Rose noted that:

> Art performs a valuable biological function: at least it provides a normative mode or opportunity for stimulating and assimilating potentially dangerous

degrees of affect – in short, extending the limits of the bearable. Instead of
traumatic reexperiencing of affective storms, or a repression of affective signals
with regressive resomatization and fragmentation, a greater degree of integration and differentiation of affects can take place within the safe holding presence
of the aesthetic structure.

(p. 227)

Rose's thesis is highly consistent with the psychoanalytic model of aesthetic
experience that we will be discussing. He argued that there is a biological, even
evolutionary, basis for the creation of art and the sense of beauty (which he
defined as the most refined and perfected expression of the aesthetic state of
mind). The sense of beauty arises out of the observer's need to ensure consistent orientation in a relatively fluid reality and to regulate disruptive affective
states. This view supports the notion that aesthetic experience integrates and
binds potentially traumatic and disintegrative affective states, as well as facilitating the adaptation to and attunement with reality – and, most significantly,
the complex interpersonal environment of the parent/child relationship. Rose
wrote:

The controlled ambiguity of aesthetic form highlights and magnifies the interaction of primary and secondary processes. Aesthetic experience has more to do
with this congruence than with emotions per se. Ambiguity eases the tension
of maintaining separate boundaries and restricting discharge; it fuses separate
moments of time changed into a sense of timeless constancy. And all this is
augmented by the distant resonance with the past, with the narcissistic fusion
with the mother. Secondary-process control, delineating spatial, temporal, and
logical distinctions, restraining feelings and impulses, builds tension moment
by moment and echoes the first building of reality in the separation from the
mother.

(1992, p. 201)

For Rose, aesthetic experience is a complex psychological activity. This includes
oscillations between primary and secondary processes, as well as between fusion
and separateness. He argued that, in aesthetic experience, a triangulation exists
between the present self, the evoked memory of archaic states, and the art object.
This, he felt, resonates with the basic structure of the mind itself, reflecting the
mind's imaginative activity or movement. Aesthetic experience recapitulates the
mind's fusion with and emergence from the maternal bond. But the problem is that
many psychological phenomena might have these functions and characteristics,
and what is it that makes aesthetic experience distinct? In the chapters that follow,
I will discuss my belief that it is the idealization of the formal aspects of experience
that underlie aesthetic processes.

Like Rose's work, other developmental approaches to psychoanalytic aesthetics have focused on the problem of merger and de-differentiation that is

commonly associated with aesthetic experience. This has been noted by philosophers not directly connected to psychoanalysis, such as John Dewey (1934), who wrote:

> The uniquely distinguishing feature of [a]esthetic experience is exactly the fact that no such distinction of self and objects exist in it. . . . [T]he two are so integrated that each disappears.
>
> (p. 249)

Some psychoanalysts have approached this problem in terms of archaic mental states, particularly regarding the child's first experiences of connection to the mother. They argue that the adult's experience of art is a form of regression to the powerful, emotionally charged, and psychologically ambiguous way in which the infant experiences the caretaking mother. These analysts have utilized the aesthetic approaches of the British Middle School, especially the writings of D. W. Winnicott. Unlike the Kleinians, who stressed the vicissitudes of defense against aggression, Winnicott emphasized the positive developmental thrust of illusion and creativity. Rather than viewing the mother/infant bond as a cauldron of rage and envy, he argued that the child enters the world eager to create, not to destroy. Winnicott saw this creativity as arising out of an original state of pleasurable and omnipotent nondifferentiation.

Building on this idea, Ellen Handler Spitz (1985) argued for the importance of idealization in these preoedipal merger experiences in aesthetic experience. In *Art and Psyche*, she wrote:

> The aesthetic ideal, then, is like symbolic fusion in that encounters with the beautiful may temporarily obliterate our sense of inner and outer separateness by drawing us into an orbit in which boundaries between self and other, and categories into which we divide the world, dissolve. This occurs, perhaps, with the return to consciousness, the reavailability to us, during moments of creativity or responsiveness in the arts, of aspects of our preoedipal life, with its pleasurable sense of merging and union.
>
> (p. 142)

For Spitz, aesthetic experience recaptures early memories of the preoedipal relationship with the mother. Most important is the experience of the maternal bond as a special and highly valued state that possesses a profound quality of perfection. In addition, aesthetic experience possesses intense affective qualities, such as pleasure, security, and fulfillment. Spitz describes a type of symbiotic relating that is evoked in the aesthetic response, in which the relationship to the object is invested with qualities that hark back to the archaic bond with the mother. Spitz believed that this reexperience is the source of aesthetic pleasure.

In a more recent paper, Patricia Lipscomb (1997) extends the discussion of the developmental basis of aesthetic experience into the realm of Winnicott's transitional phenomenon:

> Aesthetic experience functions as a transitional process, allowing the viewer of a work of art to enter a transitional space between reality and fantasy that is suggested by the various dialectics involved in aesthetic experience (past and future, concrete and abstract, passive and active, near and far), but is illustrated most clearly by the sense of ambiguity about fusion versus separateness that is typically induced in the viewer as part of aesthetic experience.
>
> (p. 154)

Lipscomb argued that aesthetic experience induces a revisiting of "the developmental phase in which the young child first began to achieve a sense of psychological separateness from mother and the rest of the world" (p. 154). She asserted that the viewer experiences two sources of pleasure: (1) the temporary experience of boundarilessness and fusion, where opposites coexist and harmony reigns, and (2) the return to a sense of one's psychological separateness and the recognition of one's capacity to withstand loss.

This approach to understanding aesthetic experience emphasizes the sense of nondifferentiation in which fantasy and reality seem to interpenetrate, even to codetermine each other. The argument goes that this experience in maturity essentially recapitulates the developmentally primitive self and object relations and that the type of emotional resonance and unconscious communication that seems to occur is directly linked to the psychological processes in the mother/infant bond.

Lipscomb directs her attention to the area of transitional experience, arguing that the work of art is like the transitional object in that the viewer is psychologically inseparable from the object. "There is no such thing as a work of art," Winnicott might say; there is only the viewer and the art as they share a co-constructed psychic reality, an area of illusion. I would elaborate this viewpoint by pointing out the oscillating positions of the viewer and the artwork. The viewer experiences him- or herself at times as the active creator and, at other times, as the receptive subject of the aesthetic illusion. This shifting identification contributes to the dynamic tension in aesthetic experience.

While I feel that developmental theorists such as Spitz and Lipscomb have much of value to contribute, their emphasis on the experience of fusion seems to ignore the fact that experiences of fusion can also be a source of terror and fragmentation. And it is well recognized that separation can result in feelings of loss and abandonment, so the fluctuation or ambiguity between fusion and separateness may not necessarily be a source of aesthetic pleasure. This is an area that has been amply explored by object relations theorists in their discussions of borderline phenomena. Since aesthetic experience is almost invariably positive and self-confirming (no matter what its content may be), I would argue that the experience of fusion and separateness is not just with any type of parental object, but with an idealized one.

In this regard, self psychology offers a model of aesthetic experience that emphasizes the loss and recovery of the tie to the idealized parent. In his paper entitled "The Artist and Selfobject Theory," Charles Kligerman (1980) noted that the psychology of the artist is linked to idealization and aesthetic experience, describing how the artist's self-crisis leads to the development of lifelong efforts to recapture a lost state of perfection. One of the important qualities of idealization is the sense of "formal" perfection and value known as beauty. The idealized object or the grandiose self is experienced as possessing in essence a perfection of form and mode of being that is beautiful; therefore, aesthetic experience forms a part of idealization. In his formulation, Kligerman speculates that the prototypical artist is someone who experienced consistent mirroring of his or her grandiosity in childhood. Inevitably, this archaic selfobject experience fails and the artist-to-be is cast out from this state of perfection. Kligerman noted:

> The ensuing fall from grace is followed by a passionate need to recover the original beauty and perfection and later to present the world with a work of beauty (really the artist himself) that will evoke universal awe and admiration. There are thus at least three main currents to the creative drive.
>
> (pp. 387–388)

> An intrinsic joy in creating, related to what has been termed "functional" pleasure. This is perhaps the most important factor, but the one we know the least about: the exhibitionistic grandiose ecstasy of being regarded as the acme of beauty and perfection and the nearly insatiable need to repeat and confirm this feeling: It is the need to regain a lost paradise – the original bliss of perfection – to overcome the empty feeling of self-depletion and to recover self-esteem. In the metapsychology of the self, this would amount to healing the threatened fragmentation and restoring firm self-cohesion through a merger with the selfobject – the work of art – and a bid for mirroring approval of the world. We can also add a fourth current to the creative drive – the need to regain perfection by merging with the ideals of the powerful selfobjects, first the parents, then later revered models that represent the highest standards of some great artistic tradition.
>
> (pp. 387–388)

Selfobject experience in childhood inevitably leads to failures in attunement and self-crisis. The child confronted by the loss of the sustaining, developmentally essential tie to the parent responds psychologically by taking into the self-structure the selfobject functions of the parent. This transmuting internalization is repeated innumerable times as the ongoing, normal selfobject failures accumulate. In his discussion of artistic creativity just quoted, Kligerman pointed out that art is an attempt to restore a lost self-state prior to the empathic failure of the parent(s). Aesthetic experience is the restoration of the early selfobject tie to an idealized parent and thus of a renewed sense of self.

I believe that Kligerman's perspective adds an essential component to the developmental model of aesthetic experience – that its sources lie not only in the evocation of early experiences of psychological connection with the mother, but also in the idealized nature of that relationship and accompanying self-states and that these are central to the aesthetic sense. In other words, a key aspect of aesthetics is an intuitive judgment (an appreciation) of quality, and this type of judgment is linked to the most elemental memories of idealization. This point will be discussed in greater depth in chapter four.

A New Psychoanalytic Model of Aesthetic Experience

> Man is, then, alone of all objects in the world, susceptible of an ideal of beauty, as it is only humanity in his person, as an intelligence, that is susceptible of the ideal of perfection.
>
> (Kant in Aschenbrenner and Isenberg, 1970, p. 187)

A Human Thing

For Kant, the source of aesthetic experience lies in the rational apprehension of man's inner goodness through perception of the human form. Thus, aesthetic pleasure is a response to the moral goodness found at the core of humanity in relation to God. Beauty for Kant was a human thing, reflecting an ideal grounded in truth beyond everyday aesthetic taste.

Later, Francis Jeffrey (1816) also argued for the human source of the aesthetic. He believed:

> It is man and man alone that we see in the beauties of the earth which he inhabits; it is the idea of the enjoyment of feelings that animates the existence of sentient beings, that calls forth all our emotions, and is the parent of beauty.
>
> (p. 286)

The depiction of aesthetic experience we have been discussing is also fundamentally human. If there is an abstract quality, it is found in the biological readiness to organize experience of the world according to certain patterns, colors, sounds, and rhythms. This inner readiness to create form is the psychological equivalent of Plato's ideal forms, but, unlike Platonic forms, those that begin as potentials in the neurons must be evoked and elaborated in interaction with the world, especially with other human beings. According to the model to be discussed in this book, aesthetic form is an emergent mental phenomenon in which psychobiological-neuronal propensities are stimulated and sculpted through relational experiences and are gradually internalized as structured expectations and organizing principals that reflect the form and particularly the quality of interpersonal experience.

Recent psychoanalytic aesthetic theories echo Kant and Jeffrey by showing that beauty has a human core, but that core is not found in some abstract inner goodness or individual affective state; rather, it adheres in the idealized experience of the parent/ child interaction that is elaborated, refined, and spread out over the individual's experience of the world. In this way, the new analytic aesthetic, a developmental-relational perspective, is a fundamentally different model from that of the philosophers we have discussed and from those of the schools of classical psychoanalysis.

A developmental-relational approach to aesthetic experience (including that of self psychology) answers several important questions that classical psychoanalysis despairs of answering, as is evidenced by the following points taken from a developmental-relational perspective:

1. Even though aesthetic experience can include symbolic content, it is not limited to this; rather than precluding analytic investigation, however, this factor demands an expanded paradigm. Such a paradigm views aesthetic experience not in terms of content, symbolic or otherwise, but according to its structure, form, and quality.
2. Aesthetic experience is evocative of archaic, preverbal experiences of self-in-relation. Thus, it is prereflective and involves procedural forms of knowing (an attribute that led to Freud's frustration).
3. Aesthetic experience arises not from defensive motives, but from strivings to experience developmentally healthy states of self-experience and relationship.
4. Aesthetic experience expresses, rather than conceals, fantasy and perception. It seeks to capture and concretize many things that are most frightening or otherwise stimulating to us. It does this by expressing and/or containing these intense affective states in formally structured and perfected forms. In this way, rather than being disguised, fantasy and drive are experientially heightened, even as they are modulated and purged of the acute sense of threat or unbearable arousal.
5. The core quality of perfection that virtually defines aesthetic experience is derived from the developmental vicissitudes of archaic fantasies of idealization that are tied to equally grandiose self-states. This is the only way that we can explain the supreme value we grant to aesthetic experience, as well as the accompanying heightening of self-esteem and well-being. We do not simply reexperience an early state of oneness with the mother; rather, in aesthetic experience, we relate to something of fantastic value and exquisite form, something that evokes the type of enthrallment that we felt (or longed to feel) as infants with our parents.

The new authors whom we have discussed see aesthetic experience as involving processes and psychological states that are grounded in early infancy. In this context, aesthetic experience does not arise fully formed in adulthood. In fact, if we posit that the capacity for aesthetic experience is an important psychological phenomenon – not just a later-acquired affectation or regressive condition – then we should assume that some developmental elaboration of the experience occurs during an individual's lifetime. E. Jacques (1965) has discussed specific elaborations in aesthetic experience and creativity that occur because of midlife psychological developmental changes. While object relational and self psychological theorists argue convincingly for the presence of an archaic substrate in adult aesthetics, they have not yet explored the possibility that aesthetic experience may have its own developmental line – one that is intertwined with other early childhood processes, but that can also be identified and discussed on its own terms.

Aesthetic experience, as noted at the beginning of this chapter, is a basic way in which we organize and experience ourselves and our world. Artists manipulate aesthetic experience; they play with its manifestations and familiar forms and use it secondarily as a medium for communication. The meanings of art (those characteristics that interested Freud) – while important to the purpose of art – do not explain it. What makes an aesthetic experience different from other psychological phenomena is the centrality of form and quality/value, not its content. This is an area of human psychological life that is preverbal, somatically grounded, and powerfully related to the earliest forms of psychological organizing activities and attachment motivations.

To further elaborate this viewpoint, we will now turn to a discussion of how the capacity for aesthetic experience comes to be elaborated during psychological development.

Chapter 3

The Development of Aesthetic Experience

In this chapter, we will examine in detail aspects of psychoanalytic developmental theory that support a new understanding of aesthetic experience. It will become clear that taking a developmental approach has significant advantages to a purely philosophical approach or to the classical psychoanalytic perspective that emphasizes individual psychic mechanisms.

Looking back at the early development of the aesthetic sense, we can explain several things that have eluded prior theorists. These are some of the remaining unsolved problems: the origin of aesthetic feeling, the psychological basis for the experience of disinterest, the sources of the sense of beauty and of the sublime, and vulnerabilities to ugliness, among others. Because a developmental/relational approach can pinpoint the psychological processes of early human relatedness, it can be a powerful new tool in the understanding of basic problems of human aesthetics and the psychology of art.

Let us start our discussion by examining one of the primary characteristics of aesthetic experience that is crucial to all modern conceptualizations – that is, disinterestedness. Freud explained this emotional state through the concept of sublimation, the desexualization of drive, and its neutral expression through socially valued behaviors, such as art. One way to conceptualize aesthetic experience that is consistent with contemporary relational and self psychological approaches, while at the same time remaining linked to the classical theory of psychoanalytic aesthetics, is through a reworking of the concept of sublimation. This may seem strange, given that sublimation was one of the cornerstones of drive theory and later of ego psychology, but what I intend to show in this chapter is that the classical approach to sublimation can be usefully updated when the intersubjective context of this important psychic process is fully appreciated.

As we have seen, Freud's understanding of sublimation accomplished two objectives: (1) it explained the sources of motivation that underlie normal activities, such as work, play, art, and other cultural pursuits, and (2) it explained why these activities, driven by libidinal energy as they are, do not exhibit obvious sexual characteristics (in fact, the failure of sublimation often results in inhibition due to the flooding of the activity with sexual fantasy and feeling). Thus, sublimation could be viewed as both a defense mechanism and a normal, inevitable vicissitude of libidinal drive.

DOI: 10.4324/9781003532484-3

In fact, one might argue that sublimation as a healthy process might have its own developmental line by which a person develops from a self-centered, id-driven, savage child to a civilized adult. Clearly, much more is involved in this process, but sublimation would play a key part. Regarding aesthetic experience, the familiar sense of pleasant calm and security is easily explained by sublimation. However, sublimation has also been vulnerable to serious criticism.

Hans Loewald developed an important new perspective on the problem of sublimation that is especially significant for the current study of psychoanalytic aesthetics. Loewald argued that the classical model of sublimation did not relate just to the fate of the drives (redirecting their aim and neutralizing them); it also affected the individual's fundamental relationship to the world. Specifically, he felt that sublimation played a key part in bridging the gap between self and world in early childhood and in sustaining the relationship between these domains throughout life. Loewald (1988) wrote:

> The polarization that arises in the differentiation of primary narcissism into narcissistic and object libido is counterbalanced, modulated, tempered by sublimation. Relations with external objects change into internal "narcissistic" relations, and these desexualized libidinal bonds are instrumental in molding aims and relations with external objects, so that these themselves are likely to become desexualized. Freud said that the shadow of the object falls on the ego. Equally, the shadow of the altered ego falls on objects, and object relations. Sublimation is a kind of reconciliation of the subject–object dichotomy – atonement for the polarization (the word atone derives from *at one)* and a narrowing of the gulf between object libido and narcissistic libido, between object world and self.
>
> (p. 20)

Thus, it is by means of sublimation that we enter object relations. Drives are no longer just seething, amorphous bodily states, but gradually become linked to experiences of objects that are internalized as structured fantasy that contains elements of both passion and actuality. Loewald (1988) elaborated:

> Sublimation then brings together what had become separate. It plays a decisive part in the "mastery of reality" (Hartmann, 1955) – a mastery conceived not as domination but as coming to terms – as it brings external and material reality within the compass of psychic reality, and psychic reality within the sweep of external reality. In its most developed form in creative work, it culminates in celebration. This "manic" element is not a denial, or not only that, but an affirmation of unity as well.
>
> (p. 22)

The mastery of reality that comes with sublimation is not simply externally directed adaptation but is also the maturing capacity to permit fantasy and reality to enter dynamic relation. Thus, we allow for our subjectivity to affect the world, but also for the world to affect ourselves. Through this process, we encounter the world "in itself," but we also discover ourselves in the world. And no longer opponents or strangers, we can enter active relations with reality while feeling joy rather than suspicion and dread. To again quote Loewald (1988):

> In genuine sublimation this alienating differentiation is being reversed in such a way that a fresh unit is created by an act of uniting. In this reversal – a restoration of unity – there comes into being a *differentiated unity* (a manifold) that captures separateness in the act of uniting, and unity in the act of separating.
>
> (p. 24)

This is another way of conceptualizing the crystallization of the transitional zone of experience that we will soon address in discussing Winnicott's work.

Loewald's model of sublimation describes a truly relational perspective on what was originally a purely individual, intrapsychic process. It is not a psychic mechanism, but rather a process that emerges and is articulated between people, in which the caretaker, being of an organizationally more advanced state, engages with the child, and by means of interaction and communication, co-creates a dialectic in which a new self-organization is elaborated and refined. Loewald argues that the child's passionate investment in the other, as well as internalization by means of fantasy (conscious and unconscious), permits the channeling of affect and desire into a new self-structure in which psychic reality and external reality are interpenetrated and enriched. We will again discuss Loewald's model of sublimation later in this book, in considering the themes of beauty and ugliness.

I will now turn to a detailed discussion of the developmental processes out of which aesthetic experience crystallizes. In doing so, I will rely on the work of Winnicott, who, as previously stated, conceptualized a developmental process quite compatible with the model of early psychic life put forward by Loewald. But for our purposes, there are two advantages to Winnicott's work: (1) he was always grounded in first-hand experience of the mother/child unit, and (2) he emphasized throughout his work the importance of creativity, aesthetic experience, and the cultural realm of human life – which he (unlike most analysts) saw as not external to the self or as a later acquisition, but as one of the core domains of self-experience.

> The mother's idiom of care and the infant's experience of the handling is one of the first if not the earliest human aesthetic. The uncanny pleasure of being held by a poem, a composition, a painting, or for that matter, any object, rests on these moments when the infant's internal world is partly given form by the mother since he cannot shape them or link them together without her coverage.
>
> (Bollas, 1987, p. 32)

At the heart of aesthetics is the sense of form that includes physical gesture, sensations, arrangements of color, sound, and physical space, and most important for our discussion, of bodily interaction, various modes of communication, and self-expression. Bollas (1987), in a valuable contribution, argued that it was the mother who gives form to the initially formless child, but I will show that it is the intertwined experience of the infant and mother's relating – their shared gestures, rhythms of response and counterresponse, and mutual mirroring – that determines the basis of form, and that, over time, is elaborated into aesthetic experience. So we will start with a brief discussion of the issue of form and its connection to infancy. I hope to show how the early emergence of psychological forms – from innate, potential (but still poorly differentiated), organizations of perceptions of self and other – provides the foundation for mature levels of aesthetic experience.

Winnicott conducted the most complex and credible theoretical description of aesthetic processes that occur in infancy. He described the normal transition from formlessness to integration that characterizes the child's passage from neonate to person. In fact, the emergence of the self, of the experience of *going on being*, is a developmental achievement that is always precarious and vulnerable to failure in attunement as well as impingement. The maturing self-experience of the infant must find a psychical bridge by which the disruptions in self-experience can be endured and by means of which the self can be made whole again. The gradual elaboration of form provides continuity and vitality in the face of impingement and failure. Winnicott (1971) wrote:

> There are long stretches of time in a normal infant's life in which a baby does not mind whether he is many bits or one whole being, or whether he lives in his mother's face or in his own body, provided that from time to time he comes together and feels something.
>
> (p. 150)

The infant's experience is initially relatively unintegrated; in other words, it does not have the degree of formal organization that characterizes maturity. This period can be described as *preaesthetic* because the child's experience of self and world has not yet developed structure or organization, let alone value or the quality of perfection. The development of the capacity for aesthetic experience depends on the gradual elaboration of the capacity to give form to thought, sensation, and affect. Winnicott talked about the importance of the *spontaneous gesture* that arises out of the true self, embodying the unique subjectivity of the infant. This spontaneous gesture is responded to and takes on aesthetic form as it is sculpted through interaction with the mother. It is this relationship that provides experiences of form and value. Winnicott (1971) wrote:

> The infant comes to the breast when excited, and ready to hallucinate something fit to be attacked. At that moment the actual nipple appears, and he can feel it was that nipple that he hallucinated. So, his ideas are enriched by actual details of sight, feel, smell, and next time this material is used in the hallucination. In this way he starts to build a capacity to conjure up what is available. The mother must go on giving the infant this type of experience.
>
> (pp. 152–153)

The transitional experience becomes structured according to instinctual desire intertwined with what is available. This occurs during experiences of pleasure and satisfaction. The reliable recurrence of these experiences (which are shared with the mother) leads to an increasing elaboration of formal qualities within the potential space between the infant's psyche and the object world. This space becomes the area of play – the matrix of aesthetic experience. Initially, playing involves the "marriage" of the infant's omnipotence of intrapsychic processes to the baby's engagement with the real.

"The thing about playing is always the precariousness of the interplay of the personal psychic reality and the experience of control of actual objects" (Winnicott, 1971, p. 47). Playing can only develop when mother and infant share the experience of security and reliability, so that the latter can experience the "capacity to conjure up what is actually available." "Baby and object are merged in with one another. Baby's view of the object is subjective, and the mother is oriented towards the making actual of what the baby is ready to find" (p. 47).

Although the baby hovers between omnipotence and recognition of the real, when all goes well, this transition is seamless and magical. But it would not occur without the attunement and responsiveness of the mother, whose ministrations engage, mold, and are molded by the baby's spontaneous gestures and desires. "It is in playing and only in playing that the individual child or adult is able to be creative and to use the whole personality, and it is only in being creative that the individual discovers the self" (1971, p. 54).

The development of play begins with the child's relating to objects as though they were omnipotently controlled, a part of psychic reality. The object is altered and manipulated according to fantasy and desire; thus, the object (still not experienced as separate) begins to mirror the self. The baby may at times play alone, but this is because the baby has had no reason yet to question the mother's availability. However, over time, the area of potential space begins to include the other, beginning with the recognition that the other can be gone and will return. According to Winnicott (1971):

> The next stage is being alone in the presence of someone. The child is now playing based on the assumption that the person who loves and who is therefore reliable is available and continues to be available when remembered after being forgotten. The person is felt to reflect what happened in the playing. The child is now getting ready for the next stage, which is to allow and to enjoy the overlap of two play areas. First, surely, it is the mother who plays with the baby, but she is rather careful to fit in with the baby's play activities. Sooner or later, however, she introduces her own playing, and she finds that babies vary according to their capacity to like or dislike the introduction of ideas that are not their own. Thus, the way is paved for a playing together in a relationship.
>
> (pp. 47–48)

At this point, the aesthetic of play begins to become intersubjective (meaning that there is mutual recognition and engagement). The child can accept, enjoy, and cherish the other, recognize the other's subjectivity, and engage in a dialogue that creates form in the shared psychical space, the potential space, between the two subjectivities. This is the source of dance, ritual, and other communal arts. The intense pleasure of play results from the idealized experience of responsiveness and attunement. The two people conjure up an elaborate structure of sound, affect, gesture, and meaning that is vitalizing and that can be repeated over and over, often increasingly elaborated and enriched through dialogue.

The aesthetic dimension of early experience (what the cultural anthropologist Dissanayake (1992) referred to as *protoaesthetic experience*) is imbued with the quality of the parent/infant interaction. In their recent summation of years of empirical reporting, Beebe and Lachmann (2002) elaborated on a model of self- and object representations that emphasized their relational nature:

> Representations are persistent, organized classifications of information about an expected interactive sequence. Basic to representation is the capacity to order and recognize patterns, to expect what is predictable and invariant, and to create categories of these invariants. The ability to categorize experiences provides the organizational framework for memory, language, and the symbolic function. These representations are encoded in a non-verbal, implicit mode of information, which may be motoric (procedural), imagistic, acoustic, or visceral. Implicit processing, such as motoric or imagistic schemas, may under certain circumstances be inaccessible to attention or language, but may nevertheless continue to operate and affect how we act and feel.
>
> (p. 149)

These implicit, procedural relational representations have form, sequence, rhythm, tone, and color. That is, they possess an aesthetic quality that is formally complex, diverse, and affectively rich. It is by means of elaboration of these representations that one's inner life, the experience of self and other, takes on a pervasive aesthetic structure. For example, the music in the vocalizations of mother and child, the sharing of warmth, the rhythmic interaction of mutual touching, the attunement of affect in facial interaction (especially lips and eyes) – these experiences singly and in concert become, over time, an ongoing, internal sensibility, which in the course of development is elaborated and extended into virtually every corner of the child's experience of the world. It becomes the archaic wellspring not only of meaning and fantasy, but also of quality, value, and beauty.

From the self psychological perspective that I am proposing, protoaesthetic experience is the experience of the formal perfection of archaic selfobject experience prior to the development of mature levels of other recognition and transience. In other words, it is an aspect of archaic idealization. Traditionally, idealization is viewed as a quality of our experience of an other. I believe that idealization does not occur only in relation to the object but is also present and elaborated within a process of interaction. The form(s) of the interpersonal transaction is or are invested with aesthetic value (see chapter four).

An area in which this protoaesthetic experience is most clearly realized is in the sense of fascination and engagement with the mother's face. Psychological researchers Beebe and Lachmann (2002) argued that "facial mirroring" between parent and infant is "one of the foundations of intimacy throughout life" (p. 98). They pointed out that there is an enormous degree of modulation and subtlety in facial interactions, which influence the internal representations of time, space, affect, and arousal. The experience of engagement with the parent's face is a primary source of affectively charged, formal organization in which space, rhythm, sound, color, and responsivity all come together into a powerful, engrossing, and recurring aesthetic experience.

In his discussion of Natkin's *Face Paintings*, art critic Peter Fuller (1988) described aesthetic form as an experience of interaction with the ideal, responsive face of the actual and/or fantasized mother:

> Here, one suspects, is the mother's face (and not only he [the subject]) would have liked to have stared: this is the ideal of that which he was denied, or which he perceived only in glimpses, a face suffused with subtle tenderness, apperceived more than perceived, a face whose features are, in one sense, bound, yet in another fluid and mobile, a face that can transform itself infinitely in response to our gaze, which certainly has a skin which separates it from us but which, in the next moment, can engulf and enfold us into itself.
>
> (p. 156)

I believe that the psychological foundation of the sense of beauty is often the archaic experience of the infant who is joyously caught up in interaction with the responsive mother's face. The combined qualities of both symmetry and unique expressiveness in the mother's face are progressively elaborated over the course of development with other experiences. However, the mother's face is not beauty (though she may indeed be beautiful); rather, it is our sense of the experience's perfection that is beauty. The maternal face is a content or occasion of the sense of beauty that may underlie many (perhaps most) mature experiences. The reciprocal nature of pleasurable, satisfying, and secure interactions is linked to all later experiences of beauty, and the search for and cultivation of beauty becomes a lifelong human motivation. From a self psychological perspective, the sense of beauty can be understood as a selfobject experience that optimally combines the experience of being in the presence of an idealized other and of having one's perfection mirrored.

The source of the feeling of beauty lies in the cumulative integration of experience. For example, although the unconscious source of the sense of beauty may lie in memories of the mother's face, it is the way in which new experiences both duplicate and elaborate on these archaic sources that determines what is considered beautiful.

However, Fuller (1988) points out that such memories/fantasies of the mother's face are composite, merged representations of the "mouth-hand, labyrinth-skin, unified situational experience" (see Spitz, 1985). Thus, the wellspring of aesthetic experience is not one specific aspect of relationship with the parent, but the whole, complex, and dynamic set of interactions in which aural tone, rhythm, temperature, touch, and gaze become associated with archaic selfobject experience that eventually functions to organize the infant's ongoing experience of self and self-in-relation-to-world.

Mother's beauty goes beyond her physical appearance. It includes all aspects of mother/child interaction, such as rhythm of breathing, shared warmth, quality of touch, and facial responsiveness. The "good feed" that Winnicott talks about is not just about appetite and holding; it is also an aesthetic experience. The child experiences a confluence of interactions that possess formal qualities, such as temporal sequencing, vocal pitch, visual balance, and vibrancy. In an encounter with the idealized object, the experience of the meeting is intensely affective, profoundly meaningful, and felt to be perfect. The "good feed" becomes the "ideal feed," in which all aspects of the experience are idealized.

The protoaesthetic form of the mother/infant interaction becomes the prereflexive template for an individual's formal experience of the world. At the heart of aesthetic experience is the infant's interaction (playing) with the mother's face and body (and her playing back) that symbolizes the primordial processes of multimodal communication, with its location in the earliest relationships. It consists largely of implicit knowledge and prereflective, internalized representations of self-in-relation. This knowledge is extended and elaborated to other aspects of one's lifeworld. The sense of quality of experience becomes a crucial dimension of living. The inchoate and inert reality is invested with feelings of form and value.

Thus, aesthetic experience is the residua of the experience and expectation that rhythm, fittedness, colors, and sound possess meaning and a transcendent sense of value, grace, and beauty. These formal aspects of vital attunement, a state of actual or fantasized perfection, become the foundation for aesthetic experience of the social and natural world. Hence, the world becomes infused with subjectivity; these representations are not limited to visual or otherwise descriptive memories, but are in fact complex, coordinated, and generalized cognitive/affective experiential states that are felt to capture idealized qualities of self and/or world.

Over time, the young child's sense of attunement and fittedness with the ideal and beautiful becomes riddled with impingement and failure. Breakdowns in empathy and experiences of unresponsiveness and/or distress disrupt the child's aesthetic experience and necessitate strategies to protect and repair the sense of self and world. This process includes the maintenance of a relationship with the beautiful/the ideal, along with a growing recognition of the hard realities of living. In fact, aesthetic experience can become a means to mitigate failure and loss, transcending grim reality through the transformation of the real into the beautiful. In this way, mature aesthetic experience comes to include the recognition and even celebration of the tragic as well as the sublime. It is that aspect of our experience in which the sense of quality, formal value, and beauty combines with the recognition of failure and mortality.

There is a mature level of awareness of the tragic nature of life and of one's own humanity, but this awareness is articulated in a form (visual, verbal, linguistic, musical) that is of such a refined quality that tragedy is given beautiful expression. Thus, tragic man transcends his or her vulnerability and mortality through aesthetic experience. It is pleasurable, vitalizing, and accompanied by a feeling of "fittedness" and positive self-experience. But, in addition, the individual encounters the reality of disjunction, transience, and even death. We are aided in living with the recognition of our vulnerability, our tragedies, and our mortality.

In mature aesthetic experience, there is recognition that all things are temporary, limited, and will ultimately fade and be lost. For mature adults, this can be said to be an ever-present aspect of all experience; however, in instances such as art appreciation, aesthetic experience achieves a heightened, even transcendent level. The sense of reality is organized according to processes of idealization amalgamated with the recognition of the other in the world. Otherness includes acceptance of the inevitability of failure of reality to meet the needs of the self in fundamental ways. In addressing the experiences of failure, loss, and death, great works of art often possess beauty even as they express terrible truths.

Another way to put it is that ideal aesthetic resonance between mother and child does not occur under normal conditions. For most of us, all that is needed to develop an adequate aesthetic sense is "good enough mothering," as described by Winnicott (1971). Given this, the child and mother engage in an adequate amount of aesthetically resonant interactions to facilitate the internalization of a good enough formal experience of self and self-in-world. Thus, most of us are not great artists, brilliant critics, or refined aestheticists, but most of us do experience an ongoing and consistent sense of our world as generally pleasing and potentially beautiful. In extreme instances of psychopathology, deprivation, or trauma, the aesthetic experience may remain undeveloped or suffer disruption, leading to acute or chronic perceptions of ugliness (see chapter seven).

But many artists, often quite talented ones, had deprived or traumatic childhoods; how is it that they still developed such a refined aesthetic sense? In these people, the need to idealize, to seek, and to perfect a formal organization of experience, even when unresponded to in childhood, may persist as a potentiality, especially for those with a talent around which intense gratification, feelings of efficacy, and social validation become possible. There are many accounts of deprived or traumatized persons who discover in art or other creative activity an opportunity to repair or compensate for self-deficits and to create a substitute for what was missed in the infantile tie. These acquired aesthetic relationships, while not possessing the transformative power of actual love relationships (many successful artists suffer greatly, despite the success of their work) nonetheless function psychologically in important ways. With sufficient talent and effort, the organizing impact of the experience or activity can be compelling, and at the very least, it helps compensate for self-deficits or vulnerabilities.

Of course, it is impossible to fully understand anything human outside its cultural context. The deprived or traumatized person has a wide range of resources that the culture makes available to assist with living and survival. A major psychological resource is to be found in art, creative opportunities, and the aesthetic attitude in general. These resources exist in all cultures and are part of humanity's aesthetic orientation toward the community and the world. An individual person, in seeking the means to repair, augment, and sustain self-experience and relatedness, may choose some form of aesthetic resource and make use of it psychologically and socially.

In fact, it is possible, given the exquisite refinement of many of the arts and the psychological meaning inherent in them, for even the most deprived and damaged person to wrest some benefit. In these cases, the aesthetic activity acts as a scaffold for a fragile, precarious self. Many artists are driven to engage in aesthetic relating and creativity because of the powerful defensive and compensatory function that art serves for them. They become addicted to the search for ideal aesthetic form and may even feel that their very existence is dependent on the successful creative process.

Aesthetic experience holds us in its embrace as we both create and discover the world. We are sustained psychologically by the formal perfection of the work, object, or experience. This perfection is not superficial. The real is both conjured up and confronted in an ideal form. It is beautiful while it is also terrible. Our fearful imaginings are reconciled with the dreadful truth – they are merged within the perfect image.

The fragments of our inner lives, of our self-experience, are gathered up, coordinated, and held together in and by the aesthetic experience. The terrors of unconscious fantasy and desire are made manifest to consciousness and enter communal life. Many of us, when we enter the Sistine Chapel – a crowd of vulnerable beings – find that we become like gods, our humanity both acknowledged and elevated. The most powerful and terrible fantasies of our culture (the creation and fall of man and his final judgment) are expressed through forms of such an ideal nature that we transcend our fragile humanity and mortality, and, strangely, we become hopeful.

Given the central role of idealization in aesthetic experience – and, as we will see, its primacy later in the creative process (chapter five) and in the sense of beauty (chapter six), the next chapter will examine the problem of idealization in some depth. To accomplish this, we will have to backtrack a bit, going over some of the same developmental ground from a different perspective. As we shall see, idealization is a fundamental component of the motivation for attachment, becoming elaborated throughout life as a key aspect of certain important types of relationships. Its most exquisite manifestation is found in aesthetic experience and in the creation and appreciation of art.

Chapter 4

Idealization and Aesthetic Experience

This chapter explores the place of idealization in human psychological life, in psychoanalytic treatment, and in aesthetic experience. Though traditionally viewed as a defense, a displacement, or a protection from one's own or the other's aggressive wishes, idealization is fundamental to our valuation of self, our relationships, and our experience of the world. Its source lies in the early affective connection between infant and caregiver, during which the communication of mutual idealization arises and is elaborated. It is the extension of idealization beyond the dyad that contributes to our feelings about life's value, being part of the foundation of self-esteem, love, and moral judgment. The most elaborated and refined embodiment of idealization is in our aesthetic sensibility, reflected in our creation and appreciation of art.

Idealization is the psychological investment of an object, event, or experience with a high degree of value. The thing is felt to be exceptional, the best of a group, perhaps even perfect. Even though idealization is recognized by most as a subjectively based judgment, the idealizer experiences it as a trait of the object, not as an illusion. Idealization is both a healthy developmental need, fueling the early parent/infant tie, and a psychological strategy that can function in both a defensive and compensatory manner. In maturity, idealization is a source of loving feelings and a general sense that life has value; it can also be used in a narrow sense to fend off aggressive fantasies or feelings of helplessness.

Psychoanalysis has traditionally viewed idealization as a misrepresentation or a pathological distortion of reality; in other words, idealization makes a person unable to judge something (or some person) for what it really is. This presupposes that there is an actual value that the world possesses apart from what we grant to it. Stephen Mitchell (2002) pointed out that this notion (supported by Freud) has its roots in naturalistic science and modernism. One of the assumptions of the present chapter is that we are the ones who grant value to what we experience and that idealization is a construction whose sources, determinants, and functions are both interpersonal and intrapsychic.

Another assumption here is that our idealization of the world is not necessarily good or bad, functional or dysfunctional, appropriate or inappropriate – however, it is essential. I will show that idealization is a motive for human attachment and

DOI: 10.4324/9781003532484-4

relatedness and that it is elaborated over time into other forms of healthy and pathological valuations.

Some readers may feel that I am "idealizing idealization," that I am going
light on the areas where idealization can be faulty or pathological, as in the over-
idealization seen in sects, in some religious or political ideologies, or (in the relational area) where people over-idealize others at the expense of their own welfare.
Admittedly, idealization can have various functions in psychopathology, even in
extreme pathology such as delusional disorders or narcissistic attachments, where
one murders or rejects another because life is felt to be unlivable without that person. However, to say that idealization may be enlisted to serve certain pathological
functions is not to say that pathology is inherent to it.

In this way, idealization might be seen as analogous to sexual desire. Although
sex is involved in many different forms of psychological conflict, I would not
claim that sex is in any way inherently pathological, although it can be involved
in pathology, as can numerous other normal psychological phenomena. Considering this, I will not deny that there are many forms of disorders in idealization, but
those are not my focus here. Rather, I want to emphasize the healthy elaboration of
idealization as an important component of human experience and its place in our
relationships and our aesthetic sense.

This chapter is, therefore, an exploration of the developmental line of idealization. In agreement with Tyson and Tyson (1990), I believe that the concept of
developmental lines is "a useful metaphor to convey the interwoven, overlapping,
branching network of simultaneously evolving psychic systems that constitute
developmental processes" (p. 36).

Inevitably, the discussion touches on other developmental areas, such as object
relations, the ego and superego, the self-structure, and affect; however, the focus
here will be on the source of idealization in early attachment and its elaboration
into mature forms of valuation. To examine these, I will start with a review of the
literature, leading up to recent proposals to view idealization as a normal mode of
relating to important others. Next, I will discuss the vicissitudes of idealization
in the early parent/infant interaction and its elaboration and extension over time.
I will then briefly discuss a case report in which the restoration of a patient's capacity to idealize led to a revitalization of adult development. I will close this chapter
with a discussion of the connection between idealization and aesthetic experience.

Freud (1914a, 1923) claimed that idealization was an unrealistic exaggeration
of the positive qualities of an object. The prototype of idealization is the act of falling in love, when the object and, by association, the self become elevated in value,
felt by the lover to be perfect and even sublime. The subject feels excitement, awe,
veneration, and enthrallment toward the idealized one. The self is experienced as
more powerful, cohesive, and continuous as it shares in the object's grandeur.

A key point in Freud's thinking is the notion of idealization as inappropriate to
the true nature of the object. Freud's working assumption was that there was a reality "out there" that possessed some inherent value. This approach was related to his
grounding in rationalism and scientism. Thus, the "exaggeration" of idealization

could only arise from non-normal psychology. Freud grounded idealization in narcissism, the early state in which the infant feels merged with the omnipotent mother. Over time, the child's growing recognition of powerlessness and vulnerability leads to the projection of omnipotent fantasies onto the parents, who then become objects not just of external support and protection (an *anaclitic* relationship), but, through internalization, they also serve as the energy reservoir for internal psychic structuralization.

In *On Narcissism: An Introduction* (1914a), Freud discussed the internal creation of the *ego ideal* as the repository of the original infantile narcissism. Identification with the ego ideal results in a sense of values, positive role modeling, ambitions, and aspirations. A later, more important elaboration of this idea was the concept of the superego. The superego, unlike the ego ideal, is charged with aggressive energy, and in addition to its ideal attributes, it is also the source of internalized authority, fear, and punishment. Eventually, psychoanalysts began to differentiate between the hostile superego and the loving ego ideal. (See Roy Schafer's *The Loving and Beloved Superego in Freud's Structural Theory* [1960] for an additional discussion of the libidinal components of superego functioning and the importance of the idealized parent in the healthy development of the mature superego. I will discuss Schafer in the final section of this chapter.)

In addition to their recognition that idealization plays an important role in the initial internalization and structuralization of the superego and ego ideal, classical analysts recognized that the idealization of external objects continues to be important throughout life. For example, adolescents have a developmentally appropriate need to idealize role models and mentors, who then become the sources of real-life choices and ambitions. But even in adulthood, the use of idealized relationships can function to support and guide people, granting to the external world some of the power and perfection of the archaic anaclitic relation with the parent. In addition to this normal role, idealization can also play a role in psychopathology, most commonly with the projection of superego fantasies, resulting in external objects that are not only aggrandized but charged with aggression, perhaps tormenting and restrictive.

Joseph Sandler (1987) argued that Freud never clearly distinguished between the superego and ego ideal in his writings. Sandler saw this as a problem, since the superego is essentially a prohibitory structure and ultimately hostile to the ego or self. He believed that there was a need to posit another internal structure, the *ideal self*, which exists as a representation within the mind. He wrote that the sources of the contents of the ideal self could be categorized as:

1. Identification with aspects of loved, admired, or feared objects.
2. Identification with the image of the "good" or "desirable" child as conveyed by the objects.
3. Identification with previous shapes of the individual's own self. By this is meant the construction of ideals based upon the wish to attain "ideal" states previously experienced or in fantasy

(p. 87).

Unlike the superego, which results from the internalization of representations loaded with the aggressive fantasies that characterize the dynamics of the Oedipus complex, the ideal self develops in interaction with the idealized parents, both real and fantastic. Sandler noted that these ideal images of self and object exist at all levels of consciousness, and thus can influence multiple aspects of psychological life. He argued that the function of the ideal self is not limited to self-esteem regulation, but, in a broader sense, it also bears on the well-being of the entire organization of self-images that populate the representational world. He wrote:

The establishment of an ideal self within the representational world of the child provides him with a potential source of well-being. Some of the libido attached to the objects can now be transferred to the ideal and the child becomes more independent of the love, praise, and encouragement of his objects, attempting to avoid the disappointment and frustration by living up to his ideal self.

(1987, p. 88)

Unlike the prohibitive and restrictive function of superego representations, the ideal self and ideal objects have a positive impact. They offer the child the opportunity to achieve increasing degrees of self-refinement and even perfection. The projection and internalization of these ideals create the feeling of the world's value and, by association, the self's worth.

Heinz Kohut (1971) placed idealization at the center of his model of the self. He argued that the internalization of selfobject experiences is essential to the structuralization of the self. Specifically, the functions of the idealized parent imago and the grandiose self are broken down and taken in as self-structure. The essence of any selfobject experience is idealization. Parent representations, self-representations, and the relationship with the twin-other are all idealized. Empathic failure creates crisis in idealization, the sustaining connection in which the individual feels known and valued is broken. Transmuting internalization converts the idealization embedded in the selfobject tie into a self-reflective sense of one's own worth.

Of course, other functions are internalized, but they are nothing compared to the experience of oneself as being of value. In normal instances, the capacity to idealize the other is also maintained. Even with the recognition of the other's subjectivity (warts and all), the capacity to value and love the other endures and colors the emotional tone of one's attitude toward the social world. In addition, the sustained idealization of twinship ties matures into an ongoing valuing of friendships and love relationships.

Joseph Lichtenberg (1989) took issue with Kohut's idealization model. He argued that the keys to the infant's experience do not lie in the preservation of idealization, grandiosity, omnipotence, or any version of these reified concepts. Rather, he noted:

The experience of the baby is best conveyed by visualizing a scene in which a smiling infant's whole body becomes taut and vibrant as his mother smiles back and exclaims, "Oh, what a beautiful smile!" A 10-month-old baby conveys the sense of sharing an intersubjective state and her mother who is being entertained by father making funny faces, looking at each other laughing, almost simultaneously pointing to "the clown," and looking at each other. Or the expansive joy of the child securely riding on his father's back or shoulders or being tossed in the air.

(p. 265)

Lichtenberg believed that, rather than abstract notions like idealization and grandiosity, it is these types of intensely affective, intersubjective, and complex relational experiences that are internalized as components of the child's representational world. It is the internalization and generalization of these types of relational model scenes that form the root of later behaviors. He concluded:

I regard the mirror, alter ego, and idealizing transferences, and the experiences beginning in infancy and continuing throughout life from which they are transformed, to be nuclear model scenes of the attachment and affiliative motivational system. When the appropriate lived experiences are present in infancy, the self will throughout life be motivated to repeat them, improve on them, and adapt new versions to new challenges and opportunities. When these experiences are inadequate at any time of life, the self will want to seek or restore them.

(1989, p. 266)

Lichtenberg emphasized the interactive and intersubjective experiences that lie at the core of idealization. As in the examples given in the preceding quotation, the child and parents are engaged in mutually enhancing interactions that lead to physical and psychological states of mutual appreciation and enjoyment. In fact, it is precisely these types of compelling and complex engagements in which the experience of idealization is stimulated, elaborated, and structuralized. The mother's statement about the child's "beautiful smile" and the child's nonverbal response – "such a beautiful mother" – repeated over and over, in an increasingly amplified and mutually confirming process of communication, lead to a sustained expectation of shared valuation. Idealization is a conceptualization of this process of mutually amplified idealization.

Others have argued to expand our view of idealization. These psychoanalysts view idealization as a broad, ongoing human need, more central to human psychological and relational life than was thought to be the case by earlier analysts. Let me briefly note the views of Person and Mitchell.

Ethel Person (1992) believes that idealization is a means by which people give meaning and value to their lives in an increasingly multicultural, nontraditional social world. She has described the phenomenon of "sequential idealization" (p. 94), which occurs throughout a person's life as various objects are invested with high value. The role of idealization in love, work, and self-experience becomes even more important when traditional values and prescribed social roles no longer hold such a compelling place in life. It is through idealization that we establish highly valued, psychologically meaningful relations to the object world, both internally and externally. In a shifting, decentered, nonauthoritarian world, the establishment and sustaining of ideals and relationships with ideal objects is essential to a healthy life and to optimal self-esteem.

Additionally, Stephen Mitchell (2002) argued that idealization is an essential human capacity that allows us to experience a powerful and passionate sense of the value of the self and of our loved ones. He disputed the notion that idealization is an undesirable distortion of reality, placing it squarely at the center of the human desire to give meaning and value to life. In his posthumous book *Can Love Last?* he argued that romance is a form of idealization that enhances intimacy, and rather than unrealistically distancing people from one another, it is romance that creates the most intense and therefore vulnerable potential for human connection. Mitchell refuted the idea that idealization was inevitably linked to archaic forms of self-aggrandizement arising out of infantile self-states of omnipotence. He viewed idealization as a lifelong phenomenon that has its source in the relational matrix:

> Grandiosity and idealization function as interactional modes, arising as learned patterns of integrating relationships, and maintained as the vehicle for intimate connections (real and imagined) with others.
>
> (p. 200)

Mitchell believed that analysts, in their emphasis on narcissism, have viewed only half of the puzzle in their discussion of idealization. The other half is relatedness and its incorporation of idealization as a learned mode of connection with others. (Unfortunately for our purposes here, Mitchell's discussion of idealization was brief and presented as part of his consideration of other subjects.)

Psychoanalysts have traditionally viewed idealization as a regressive or defensive psychological process. The assumption has been that idealization distorts and misrepresents reality, and therefore needs correction. An objective of analytic treatment is the reduction of idealization, as part of the eventual full recognition of true reality. However, analysts like Sandler and Person have argued that idealization is a normal and even desirable process that not only plays an important part not just in childhood, but also in mature forms of love, morality, and self-experience.

I believe that Lichtenberg and Mitchell offer the most significant revisions of the concept. Both these analysts argue that idealization is best understood as a mode of relatedness. Lichtenberg sees idealization as synonymous with the experience of attunement and fittedness that characterize the experience of the parent/infant dyad.

The intent of this chapter is to further expand on this new view of idealization. Backed by data from infant research, I will show that idealization plays a part in attachment and in the development of internal representations of self and other. Also discussed are the role of value affects in idealization, and I suggest ways in which idealization is elaborated into adult relationships and self-experience.

Idealization: A Developmental/Relational Model

Idealization begins in earliest infancy, but unlike Freud, who located its source in the infant's self-aggrandizement, I believe that idealization crystallizes within an intersubjective dialogue in which a shared sense of valuing results in the capacity to develop and sustain connection. There is a process of shared idealization in the normal and healthy mother/infant interaction: mutual pleasure, excitement, and joy at the sight of each other, the thrill of touching and vocalizing – this is the stuff of idealization. But this is no accident; I believe that the need to idealize is one of the driving forces in the motivation for attachment. Thus, idealization becomes psychologically structured; and as the tendency to idealize is extended beyond the early relational context, it becomes a source of motivation to seek out, create, and engage with objects and experiences that are highly valued and gratifying, such as in the production and/or enjoyment of art.

According to attachment theory, there is a biological need for the infant and the parent to get physically close to each other, thus facilitating essential caretaking behaviors. In this way, closeness increases the probability of survival for the dependent (and for the species in general). The quality of attachment is crucial, not only for physical survival, but also for psychological security and well-being and the general capacity to engage effectively in life and relationships.

I suggest that shared idealization of parent and infant, each for the other, as well as idealization of the relationship, is important to the strength of the desire for attachment, and to the quality of the experience of the other and of the relationship. The child does not seek out just anyone; he or she is drawn to and desires to get close to a special object that is felt to be ideal: "my beautiful, perfect, irreplaceable mother." And the same goes for the mother's need for the child, who, she feels, is "the best baby, my most beautiful little one."

In fact, this adds an important dimension to the phenomenon of bonding in which the mother begins to value the newborn. At the core of bonding is the idealization of the child by the mother and vice versa. The pleasurable experience of engrossment with the perfect object increases the parent's attunement to the infant, which results in greater emotional health as well as increased survival probability. The experience of the ideal relationship makes each partner want to protect, pursue, and cultivate the ideal tie. I believe that it is this biologically based drive to idealize that contributes to the motivation to form, maintain, and even intensify attachment. Therefore, in parent/infant interaction, the observer should see behaviors and communications that reflect idealization in action. (See Emde et al. [1987] for a discussion of "positive affect sharing" as the basis for the development of morality in young children.)

Confirmation of this can be found in recent infant research. In *The Interpersonal World of the Infant*, Daniel Stern (1985) demonstrates that it is the parent's attunement to the infant's changing affect states that contributes most to the development of self-experience. Stern stresses that it is not only just awareness and remediation of negative affects that are important, but also attunement to the sharing of positive affects. He highlights these *vitality affects* as reflecting the infant's spontaneous and lively response to experience. The parent's mirroring and resonance with these affects play a major part in the child's sense of aliveness and vitality.

In addition, Robert Emde (1992), in his research, discovered the central role of positive affects in development, and, like Stern, Emde emphasized the developmental importance of positive affect sharing and emotional availability in infancy. (See also Schore [2004, pp. 8–11] for a review of research concerning the crucial role of the sharing and amplification of positive affect states in early brain development.) Building on the ideas of both Emde and Stern regarding positive affect, I suggest that there is an aspect of affect sharing that has not yet been articulated: the dimension of *value*. These affects reflect the personal significance and value that certain experiences, objects, and people have to the infant. They can be expressed noisily – for example, pleasurable laughter at the unexpected entrance of a loved one – or quietly, such as in the gentle cooing of a mother while rocking her child, or in a woman stroking her lover's body.

Most important, these *value affects* are communicative – they convey how one feels about the other. Affects such as love have internal referents, but they are ineluctably tied to the other; "I love" is only half of the equation, while "I love you" is a value affect. A familiar value affect is what Kohut (1971) described as *the gleam in the mother's eye*. The best way to categorize this affect is that it communicates the parent's pleasure, joy, and pride at the sight of his or her child.

Within the relational matrix, these affects mutually communicate the experience of shared value. Admiration of the father, joy at the sight of the mother, pleasure about playing with a child, excitement about the proximity of a lover – all these communicate in a visceral and compelling way a sense of valuing and idealization.

Value affects can be observed in many interchanges between mother and child. Most models of affect view them as endogenously arising, semi-somatic eruptions of feeling states, although there may occasionally be an external stimulus. On the other hand, value affects are usually both elicited and reciprocated. Amplification and elaboration of the affective exchange result in a state of shared idealization for the dyad.

In examining the infant research studies of Stern (1985) and Beebe and Lachmann (2002), one finds interesting observational support for the notion that idealization arises and is elaborated in the dynamic interchange between parent and child. These researchers focus on the issue of affective attunement between mother and infant; however, I think it is also important to consider the nature of the affects being shared. In positive interactions, it is obvious that both members of the dyad are resonating with each other's value affects. That is, mother and child are communicating through affect the feeling of valuing each other. There is the gleam in the mother's eye, the smile on her face, the excitement in her tone of voice, all of which say, "I love you. You are special to me. You are the best little baby in the whole wide world." And then there is the child's simultaneous communication that "You are the best, most beautiful mother in the world."

These affects are mutually confirming responses between individuals who value each other. Repeated over time, such interactions increase idealization, which becomes structuralized and sustained in the relationship. As a result, the affective state of the other (for example, their valuing of the subject) becomes incorporated into the complementary value affect. My love for you increases in intensity as I accept your love for me. Each value affect adds to the other and vice versa.

To summarize this point of view, then, the infant is hardwired to seek out the special object and respond to it. The parent, in bonding, experiences the child as ideal and treats the child accordingly, as "my precious darling." The infant reciprocates in increasingly specific and idiosyncratic ways, and, over time, as recognition of the mother increases, the infant returns her joy. Each member of the couple stirs up in the other an exciting, confirming sense of shared idealization: "we are a wonderful couple." Value affects are consistently resonant and increasingly amplified. Thus, the child gradually develops internal representations of the ideal parent who will protect and mirror him or her – the ideal self that is important and worthy of self-care and autonomous efforts at survival. The mirrored idealization results in the child's experience of the self as ideal, thus leading him or her to feel more integrated and loved.

Over the course of development, idealization is both refined and reconciled with reality. Most important, the ability and willingness of the child to recognize the subjectivity (and real flaws) of the mother, while at the same time maintaining an idealized valuation of her, is an achievement that permits the maintenance of idealization in the face of impingements and failures. Of course, as Kohut showed, this maintenance of idealization can only occur when there is nontraumatic failure and gradual recognition of the mother or parent as a separate human being. This process is an enriching one for the child, provided that the real-world parent can be both known and idealized, allowing idealization to expand from fantasy and archaic wish fulfillment to a valuation that survives reality testing.

In addition, over developmental time, the urge to idealize is expanded and extended beyond the parent/infant dyad to other objects and experiences in the child's life. Winnicott's (1971) model of the transitional object is useful in understanding this process. The transitional object was primarily viewed as a psychological space between the subjective and objective realms. The object, both created and found, functions to facilitate the child's sense of the self as embedded, which, at least regarding the object, interpenetrates fantasy life. But the transitional object is also an object of value; it is the first idealized object other than the parent. It is the gradual recognition of the object's existence outside the omnipotence of the self – *and* the object's continued idealization by the child – that contribute to the extension of idealization beyond the dyad.

Furthermore, the developmental model of idealization has important implications for the view of idealization as a distortion or an unrealistic valuation of reality. As noted earlier, Mitchell (2002) disputed the idea that idealization was inevitably illusory. He argued that contemporary psychoanalysis, grounded as it is in a postmodern worldview, saw the human world as a construction in which meaning and value arise not out of inherent qualities of objects, but as modes of relatedness that crystallize in interaction with important others and are elaborated and expanded across the relational world. In this light, to say that idealization is illusory is perhaps an oxymoron; a negative judgment would therefore be implied about illusion as opposed to "reality."

However, I would argue that all value judgments are illusory because they are not qualities of reality, but rather statements about the worth of objects or events to human desire and need. On the other hand, paradoxically, idealization – rather than blocking recognition – seems to enhance perception and the cognitive and emotional significance of the object. For example, the gaze of the nursing child is not typically languid or dulled by the closeness of the ideal mother; in fact in most instances, one is struck by the child's alertness – the way in which he or she appears to search the mother's face, watching intently and appearing to be vividly aware of each expression, each line, and each passing mood on the mother's face. And in an adult's love, either for a child or for a lover, the idealization of the cherished other does not typically lead to lack of awareness; rather, there is an intensified recognition, an alertness to the internal and external state of the object, its mood, health, and gestures. Love is only blind in certain pathological relationships that require the denial of the other's subjectivity. But in normal love relations, love opens the eyes and other senses, reality becomes more vivid, and the true nature of the other (and self) is more apparent and meaningful.

Parent and child experience idealized attachment in terms of fantasy and desire (as all later idealizations are also experienced). The most important fantasies are derived from sexual and aggressive wishes. One of the least discussed aspects of Oedipal relating is the idealized nature of these fantasies. As part of their relationship, the child and parent experience wishes for sexual involvement that are elaborated in fantasy, consistent with the highly valued nature of the idealized attachment. Given this, the sexual and aggressive fantasies take on an idealized nature, with the mother's being experienced not simply as a person but as a queen, the father a king, and the child as usurper to the throne (the regal nature of the original oedipal triangle was not simply a dramatic conceit, but a reflection of archaic idealization). Thus, sexuality within the child's internal world is elaborated not only as physical desire, but also as representations of a wonderful, powerful, and exalted nature.

Of course, these fantasy wishes are not realizable within the context of family relationships and must be repressed. The typical resolution of the Oedipal complex involves the internalization of these sexual and aggressive fantasies that are exceedingly idealized. Optimally, under conditions of normal development, the child develops the capacity to sublimate these wishes through activities of a socially acceptable nature, such as in later adult love relations and in artistic activity.

In addition, parent/child relations are not limited to mutual affection and idealization; clearly the adult's capacity to discipline, modulate, contain, and channel the child's aggression and sexuality is an essential part of the parenting role. Roy Schafer (1960) argued the following:

> There is a necessity to examine the parent's superego to understand the child's. Much will depend on how right or conflict free the parent feels in his role of moral guide, how much he can genuinely and realistically act "in the divine conviction of doing the right thing. . . . Unconflicted gentleness is likely to go hand in hand with unconflicted firmness.
>
> (pp. 184–185)

Schafer believed that the optimal parent disciplines and even punishes the child without a loss in idealization. In fact, he argued that the child may experience some punishments as acts of love and protection from a powerful and protective parent. In other words, healthy idealization survives and may even be strengthened by the parent's efforts to instill in the child internal superego values that are important to self-regulation, adult relationships, and socialization. The essential thing is that the parent be able to communicate affection and admiration for the child, despite the need to set limits and even to punish. In this case, the reciprocal idealizing processes may be suspended but quickly restored, allowing for a sense of continuity in idealization and the maintenance of the fundamental integrity of the parent/child bond and sense of self (of child *and* parent).

However, in instances where the parent's own superego is impaired or untempered by healthy idealization, the parent/child interaction may be disrupted and the idealizing processes collapse. During acts of discipline, the parent may not only be uncertain of his or her own goodness, but also unable to sustain idealization of the child in the face of frustration and anger, or the parent may be unable to modulate aggression inherent in the moral structures that there is a wish to enforce. In these instances, the bond of idealization is broken and experienced as lost. All that remain are hostility and negative judgment. The child comes to feel shame, guilt, or hatred (or a combination of all three); the result is the classic Oedipal conflict and a severe superego.

I would add that in such cases, there is also a profound rupture in the relational tie with the parent. The child and parent are estranged by acts of discipline, rather than united, and the child's sense of human connection may be broadened to an internal sense of being unfit or unacceptable, due to wishes and needs that have been attacked and repudiated by the parent. Ultimately, the collapse of idealization processes, as they have been both internalized and enacted, leads to clinical syndromes of a narcissistic or neurotic nature.

What is the fate of idealization in these instances where the normal urge for enthrallment and wonder is met with indifference, rejection, or misattunement? I suggest three broad possible outcomes: (1) the suppression of idealization through affective deadening or withdrawal of attachment, (2) intensification of idealization of self or other in an effort to restore connection and heighten security and well-being, or (3) a combination of suppression and intensification in the splitting off of aspects of self and other that are idealized from those parts that are felt to be unwanted, deficient, or damaged (Kohut's [1971] vertical split).

As an illustration of the clinical implications of these three outcomes, as well as of other vicissitudes of idealization, I offer the following case report. This patient, Dave, suffered the death of his mother in adolescence. As a result, for many years, he lacked the ability and motivation to idealize either himself or others. He experienced all three outcomes of idealization. Prior to and in the early days of treatment, Dave's capacity to idealize was repressed, and his unconscious fantasies of special or powerful parents were inaccessible to his conscious life.

As treatment progressed, he experienced a renewed capacity to idealize, and engaged in a relationship with a charismatic man. The treatment most productively focused on the unsettling relationship with the aspects of self and other that had been depressed and depleted (associated with isolation and loss), and the self with other that became vitalizing and renewing, a door to a restored life.

Clinical Illustration

Dave was a thirty-two-year-old man who sought analytic treatment due to chronic depression, academic problems, and long-term concerns about his self-worth and ability to engage in satisfying relationships. He was a doctoral student in economics at a major university and was working on his dissertation. He felt locked in a silent struggle with his advisers. His presenting concern was that these men seemed to want to attack and eliminate any expression of his self in his work. He discussed at length how he was asked to cut this or that section of his thesis, parts that he invariably felt expressed his own unique view of the problem. He complained of feeling alone, not taken seriously; he did not seem to measure up. At the same time, he complained about his superiors, whom he felt were blind to or uncaring about his talent and insights. He lived in a frustrating, depleted world, in which his subjective life languished.

Dave had grown up in a middle-class, white family that was good enough for most of his childhood. The primary problem that he remembered was the absence of his father from the family, due (overtly) to work demands. It became clear that the father rarely tried to connect to his son, and even when around the house, he was preoccupied and unavailable. Dave's closest relationship was to his mother, and he frequently recalled the times when he would sit with her in the kitchen while she cooked. She was attentive, and he would be able to discuss with her his daily experiences, concerns, and joys. To the present time, Dave remained a motivated and resourceful cook.

When Dave was fourteen, his mother was diagnosed with a cancer that would kill her four years later. The family did not talk about the mother's illness or her impending death. The children took up the slack for the mother, with Dave becoming the family cook. Over time, the family's life began to contract around the mother's cancer, and Dave remembered spending more and more time at home, losing touch with friends, escaping only for short rides on his motorcycle.

A crucial memory was when, at the age of fifteen, as his mother's illness became apparent, he confronted his father, demanding that he tell him what was happening to her. "He just looked at me as if I was doing something wrong," Dave remembered. "Then he walked away. That was the closest we came to acknowledging what was happening . . . nothing."

In our early sessions, Dave and I spent a good deal of time exploring those years, as if it were necessary to give voice to what he had observed and how he had felt. Over time, his memories, restored and more vivid, became a major part of our sessions as he tried to reconstruct what had happened to his mother, his family, and himself.

The cancer took its time, and Dave's mother died in the summer of his eighteenth year. Soon after the funeral, he left for college far away. He returned home, where his father lived with Dave's two younger sisters, only for short stays, and they never talked about his mother's death again. From that point on, Dave pursued his academic career, eventually attending graduate school and entering a doctoral program at a major school of economics. His life was that of a solitary dreamer, his most positive activities being reading and indulging in big ideas that allowed him to give full rein to his creativity and excitement about life. But, in fact, his life tended to be dreary and lonely.

A year into his twice-weekly treatment, Dave began to talk about a charismatic political figure, Solodor, who visited his school. He was excited by this man's vision and ambition and began to talk about devoting his postgraduate work to economic policy development. When Solodor took over a major foundation, Dave, newly graduated, joined his administrative staff.

Dave's relationship with this idealized, bigger-than-life figure energized his life. He felt for the first time acknowledged and empowered. When he at times felt uncertain and doubtful about himself, he would have a supervision with his boss and returned to psychotherapy sessions feeling renewed and confident. During sessions, we would discuss these fluctuations in mood and self-experience. Without Solodor, Dave felt conflicted about his ambitions and doubted whether he measured up. He longed to be taken seriously but doubted that he deserved to be. Solodor seemed to magically restore Dave's sense of self. The attention from and dialogue with this ideal man had a compelling effect, Dave's career flourished, and socially, he began to reach out to people. He married and had a child.

I considered that the idealization of Solodor was a displacement from the transference, and that it functioned partially to defend against Dave's unconscious competitiveness and self-assertion; but, as I will discuss, the benefits for the treatment outweighed any difficulties that the idealization of Solodor may have caused. Dave, for the first time in many years, experienced himself as effective and valued. His mood improved; he engaged in life more vigorously.

In sessions, we explored the ways in which Solodor functioned for Dave. I interpreted the fluctuation of Dave's self-state and mood as they were tied to variations in his relationship with Solodor. We explored the sources of Dave's inhibitions in the blocked and withered relationship with his father. He acknowledged that he had suppressed his vitality and excitement as a teenager in the face of his mother's decline and the grim collapse of his family.

> Nothing about me was important. Mom was more and more in her room.
> I would sit with her, and we would talk. My father was working.
> And did you ever talk with her about how you felt?
> No . . . we never seemed to consider that.
> She was failing. You were losing her. Both your parents were collapsing for you. You must have been terrified, but there was no one to speak to about it.
> I just shut down, I guess. I would go riding, and in the summer go down to the water and watch the sunset.

The idealization of Solodor represented the renewal of hope for Dave. The engagement with this energetic man empowered him, and Solodor's vision stimulated Dave's vision. His ambition nurtured Dave's desire to succeed.

For most of the first years of their relationship, there was dissociation between the old, depressed Dave and the new, vital Dave. However, the relation between these two selves was a rich source of feeling and fantasy to explore in sessions. With Solodor, Dave imagined that the economy of the world could be transformed, and world hunger would end. He spoke of saving the planet from catastrophe (this was, in fact, the actual mission of the foundation), while acknowledging that he was trying to overcome his own losses and helplessness.

But as Solodor became increasingly distant due to his expanding commitments, and thus less available to Dave, Dave would begin to feel small and unimportant; rather than saving the planet, he worried that he would be unable to save his job. Nonetheless, the gradual loss of Solodor did not destroy Dave. He struggled but felt that he could function alone. Over the years, he had developed a reputation and network of professional relationships that provided real support. His sense of self and his social environment were now durable enough to sustain him and to keep him from falling back into depression.

During Dave's childhood, the absence of his father appeared to have been compensated for by a close, supportive tie to his mother. This worked fine until her illness and death during his adolescent years. Then he was left with nothing: an absent father and a radically devalued mother, dead from cancer. When he came to treatment, his long-term adaptation to this loss had been shaken by the pressures of graduate education. He was forced to engage actively with an older man and to begin to compete. This resulted in powerful conflicts and resurgent depression.

At the beginning of treatment, Dave suffered from the types of distortions in superego structuralization and function that Schafer (1960) noted. These conflicts were primarily stimulated by his relationships with mentors and authority figures. He was self-blaming, felt that he did not measure up (always to a vague but nevertheless severe standard), and would chronically inhibit desires and actions that expressed his ambitions. He had no ability to recognize loving feelings from superiors and seemed incapable of sustaining any level of idealization. As a result, his sense of self and his feelings for his work were depleted, at times becoming the source of tremendous anxiety.

Loewald (1960) noted that the analyst offers him- or herself as a new object to the patient, different from the archaic figures of the transference, and that the patient may – often for the first time – experience love in the form of the analyst's interest and concern. This sense of love (at first stimulating understandable anxiety) eventually becomes the occasion for the development of trust and the activation of both disintegrative and then integrative processes. I would argue that the resulting idealization of the analyst and the treatment reflect the activation of reparative efforts by the patient.

In the case of Dave, it would not have been surprising to see an idealizing transference develop in the treatment. In fact, it did develop, unconsciously, as if to protect and preserve the tie against Dave's own feared destructiveness and Oedipal rage. He maintained a motivated and effective therapeutic relationship with me, even while his most conscious and dynamic idealization flourished in his work with Solodor.

Dave's relationship with Solodor satisfied his need for an idealized tie. As Solodor's lieutenant, he felt valued and empowered. In his admiration of Solodor, he felt stimulated and supported by a powerful man. Solodor offered a real, idealized attachment in which dialogue and interchange played a central part. It was the value of their contacts, discussions, and shared adventures that mattered most to Dave. He cherished encouragement from Solodor and hung on every word of praise and admiration that the older man expressed about him. Of course, this engagement was highly charged with fantasy.

It was Dave's active engagement in the idealized relationship to Solodor that fueled his renewed ambitions and self-esteem. He gradually came to recognize his mentor's limitations, and our work, over time, began to center on the waning of his idealization, and then on the complete loss of Solodor when the latter took a position in another town. Dave's experience of abandonment by his mentor led to the emergence of memories of his father's chronic unavailability and later rejection. He struggled to maintain his self-experience and a new, more vitalized life. Fantasies of rejection and failure plagued him. He feared being laid off, and as a new director took over the agency, he watched from a distance as this person took charge. Eventually, Dave made an appointment with him to discuss his job, and the new boss "blew off" the appointment. Dave felt crushed, crying with rage as he cursed his own weakness. "Why do I always try to look up to these guys? I don't trust any of them" – by which I assumed he also meant me.

"You feel you can't trust us, but I think that, most painfully, you feel that it is, in fact, your fault, that there is something wrong with you."

Dave stopped crying and smiled slightly. "And some people say there is no discipline in therapy."

Dave experienced this interpretation as my reinstatement of the new, mature parental object that understood and valued him. This restored his motivation to idealize me and the treatment, mitigated the primitive torments of his resurgent superego, and helped to restore his capacity for reflection and self-integration. After we discussed the relation between his damaged self and the failure of these idealized men, he spoke of a new man he had met recently; this man had just left a high-powered job and might recommend Dave for his former position.

"You know," Dave said to me, "This guy is a good guy. He's not a narcissistic asshole. He might be someone I can admire and trust."

Idealization in Creativity and Aesthetic Experience

> An artwork that is loved reflects the ideals of the self and is loved for that very reason. The artwork contains projections of the self-ideals of the artist. The press to employ the imagination to overcome reality through the construction of the ideal also reflects a longing to make ideal a reality. The need to transcend reality through the creation of the ideal is neither a delusion nor a form of pathology. It is the creative realization of the wish to refashion a lesser reality into something more . . . an act of transcendence.
>
> (Kainer, 1999, pp. 19, 28)

The model of idealization that we have been discussing, while optimal, is not always the experience of actual parent/child couples. We know that failures in early parent/child relationships are common, especially in those persons who seek clinical help. What is the fate of idealization in instances where the normal urge for enthrallment and wonder is met with indifference, rejection, or malattunement?

We know that many artists, living and deceased, experienced significant failure in early relationships. Art and creativity become an attempt to articulate an idealized relationship with a part of reality (subjectively conceived) that functions to express unconscious wishes, as well as to restore self-experience and the powerful archaic experience of self-in-relation. In the next section, we consider how this need to idealize is elaborated through mature forms of aesthetic experience found in art creation and appreciation.

Aesthetic experience involves a phenomenon (object, event, sound, or other perception) or a set of phenomena (a group of objects, a sequence of events, a melody, or complex structure of perceptions) that are felt to possess perfection or ideal form. Aesthetic experience is fundamentally subjective, but also grounded in the objective qualities of the object. As Bernard Bosanquet (1915) stated: "The aesthetic attitude is an attitude in which we imaginatively contemplate an object, being able in that way to live in it, as an embodiment of our feeling" (pp. 29–30). In maturity, aesthetic experience recaptures the state of ideal attunement and mutual valuation that characterized our archaic tie to loved objects. It invariably includes affects such as joy, sadness, wonder, and awe. The quality of self-experience is also part of it; the person feels whole, vitalized, more positive, and closely engaged with the world.

Idealization is central to aesthetic experience. Freud, who viewed aesthetic experience as the sublimation of sexual desire into cultural objects and pursuits, argued that the desexualized cathexis resulted in an overestimation of the object, an idealization that contributed to the sense of the perfection of the artwork or other object of beauty. Melanie Klein and Hanna Segal felt that the ideal nature of aesthetic experience functioned to resolve the fragmentation of the paranoid-schizoid position, facilitating the psychological integration that characterizes the depressive position.

From a similar point of view, H. B. Lee (1948) argued that the idealized nature of aesthetic experience protects the individual from destructive internal fantasies, with the sensation of beauty quelling aggression and protecting the ideal other from our hostility. Self psychologists also link idealization and aesthetic experience, as artist and audience seek to recapture archaic states of merger with idealized selfobject experiences. In short, despite differing theoretical models, analysts have agreed that idealization plays an important role in aesthetic experience. This process is manifest in the sense of beauty.

As we will see in chapter six, the aesthetic experience of beauty duplicates the actual or longed-for perception of the ideal. The affective states associated with beauty – enthrallment, optimism, and vitality – are similar responses to what is felt in childhood when one is close to the ideal parent, or in adulthood when one is with one's lover. In the appreciation of beauty, the form of the beautiful thing is experienced as expressive of value affects. Its form resonates with the enjoyer's affective readiness and response. The joy and excitement that the enjoyer feels toward the beautiful thing is confirmed and mirrored by the object's beauty. The richer and complex the meanings of the object or piece of artwork, the more stimulating and elaborate the response and the more enduring the aesthetic experience.

I am sure we have all felt an immediate rush of aesthetic enjoyment at the first glimpse of a piece of art, only to find it fade rapidly when the depth of meaning fails to unfold beyond a superficial level. The responsiveness that we find in a great work of art involves a feeling of revelation that is renewed with each viewing. Our valuing of it is confirmed and even amplified as we discover hidden beauties and exciting formal possibilities. It is a dialogue with the concretized imagination of the artist in a dialectic with our own sensibility, but it is also a dialogue fueled by the excitement with and hunger for an ideal creation, the sense of life refined and elaborated into its most exquisite and complex formal arrangement.

The creation of art is one of the most dynamic and refined forms of sublimation. Through creative activities, the artist attempts to do three things simultaneously: (1) to produce an object that, through its symbolic content, allows for the expression of forbidden fantasies of a sexual and aggressive nature (we are familiar with this process as described in traditional psychoanalytic theory), (2) to express these wishes in an ideal form, which re-creates the original experience of the relationship with the original idealized objects of childhood, and (3) to externalize aspects of self-experience that, also possessing an idealized form, mirror the self's grandiosity, in a manner similar to that experienced in interaction with the parent.

It is the process of idealization that distinguishes artistic creativity from dreamwork and from other forms of sublimation. The creative process is a dialectic in which the artist engages a subjectively produced object and refines it. In other words, subjectivity is externalized and its expression perfected. More specifically, the creative process is an attempt to re-create the early experience of the ideal relationship (as it was or fantasy), but this time with an externalized part of the self. That part, concretized in the artwork, is refined and perfected as the artist seeks to create or restore a perfect state of resonance with an ideal other – the other being in this case, both object and self simultaneously – a "perfect match."

Part of the artist's aesthetic experience is value affect resonance, as the beauty/ perfection of the creation mirrors the emotional state of the artist, articulating the artist's self-experience in an ideal form. Value augmentation, which we discussed in relation to the parent/infant relationship, also characterizes the artist's engagement with the artwork. In other words, the artist, through skill and vision, refines the artwork, perfects the expression of his or her subjective experience, and the sense of the object's increasing quality results in an enhanced vitality for the artist, who becomes further engrossed in the work and further motivated to perfect it.

Creativity and aesthetic experience involve the idealization of self-experience as mirrored in the perfection of the object. Lee (1948) describes the state of being "love-worthy" as one stands before the beautiful object. We are close to the ideal one, but the other responds, it mirrors our own perfection, and the dialogue that follows results in a reciprocal value affect augmentation. We *love* – we accept love, and both object and self increase in value. The extent to which the appreciation of the beautiful object evokes actual or fantasized experiences of value resonance will determine the enhancement of self-experience. This accounts for the pronounced sense of inner vitality and goodness that we feel as we enjoy art or beautiful things in general.

In conclusion, we have seen that aesthetic experience involves the externalization of value affects. Specifically, it is the creation of or encounter with an object whose formal qualities elicit value affect resonance, or, more simply, *aesthetic resonance*. Aesthetic experience is most pronounced in relation to something that is felt to possess ideal form. By form, I do not mean simply shape or configuration, but rather all the inherent qualities of its being – that which makes it what it is, its essence.

We feel excited by the appearance of this ideal form. We are entranced, in awe, fascinated by its perfection, its balance, its rhythm, its color, shape, and texture. Its meanings are exquisite, complex, and resonant with our most unconscious knowledge. We are eager to engage it, to get close; we have an urge to make it part of us. The earliest, most archaic qualities of enthrallment with the essential other are evoked in aesthetic experience. In the best of cases, it is a feeling of relatedness without comparison, until we recognize its link to the stirring wonder of engagement with the first objects of childhood.

Chapter 5

The Creative Process

An area of human psychology where idealization and aesthetic experience combine is in the creative process, and most exquisitely in the creativity of the artist. Since Freud's (1908) early writings on the subject, the psychology of the artist has fascinated psychoanalysts. The analytic literature on art is large and varied, and each school of psychoanalytic thought has attempted to develop its own understanding of the artist and his or her work (for example, Ehrenzweig, 1967b; Freiberg, 1965; Freud, 1908, 1910, 1925a; Klein, 1929; Kris, 1952; Noy, 1979; Rank, 1932; Rose, 1992; Sachs, 1942; Segal, 1991; Stokes, 1963; Winnicott, 1971).

One crucial area of the psychology of the artist that has continually challenged and eluded analytic theorists is the psychodynamics of the creative process itself. In this regard, Freud (1925b) complained that, although his theory helped him understand the unconscious meanings of art, he despaired at unlocking the secrets of the creative act. In fact, subsequent analytic theories of creativity, while offering interesting observations, also failed to develop an adequate model of the psychological process that makes artistic creativity unique (Noy, 1979). In this chapter, I will show how contemporary psychoanalysis, and in particular self psychology, offer just such a model of the creative process.

I have developed the ideas presented in this chapter from several sources: First, my own experience as an artist, a vocation I pursued intensively for ten years and have continued to be involved with for the past twenty years; second, my knowledge of the experience of other artists, as patients and friends; third, a study of the writings of artists regarding their creativity; and fourth, a review of the psychoanalytic literature (particularly that of self psychology) on the creative process.

My definition of the creative process is the following: the psychological processes of the artist that result in the creation of new, aesthetically legitimate works of art. I will not discuss the concept of creativity as a general psychological principle or as an aspect of our relationship to the world. It is not that I do not consider creativity in the broad sense to be important, or as something unrelated to the issue at hand; rather, I wish to focus on the creation of artworks. Is there a fundamental process that can account for the artist's ability to produce the extraordinary and sublime creations that we call "fine" art? Throughout this chapter, I will use the painter as my prototype of the artist for purposes of discussion and illustration;

DOI: 10.4324/9781003532484-5

however, the perspective I take is, I believe, applicable to most forms of art, and perhaps to other forms of creative endeavors as well.

As we have seen, classical drive psychologists emphasized the dreamlike nature of art. Freud himself (1908, 1910, 1925a) pioneered the application of dream interpretation and genetic reconstruction to the analytic study of art and artists. His focus was on the interpretation of artistic symbols and the uncovering of unconscious meanings. In fact, the interpretation of the creative process as a type of dreamwork became the primary focus of psychoanalysis for many decades. Albert Rothenberg (1979) describes the limits of this approach:

> Although Freud was surely correct in suggesting that daydreaming or fantasy plays an important part in creation, he was incorrect in assuming that creative thinking consisted merely in disguising these fantasies in an acceptable form.
>
> (p. 130)[1]

Nonetheless, the notion that creativity has deep sources in unconscious processes is a profoundly important insight, which has direct implications for a self psychological model.

With the ascendance of ego psychology, the emphasis began to shift to creativity as an activity of the ego (Kris, 1952; Sachs, 1942). Nonetheless, although there was an increasing focus on the role of the ego in art, creativity continued to be linked directly to the dynamics of the primary process, albeit now altered by defense mechanisms. For example, Louis Freiberg, in his paper, "New Views of Art and the Creative Process in Psychoanalytical Ego Psychology" (1965), summarized this model:

> Creation may be characterized psychoanalytically as a process having two phases, inspiration and elaboration. In the first (inspiration), impulses from the Id attained a high degree of expression, but this occurs only under the close control of the ego that receives their powerful manifestations, shuts off the supply when it chooses, and turns them to its own uses. The artist builds upon the partial alteration of the fantasy, which has occurred unconsciously, but at least as significant a part of the work is conscious. The impulses, having achieved partial expression, are no longer in the position to exercise control, and the work of art may acquire greater independence from their demands, i.e., secondary autonomy. The elaborative phase of creation follows, and it is then that conscious relationships may be established. Connections are made, patterns are created, and communication is possible. A product emerges which is modified or even transformed into something, which can be received and understood by another person. The material is now subjected to an entirely different set of rules, the requirements of society, of communication, of art.
>
> (pp. 239–240)

According to ego psychologists such as Freiberg and Kris, the creative process involves a *regression in the service of the ego* (Kris, 1952) in which primitive drive impulses in the form of fantasies are consciously channeled and organized according to the rules of communication and art. To them, art is primarily a product of the secondary process acting upon primary process fantasies.

In an interesting variation of this model, Albert Rothenberg, in *The Emerging Goddess* (1979), viewed creativity as the mirror image of dreaming. Although appearing to have similar dynamics as primary process, the creative process begins and ends with consciousness and the drive for progressive discovery. Rather than channeling drive fantasies, the ego makes use of primary process thinking not as an end, but to an end. Thus, the creative ego moves freely between conscious and unconscious modes of thinking in pursuit of the exciting prospect of discovering something new and personally meaningful.

The work of the ego psychologists, most especially that of Kris, contributed an important facet to the psychoanalytic model of creativity – that is, that the creative process involves a dynamic interaction between conscious and unconscious thought processes, between fantasy and reality. This is crucial, given that successful art must "work" according to conditions and terms that are radically different from those of the unconscious or asleep. Art exists for the real world, and ego psychologists understood this.

At the same time, from the perspective of object relations theory, Melanie Klein viewed creativity as a function of the psychological dynamics of the depressive position. In a model later extended by Hanna Segal, the Kleinians viewed the search for order and beauty as an attempt to reconstitute and preserve an internal good-object world, threatened with permanent disintegration because of the aggressive forces of the paranoid-schizoid position. What is important for us to note in this approach is the notion that creativity and art have a dynamic, integrative function in which the artist works to achieve a form of self-experience by means of creative activity. In his monograph In *the Hidden Order of Art* (1967b), Anton Ehrenzweig presented a three-stage model of the creative process, using a Kleinian framework:

> The creative process can thus be divided into three stages: an initial ("schizoid") stage of projected fragmented parts of the self into the work; unacknowledged split-off elements will then easily appear accidental, fragmented, unwanted, and persecutory. The second ("manic") phase initiates unconscious scanning that integrates arts substructure, but may not necessarily heal the fragmentation of the surface gestalt. In this stage all accidents seem to come right; all fragmentation is resolved. In the third stage of re-introjection part of the work's hidden substructure is taken back into the artist's ego on a higher level. Because the undifferentiated substructure necessarily appears chaotic to conscious analysis, the third stage too is beset with often-severe anxiety. Who has not experienced the gray feeling of the "morning after" when having to face the work done the day before? Part of the creative capacity is the strength to resist an almost anal disgust that would make us sweep the whole mess into the waste-paper basket.
>
> (pp. 102–103)

In this model as described by Ehrenzweig, according to object relations theory, the dynamics of *projective identification* are applied to the creative process. I believe that the most relevant parts of the Kleinian model are: (1) the notion that aspects of self-experience become part of the artwork, and (2) a primary motive of creativity is reparation and the representation of the ideal. These points have direct relevance to self psychology, in that they presaged the notion of art as involving self-experience and the belief that the goal of creativity is the production of an experience of perfection and wholeness.

On the other hand, D. W. Winnicott (1971), starting from but diverting greatly from the Kleinian viewpoint, proposed a special relationship between the inner world of the artist and the object of his or her creation. For Winnicott, an artwork can be understood as a type of *transitional object*, which is experienced by the artist as a part of the self, an object invested with fantasy. Creativity arises from the fluid relationship between the fantasy life of the artist and the plastic nature of the potential artwork. Creativity occurs in the transitional or potential space between the artist's inner fantasies and the world of objects. This is where the capacity to play is important.

Once again, for Winnicott, consistent with classical tradition, unconscious processes (fantasizing, in this case) impact on the artist's relationship with the world, altering the formal structure of reality to express subjective processes. Unfortunately, despite the richness of Winnicott's model, he does not differentiate between the creativity of the artist and the everyday creative engagement of an individual with his or her world. Given this limitation – although Winnicott offers us a stimulating view of human psychology – we remain disappointed by his failure to speak to the special quality found in the creation of art.

In 1980, Gilbert Rose published the first edition of his monograph *The Power of Form* (all quotes will be from the expanded 1992 edition), in which he offered a model of creativity as a distinct psychological process. Most important, Rose's work is a transition from the ego psychological and object relations perspectives toward a self psychological model of the creative process. This is due to the emphasis that Rose places on the role of narcissism in creativity. He wrote:

> Unconscious remnants of the so-called omnipotent feelings of infancy can be seen to play an important role in the impulse to create. Whereas before, they were grandiose notions of the person the child thought him- or herself to be, they have become transformed into perfectionistic goals to which the child aspires to earn self-respect. The artist endows his or her work with this ego ideal of perfection.

(p. 63)

Echoing the Kleinian model, Rose believed that the artist is seeking to recover the experience of early states of perfection in which the child feels at one with an idealized, all-powerful mother. This is not to say that creativity implies psychopathology or developmental deficit. Rather, Rose (1992) believed that:

> Everyman has undergone separation from what was the primordial, unitary pre-self, each of us is, so to speak, bereft of our original partner. Our *imperfection*, then, is our *incompleteness,* and seeking self-completion is the route (back) to perfection.
>
> (p. 67)

Unlike Klein, Rose did not think that aggression played a central role in creativity. To him, the loss of perfection formed a part of individuation and the establishment of self-experience.

The artist, according to Rose, is someone who turns inward to reexperience the early state of fusion, and thus to "gain an increased apprehension of the nature of reality" (p. 69). This is not just a private fantasy, but also an exploration of primitive fusion states of maternal oneness and bisexuality through which the artist "reshapes reality in new forms" (p. 69). Rose stated: "The re-emergence from narcissistic fusion and the re-establishment of ego boundaries carry the possibility of altered, perhaps even innovative, arrangements of the building blocks of reality" (p. 70). Rose continued:

> By making the work serve as a proxy, the artist can vicariously relive the primitive experiments of testing reality by repeated fusions and separations. The artwork is built up and melted down again and again, repeating second-hand the building up and melting down of psychic structure in the emergence from narcissism. In this way the artist can give him- or herself up to the artwork, sometimes with the intensity of an addiction, and impress him- or herself upon it in repeated alternations of active mastery and passive surrender, of controlled fusion, letting go and reimposing control, to rediscover depths and limits. The artist resamples the earliest body imagery, perhaps in an unconscious fantasy of fusion and rebirth. The intensity of instinctual forces is reduced as self- and object representations become further refined, more internalization takes place, and, in the process, additional psychic structure is built from further drive neutralization. In other words, the artist searches for self-completion in the work; he or she has a private dialogue with a projected part of self-mirroring, smiling, frowning, approaching, and withdrawing, until the final completion and release.
>
> (p. 73)

Here Rose described how the artist engages in a dialectical process with the artwork, which is composed of the projected contents of the artist's psyche. In this way, the artist engages in an act of self-creation through structure building, both internal and external. Rose seemed to be describing a dialogue in which the artist creates the object as he creates his self. However, it is not just the artist's own self, but the universal human self-making process that is captured in the artwork.

> The major forms of creative imagination transcend the private and restructure reality itself. A work of art simplifies but also expands and deepens the view of the world and of the self. As the ego's coordinated activity recapitulates the past in the light of the present to prepare for the future, the artwork summarizes and magnifies the process by which each of us continually tests and master reality, relating inner and outer in repeated fusions and separations. The creative work that remains behind represents the cast of a mind "reborn" and objectified in the process of thought, feeling and action.
>
> (pp. 77–78)

While Rose was publishing his psychoanalytic aesthetics, Heinz Kohut (1971, 1977) was reworking the psychoanalytic theory of narcissism and elaborating it beyond the classical model that Rose relied on. It is certainly beyond the scope of this chapter to compare Kohut's self psychology and the classical understanding of narcissism. However, I suggest that it may be interesting to keep Rose's viewpoint in mind (based as it was on the metapsychological system, which Kohut initially worked with) as we look at the self psychological perspective.

Self psychology has tried to identify the special role of self-experience in the creative process. Kohut felt that the creative person possesses a more fluid self-structure, characterized by dynamically active, archaic modes of psychological organization. He believed that the artist's relationship to the world was narcissistically driven and that the boundaries between self and object were less rigid:

> In creative work narcissistic energies are employed which have been changed into a form to which I referred earlier as idealizing libido. The creative individual is less separated from his surroundings than the non-creative one; the "I–You" barrier is not as clearly defined. The creative individual is keenly aware of these aspects of his surroundings that are of significance to his work, and he invests them with narcissistic-idealizing libido.
>
> (1966, p. 112)

At the heart of creativity, Kohut believed, the artist seeks an experience of perfection, or rather the reexperiencing of a lost, ideal self-state:

> Creative artists may be attached to their work with the intensity of an addiction, and they try to control and shape it with forces and for purposes, which belong to the narcissistically experienced world. They are attempting to re-create a perfection that formerly was directly an attribute of their own.
>
> (1985, p. 115)

Kohut envisioned a form of psychological process that characterizes the internal psychological life of the artist. This process involves movement from states of self-cohesion to fragmentation and depletion, to periods during which the self can reinvest the work with renewed energy. He elaborated these ideas as follows:

> The psychic organization of some creative people is characterized by a fluidity of the basic narcissistic configurations, i.e., that periods of narcissistic equilibrium (stable self-esteem and securely idealized internal values; steady, persevering work characterized by attention to details) are followed by (precreative) periods of emptiness and restlessness (decathexis of values and low self-esteem; addictive perverse yearnings: no work), and that these, in turn, are followed by creative periods (the unattached narcissistic cathexis which had been withdrawn from the ideals and from the self are now employed in the service of the creative activity: original thought; intense passionate work). A phase of frantic creativity (original thought) is followed by a phase of quiet work (the original ideas of the preceding phase are checked, ordered and put into communicative form, e.g., written down), and that this phase of quiet work is in turn interrupted by a fallow period of precreative narcissistic tension, which ushers in a phase of renewed creativity, and so on.
>
> (1977, p. 815)

At the present time, we understand this process as an unfolding experience of self-cohesion, selfobject failure, restoration, and renewed self-experience. Kohut's model of creativity stresses the relationship between selfobject failure and restoration at the heart of the model; later, I will further develop this idea.

Charles Kligerman was the first to devote an entire paper to the development of a self psychology of creativity. Essentially in agreement with Kohut, Kligerman (1980) described four characteristics of creativity:

> An intrinsic joy in creating. This is perhaps the most important factor, but the one we know least about.
>
> The exhibitionistic, grandiose ecstasy of being regarded as the acme of beauty and perfection and the nearly insatiable need to repeat and confirm this feeling.
>
> The need to regain a lost paradise – the original bliss of perfection – to overcome the empty feeling of self-depletion and to recover self-esteem. In the metapsychology of the self, this would amount to healing the threatened fragmentation and restoring firm self-cohesion through a merger with the self-object – the work of art – and a bid for mirroring approval of the world.
>
> We can also add a fourth current to the creative drive – the need to regain perfection by merging with the ideals of the powerful selfobjects, first the parents, then later revered models that represent the highest standards of some great artistic tradition.
>
> (pp. 387–388)

Kligerman's paper opened the way to a new perspective on creativity, in which the artist actively seeks to bring about an experience to confirm and/or repair his or her sense of self. Rather than a regressive phenomenon, creativity is a complex, high-level psychological activity that attempts to create an experience in which a fragile or precarious self is linked to an ideal object, to idealized relationships, and to ideal values. As a result of the successful creative effort, the artist experiences him- or herself as renewed, confirmed, and vitalized. Kligerman's psychology of the artist is based on a model of developmental psychopathology; however, he suggests that the drive to create may occur without serious self pathology, and that it may be engaged in as an end.

In 1988, Carl Rotenberg sought to develop a more elaborate self psychological model of creativity. Rather than viewing art from a purely clinical perspective, Rotenberg recognized the "powerful organizing influence that visual arts have for the self" (p. 195). Focusing primarily on the viewer of art, he argued for the important role of creativity and art appreciation in normal human psychology. For example, consistent with Kohut's viewpoint that selfobjects play a role not just in an archaic developmental sense, but throughout life – even in the psychological lives of emotionally healthy adults – Rotenberg noted that both the artist and the viewer seek out the confirming, vitalizing, and transformative functions of the aesthetic selfobject experience. He believed that they do so not to cope with pathology, but rather as a healthy, affirmative, and vital experience in and of itself.

In addition, Rotenberg saw the selfobject function of art as embedded in a *shared experiential space* between the subjectivity of the viewer and the artist. The point at which these multiple subjectivities come together, of course, is the experience of the artwork itself. The question is in what sense the artwork contains or reflects the subjectivity of the artist. In this regard, Rotenberg (1988) had something quite interesting to say:

> [The artist] puts his own puzzles and mental ambiguities outside of himself and then reacts to them as if they were other than his. In a sense, once the artist begins a work, he surrenders to it as though the work were dominating him, demanding the solution of its own ambiguities, and requiring completion. The artist experiences the selfobject functioning of the artwork as alive, active, interpretive and eventually having transformational capabilities, to the extent that inner puzzles of the artist are worked out through this externalization.

(p. 209)

Thus, Rotenberg had begun to identify the internal dynamics of the creative process, though not in the traditional terms of intrapsychic life; rather, he was talking about the dialectical relationship between the artist and evolving artwork, in which aspects of the artist's subjectivity are externalized as artistic form.

Here I would like to elaborate on Rotenberg's model. Rather than seeing the artist as surrendering to the work, my view is that the artist engages in a process in which internal and externalized aspects of self-experience enter a dialectical relationship that transforms both. Successful creation is determined by the symbolic articulation of feeling, of the vital experience of living made manifest through the completed artwork.

Let me add that Suzanne Langer's (1953, 1957a, 1957b) aesthetic theory is highly compatible with principles of self psychology, particularly as it incorporates her view of art as the externalization of subjective experience. Examining Langer's theory allows us to see more clearly the unique nature of the aesthetic selfobject experience, wherein the artist is linked not to another object per se, but to externalized aspects of his or her own subjective life.

Creativity and Selfobject Experience

Art brings together the real and the perfect.

(Stokes, 1963, p. 26)

Although art is fundamentally everywhere and always the same, nevertheless, two main human inclinations appear in its many and varied expressions. One aims at the direct creation of universal beauty, the other at the aesthetic expression of oneself, in other words, of that which one thinks and experiences.

(Mondrian, 1937, p. 561)

In discussing the creative process, it is important to understand just how the artwork is linked to the artist's self-experience, both in process as well as in completed form. What I would like to explore is the following question: "If the artwork exists in a borderland or transitional area between the artist's inner world and reality, what is the nature of that relationship?" I think that part of the answer can be found in Langer's work on creativity and symbolism, in which she argues that art is a type of language of human experience, of human feeling.

Langer developed a remarkable and influential theory of art, in which a new view of symbolization explains the nature of artistic expression. She suggested that art symbolizes "forms of feeling," and that there is a parallel between different arts and common forms of human feeling. And for Langer, *feeling* means far more than emotion. In *Problems of Art* (1957), Langer argued that art is fundamentally different from discursive forms of symbolism, such as written language; rather, it is how artists capture and communicate lived experience. According to Langer (1957):

An artist expresses feeling, but not in the way a politician blows off steam or a baby laughs and cries. He formulates that elusive aspect of reality that is commonly taken to be amorphous and chaotic; that is, he objectifies the subjective realm. A work of art expresses a conception of life, emotion, and inward reality.

But it is neither a confessional, nor a frozen tantrum; it is a developed metaphor, a non-discursive symbol that articulates what is verbally ineffable – the logic of consciousness itself.

(p. 26)

What does it mean to express one's idea of some inward or "subjective" process? It means to make an outward image of this inward process for oneself and others to see; that is, to give the subjective events an objective symbol. It is an outward showing of inward nature, an objective presentation of subjective reality. It is the created image that has elements and patterns like the life of feeling. But this image, though it is a created apparition, a pure appearance, is objective; it seems to be charged with feeling because its form expresses the very nature of feeling. Therefore, it is an objectification of subjective life.

(p. 9)

Langer believed that the articulation of feeling is not the same as emotional expression, affective or cathartic, although these components of experience may be used as raw material for the creation of artistic form. She stated that in art, "we don't want self-expression" (1957b, p. 25). In artistic creation, the artist attempts to objectify by means of symbolization the fullness of lived experience – the feeling not simply of emotion or affect, but of life itself. The following quotation from the nonrepresentational artist Robert Motherwell expresses some of what Langer tried to say:

I never think of my paintings as "abstract," nor do those who live with them day by day. I happen to think primarily in paint – this is the nature of the painter – just as musicians think in music. And nothing can be more concrete to a man than his own felt thought, his own thought feeling. I feel most real to myself in the studio and resent any description of what transpires there as "abstract," something remote from reality.

(Motherwell as quoted by Protter, 1997, p. 256)

For Motherwell and Langer, then, the artist's self-experience is made real to him or her through the creative process, and this experience is only partly affective. Langer argued that those emotions that we commonly identify as anger, sadness, or joy are only the most obvious and socially delimited aspects of inner life. The life of feeling, the experience of self in the world, is, according to Langer, largely ineffable and incommunicable in logical forms, such as linguistic discourse (see also Kohut's [1977] description of the unknown self). However, self-experience can be contained and communicated through the formal relations of art – in space, movement, and/or the dynamic relations of interacting forms.

The artist, through the process of creation, seeks to find objective expression of the experience of living – in other words, his or her subjectivity. The artist attempts to articulate the fullness of self-experience. In this sense, self-experience is not found in a momentary experience of joy, or in grief or anger (although these affects may have their role). Art does not simply capture how we feel; it articulates whom each of us is: a living person with an inner life, having its own rhythms and connections, crises and breaks, complexity and richness. However, more important, art expresses subjectivity through formal perfection and the realization of ideal values. Kohut (1985) saw this as an important aspect of the creative process:

> A leading part of the psychological equipment of creative people has been shaped through the extensive elaboration of a transitional point in libido development: idealization.
>
> (p. 114)

Through art, what is temporary and ineffable is expressed in terms that are permanent (even eternal), vivid, and beautiful. What is common becomes sublime. What is incomplete becomes whole. This is crucial to our understanding of creativity: the artist does not simply express feeling; rather, feeling must be expressed in an ideal form. It is the accomplishment of an idealized formal organization that gives cohesion, vitality, and continuity to the aesthetic experience, and thus to the self-experience of the artist and, by extension, to the experience of his or her audience.

What we have been discussing regarding creativity was also described by Kohut in more general terms in his psychology of the self. For example, optimal self-experience for Kohut involved feelings of self-cohesion, self-continuity, and vitality; he did not intend to promote a bland uniformity, however, but rather a vital, dynamic inner world of feeling and fantasy. The sense of self-continuity is not just of ongoing sameness; it is the meaningful flow of lived experience. And vitality is not just excitement; it is the experience of being fully and clearly alive to oneself, to other people, and to the world. Kohut described how this cohesive, continuous, and vital experience of a person's self-originated and was then maintained and/or repaired through selfobject experiences.

Put simply, selfobject experience arises because of engagement with another, and the experience of that engagement results in a psychological state of greater self-cohesion, continuity, and/or vitality. In most instances, selfobject experience is associated with relationships with other people, but Kohut was also clear that other objects, institutions, and even ideas could serve the same function. However, the selfobject experience is most significantly a transcendent one. The self is felt to be grand, the other ideal, and the companionship of the twin sublime.

Aesthetic creativity is motivated by the desire to create selfobject experience through artistic activity. In this regard, artistic creation is a unique form of relatedness. The artist creates an object, which, as previously noted, is a formal embodiment of his or her deepest experience of being in the world. The artist's relationship to the art object is a relationship with his or her own subjectivity. Not only does the artist create an ideal object, mirroring the grandiosity of the artist's self-experience, but more important to our purposes, the artist seeks that perfection through a dialectical process between self-experience and the experience of the art object, which are both merged and separate, and in which split aspects of self-experience alternately blend and differentiate. For the artist, it is never enough to sit and enjoy the fruit of his or her labor; the artist is compelled again and again to re-create a process of self-experiencing in which he or she seeks an elusive yet powerful affective event. Once the object is finished, possessing a fully separate life, the artist must return to the process, the continuing search.

It is important to note that, although the artist seeks to express self-experience in ideal form through artwork, the idealization must authentically reflect the artist's inner life. Art often depicts forms of idealization that are shallow and inauthentic: pretty pictures that defend against or avoid the articulation of true experience. On the other hand, many great artists seek to portray in the ideal forms of their art the most ugly and grotesque aspects of their fantasy life. In these instances, the creative process involves the creation of a sublime and organized image, which paradoxically articulates the actual, threatened, or imagined fragmentation, distortion, or depletion of the artist's self-experience. This is like the empathic, healing resonance of the analyst, wherein the analyst mirrors the complex and often disturbed inner experience of the patient. The great work of art must be idealized but true, expressing in objective form the depth and breadth of the artist's inner life.

The source of the creative impulse is the fantasy life of the artist. These fantasies are not simply conscious, but include multiple levels of self-organization, incorporating the most hidden levels of the unconscious. On the other hand, unlike psychological fantasy, the evolving artwork quickly takes on its own nature, which compels the artist to work to express inner fantasy in external forms. Once a mark is put on the canvas or other raw material, inner fantasy changes in response to the external image; this is followed by further action to express fantasy through increasing manipulation of the image. At this point, the distinction between inner processes and outer art object breaks down; it is replaced by a dialectic in which inner and outer processes seek a state of conjunction. Creativity from this perspective is intersubjective, however paradoxically the two subjectivities exist as aspects of the same self-experience. One aspect is concrete and alterable as a medium and a formal structure, while the other is psychical, and both are immersed in a fantastic and imaginative dialogue with each other, out of which experience is increasingly articulated.

The creative process comprises three stages, described next. However, creativity is not a linear process, and the stages do not necessarily unfold in a neat progression. In fact, as an artist develops a work, the stages may recycle many times until it is completed. Nonetheless, I believe that the following stages generally fall into the sequence described, and that it is heuristically useful to delineate the components of the creative process in this way. By way of introduction, here is a quote from Mark Rothko regarding the earliest phase of a painting:

It begins as an unknown adventure in an unknown space. It is now of completion that in a flash of recognition they are seen to have the quantity and function, which was intended. Ideas and plans that existed in the mind at the start were simply the doorway through which one left the world in which they occurred.

(Rothko as quoted in Protter, 1997, p. 239)

The first phase is *Inspiration and Self-Crisis*. Following upon the desire to create an ideal image of inner life, the artist begins to put brush to canvas. During this phase, the artwork remains fragmentary and incomplete. The artist is in what Kris (1952) referred to as the *inspirational phase*, in which unconscious fantasy and primary process thinking predominate. Beginning a piece of work is experienced as an opportunity and a risk. This is when the artist works on the *primary structure* of the piece – that is, the archaic, fragmentary elements that compose the initial phase of the work's development. During this phase, the artist tries to access every aspect of conscious and unconscious subjectivity. Doubt, uncertainty, and confusion may trouble the artist, alternating with joy and exhilaration. Kohut (1976) describes the psychological state of the artist as follows:

During creative periods the self is at the mercy of powerful forces it cannot control. It feels itself hopelessly exposed to extreme mood swings, which range from severe precreative depression to dangerous hypomanic overstimulation.

(p. 818)

The artist assesses each mark on the canvas and responds with an internal adjustment of fantasy. As Kohut noted, he or she experiences this phase primarily in affective terms; anxiety is followed by pleasure and, hopefully, by self-confidence. In most cases, the experience of crisis occurs on an optimal level. Rather than being derailed or immobilized in the face of an aesthetic challenge, the artist experiences a heightening of attention, a sense of tension and discomfort, which leads to a deepening responsiveness to the work. In some cases, the artist's self-experience is often precarious and at times threatened by the fragmented and ill-defined nature of the artwork. The work during this phase involves the manipulation of the medium and image to sustain and formally articulate a particular self-state.

A picture is not thought out and settled beforehand. While it is being done it changes as one's thoughts change. And when it is finished, it still goes on changing, according to the state of mind of whoever is looking at it. A picture lives a life like a living creature, undergoing the changes imposed on us by our life from day to day. This is natural enough, as the picture lives only through the man who is looking at it.

(Picasso as quoted in Protter, 1997, p. 202)

This quotation captures the dialectic between the inner subjectivity of the artist and the external subjectivity of the artwork. Both seem to have a life of their own, but they are also profoundly and ineluctably linked. The artwork is like a growing and changing, living thing, but it lives only through the person who looks at it.

Moreover, the observer is also altered by the work. At a certain point in the creative process, the artist begins to experience a state of aesthetic resonance with his or her creation.

The second phase is *aesthetic resonance*. Once the artist begins to experience a growing conjunction of feeling and image, this phase can begin. Here the feeling that the artwork is beginning to take form excites the artist. There is an increased experience of self-cohesion, effectiveness, and vitality. The artist feels in tune with the artwork, and there is a sense of resonance in which the piece seems to become a perfect reflection of the artist's inner fantasy life. I use the term *aesthetic resonance* in this context to describe the intensification of feeling that the artist experiences, both internally and externally, due to the conjunction between self and work. This is the most affectively charged moment of the creative experience, in which the artist feels the presence of the sublime and feels confirmed in his or her grandiosity.

Jackson Pollock described how he unrolled his canvas onto the floor and used unconventional tools to experience himself as literally "in" the painting.

> When I am in my painting, I'm not aware of what I am doing. It is only after a sort of "getting acquainted" period that I see what I have been about. I have no fears about making changes, destroying the image, etc., because the painting has a life of its own. I try to let it come through. It is only when I lose contact with the painting that the result is a mess. Otherwise, there is pure harmony, an easy give and take, and the painting comes out well.
>
> (Pollock as quoted in Protter, 1997, p. 253)

In artistic creation, the object is never experienced as fully a part of the self, and the continuing recognition of the unique qualities of the artwork is essential. In other words, during the process of creating, the experience of merger with the artwork is necessary, but this means more than the object experienced as part of the self; equally as much, it means that the self is experienced as merged with the object. The artist feels that he or she *is* the artwork, and in fact, this is true; it is not an illusion. For an artwork to be truly a new creation, it must be structured by the artist's self-experience. It must exist both out in the world and psychologically within the artist.

However, the artist must remain aware of the reality and physical nature of the evolving artwork. In fact, his or her self-experience is powerfully linked to this other, which is both a part of the artist and profoundly and significantly separate. If this differentiation were to collapse, if a full experience of merger occurred and persisted, the creative process would cease, and the artist would be relegated to the status of a common dreamer.

From the first moment of creation, the artist engages in a dialectic with the selfobject/artwork; this dialectic is the engine of creativity. The artist extends his or her subjectivity outward and alters the medium. From this point on, something new exists, which has been created out of a merger between the self-experience of the artist and the world. The work in progress comes into being. The artist observes the work, appraises it, and a dialectic ensues between that which has been created and the subjectivity and judgment of the artist. The important thing is that the dialectic occurs between two realms of self-experience: the internal/subjective and the external/objective. Each influences the other (the imaginary and the manifest), and the result is further creation.

Thus, the artwork is increasingly elaborated toward a level of refinement. In other words, the artist finds in creativity an opportunity to give form to subjective experience in an increasingly articulate and formally refined manner. There is output, feedback, response/output, dialectic within the realm of the artist's subjectivity. The artist's measure and guide for this process is the delicate sense of resonance that he or she experiences with the developing artwork. Mondrian (1937) uses the term *intensification* to describe this process, in which the artist creates "successively profound planes." Through intensification, rather than simply repeating cultural or natural forms, the artist elaborates something truly new and emotionally stirring.

> The most important tool the artist fashions through constant practice is faith in his ability to produce miracles when they are needed.
>
> (Rothko as quoted in Protter, 1997, p. 239)

The experience of aesthetic resonance, while essential to the elaborative phase of the creativity previously discussed, is not the only important factor in successful creativity. Inevitably, there is an experience of failure in resonance, of selfobject failure. Kohut (1985) put it this way: "Creative people tend to alternate during periods of productivity between phases when they think extremely highly of their work and phases when they are convinced that it has no value" (p. 114). It is the artist's response to this sense of failure that further intensifies the creative effort, compelling him or her to elaborate ever more radical formal organizations. In most cases, this stage begins when the artist's feeling of certainty gives way to sober reflection and reassessment. The artist may come to doubt the work's perfection, and it no longer seems to perfectly reflect the feelings that the artist wishes to capture. (Ehrenzweig [1967a] describes this experience as the "grayness of the morning after" when the artist must confront the flawed reality of what was felt to be sublime just the day before.)

This phase is characterized by a sense of failure, in which the resonance breaks down and the artist must use all his or her skill and resourcefulness to reassess the image and rework it to restore the aesthetic tie. The selfobject experience is restored when the work is once again felt to capture the ideal and grandiose components of fantasy. As in the first phase, the experience of selfobject failure during this phase should remain within certain limits of intensity. As with the optimal frustrations described by Kohut, the selfobject failure experienced at this point in the creative process should not be traumatic in most cases. There may be some heightened anxiety and even depression, but as with optimal frustration, the artist should be able to rally and address the aesthetic problems that he or she is faced with. The artist attempts to restore the selfobject tie not through the accrual of self-structure, but through alteration of the artwork.

During this phase, preconscious and conscious processes play a part in organizing and clarifying the elements in the artwork, as the artist attempts to bring it into harmony with self-experience. I call this activity *working on the secondary structure* of the artwork, in that, rather than relying on inspiration and primary process thinking, the artist approaches the work more synthetically, with an eye toward the total organization of the work and the relationships among its formal components. This is like Kris's (1952) notion of the elaboration phase. However, while Kris stressed the use of secondary process thinking during this period, I believe that the artist must continue to respond to the work on multiple psychic levels. Like what occurs in the case of *transmuting internalization,* the response to a break in the selfobject tie is the accrual of structure; here the artist refines and strengthens the artwork's formal organization to make it more resonant with fantasy. At the same time, the artist's inner experience changes in response to the artwork as well. The result is the restoration of the selfobject tie between artist and artwork.

> When you begin a picture, you often make some pretty discoveries. You must be on your guard against these. Destroy the thing, do it over several times. In each distorting of a beautiful discovery, the artist does not really suppress it, but rather transforms it, condenses it, makes it more substantial. What comes in the end is the result of discarded finds. Otherwise, you become your own connoisseur. I sell myself nothing.
>
> (Picasso as quoted in Protter, 1997, p. 203)

Kohut (1966) compared creativity to addiction, and in a sense, this is apt. I would, however, modify this comparison somewhat by saying that the artist's addiction is to the process of selfobject failure and restoration. The artist is driven to seek out again and again the experience of heightened, lost, and regained self-experience. Central to the addictive nature of this process is the artist's experience of doing it him- or herself; this may be what Rank (1932) referred to as the artist's quest for self-begetting and self-rebirth. As Stolorow and Atwood (1993) stated in their analysis of Rank: "The artist's own self-created differentiated self is his first creative work, and throughout his life remains fundamentally his chief work" (p. 45). (Rank argued that the artist seeks to transcend reality and mortality.)

Albert Pinkham Ryder expressed this motivation for his work:

> When I stood before my easel with its square of stretched canvas, I realized that I had in my possession the wherewith to create a masterpiece that would live throughout the coming ages. I at once proceeded to study the works of the great to discover how best to achieve immortality with a square of canvas and a box of colors.
>
> (Ryder as quoted in Protter, 1997, p. 150)

I would argue that the artist repeatedly seeks to transcend the experience of selfobject failure, and that, by means of creative effort, the artist experiences his or her own power in bringing about the restoration of self-experience. In most cases, the aesthetic resonance with the completed artwork will fade, and although the work may always hold some positive meaning for the artist, the search for transcendence and renewal must be re-engaged.

It is this complex dialectic between artist and artwork that drives the artist to seek increasingly refined and sophisticated, formal means to express subjectivity. The artist who engages in this process is driven to repeatedly seek out the wonder of the aesthetic selfobject experience; therefore, he or she must continually work to articulate and perfect a formally organized and ideal representation of lived experience. The skillful and talented artist can feel the potential for this experience in artistic activity; and this is perhaps the source of the feeling of joy that Kligerman described in an earlier quotation. In a sense, the successful artist is possessed, even driven, to seek restoration of this experience, until he or she reaches a point at which there is a conjunction between inner experience and outer image.

Matisse stated this quite simply when he was asked how he knew that a piece was finished:

[I know] when it expresses my emotion as completely as possible. It is at that point when the sense of resonance is enduring and durable. The artist assessing the work does not experience anxiety, depression or fragmentation, but sureness and calm. The artist no longer feels compelled to change the work because it feels balanced and complete. The work is done. It exists as a thing.

(Matisse as quoted in Barr, 1951, p. 286)

And Mark Rothko described the artist's relationship to the completed work:

Pictures must be miraculous: the instant one is completed, the intimacy between the creation and the creator is ended. He is an outsider. The picture must be for him, as for anyone experiencing it later, a revelation, an unexpected and unprecedented resolution of an eternally familiar need.

(as quoted in Protter, 1997, p. 239)

In summary, I have in this section made the following points about the creative process:

- Art is the externalization of self-experience. It is what Langer calls *objectification of subjectivity*, or, more simply, the symbolization of *feeling*.
- The motivation to create is characterized by the desire for idealization of self-experience.
- As a result, during the creative process, the artist engages in a dialectic with his or her own idealized subjectivity in the objectified form of the developing artwork.

- The feeling of harmony (aesthetic resonance) that the artist experiences with the work in progress is a form of selfobject experience. The artist longs to establish this form of selfobject tie.
- However, while creating a particular artwork, the artist inevitably experiences the selfobject tie as elusive, precarious, or broken. The artist is repeatedly disillusioned as to the work's perfection.
- The artist seeks to strengthen or restore the selfobject tie through its gradual refinement. By this means, the artwork is moved closer to a formal ideal.
- The repeated experience of self-restoration and creation (and re-creation) of a truly ideal object out of oneself explains the addictionlike quality of creativity. Through creation, the artist triumphs over the ineluctability of selfobject failure and the vulnerability of self-experience.
- In the end, the artist's fantasy is that he or she will surmount personal mortality through art.

In the next section, I will present the treatment of a young artist and discuss some of the typical disturbances that can occur in the creative process. This case was chosen for the way in which the patient experienced transitory problems during each phase of creativity. Childhood sources of his self-vulnerability will be touched upon.

Clinical Illustration

Several years ago, I saw a young painter, Rob, in psychoanalytic psychotherapy. He had been working as an artist for some time and was on the verge of receiving much-deserved recognition. Initially, he had come to treatment after the breakup of a six-year relationship with a woman upon whom he was extremely dependent. He continued to be despondent for several months, but his motivation to paint remained high. In fact, he seemed to use his artwork to express his despair and loneliness. For a time, his work became dominated by varieties of grays and dark earth tones.

About six months into the treatment, Rob received an invitation to hold a one-man show at a downtown gallery. Although he had exhibited in group shows frequently, this was his first solo exhibition. He was elated. Having viewed himself as a struggling junior artist for some years, he saw this as his chance to make it big. He worked at preparing the show for several weeks, day and night, and when the show opened, the reviews were generally positive, even laudatory in some cases. However, Rob was almost literally paralyzed by self-doubt.

It is not uncommon for artists to experience this type of response to success. The state of vulnerability experienced during exhibitions, especially early in the artist's career, can lead to difficult-to-manage excitement and profound disappointment. However, for the purpose of this chapter, what interested me about Rob's reaction was the subsequent impact of his success on his creative process. In general, until this point, he had been free of work inhibitions or other conflicts around creativity.

He had produced a large amount of work with a reasonable amount of effort; but several weeks after his solo show, when he had begun to work on a series of dramatic and very ambitious pastels, he started to come to his psychotherapy sessions in a state of panic.

"I can't seem to get a handle on things," Rob complained. "I know basically what I want to do. I can almost *taste* it. I feel like I'm on the verge of something different, but it's all just a mess. I can't seem to pull it together. I just sit and stare at these blotches of color. It's as if all the talent is gone, just gone. I don't know what to do."

As we talked, it became clear that Rob's expectations of himself had become extremely high, and his need to prove his talent led to anxiety as he struggled with the early inchoate phase of his new productions. "Before, I used to be able to just go with it," he explained. "I'd sit back and say to myself, *stay calm, just wait a bit and it will come together.* But now, it's like the stakes are so high; I feel like so much is expected of me. I'm no longer just a struggling artist, but also feel that I haven't really made it. It could all fall apart so easily."

In fact, Rob had begun to feel that his career *had* fallen apart. As he struggled with each new drawing, he was unable to sustain his self-confidence or his focus during the confusing early phases of his creative process. His need for a sense of confirmation, which resulted from his sense of vulnerability to selfobject failure, transformed the challenge of each new drawing into evidence of his fundamental, and now undeniable, failure.

Rob was gradually able to recover his self-confidence, but his sense of vulnerability and precarious self-cohesion remained a problem throughout all phases of his work. For example, when he was finally able to move beyond the early phase of a work in progress and had developed a sense of rhythm and renewed excitement, he began to wake up in the morning in a state of dread. A particular piece of work, one that had so inspired him the day before, would now appear to be a "train wreck." That image perfectly captured his self-experience: "It's like I'm just cruising along, and everything is coming together, and then the first bump in the road, wham, out of control, and then crash! I feel like it's all gone and it's never coming back again."

Most artists, even when a work seems to be falling into place, reach a point where the sense of harmony and perfect fit is disrupted. The challenge is then to recover and solve the problem through a reassessment, and oftentimes a reworking, of the piece. The capacity to sustain enough self-experience to repair the sense of disruption is crucial. Even the worst "train wreck" may be a necessary stage leading to creative advancement. Rob's sense of self was so tenuous that the selfobject failure typical of this phase resulted in collapse and a sense of fragmentation.

A crucial part of Rob's recovery from artistic success was his experience of me as both consistent and confident in him. He saw me as "having my feet on the ground," and explained that when he was in session, he was able to "retool" himself and get a handle on his work. Eventually, he was able to struggle through and create some interesting work, but even then, he remained afraid to show completed pieces even to close friends. It was as if he saw every flaw and imperfection. He felt ashamed of his self-doubts. He remembered that when he was a child, his father had criticized him for acting like a "big shot."

"That's it, that's it!" Rob seemed almost elated.

> I feel like I've been paying the price for being a *big shot*. I never felt with my dad that it was all right to be a big shot. I don't even think I was, but he would always criticize me as if I was doing something wrong. The show that was my undoing. I was acting like a big shot when I am just a kid trying to please my dad. But I never could. I don't remember any time when I really felt like I did anything good. One time, when I was in high school, I had just won a big race, and I was all excited. He comes up to me and all he says (in front of my friends) is, "*Put your sweater on.*" I was pissed off. Suddenly, my excitement was gone – all I felt was anger.

Rob's long-anticipated success was followed by a period of self-crisis, during which his experience of shame and selfobject failure impacted on every phase of his creative work. The precariousness of his self-experience resulted in an increased need for mirroring, as well as his craving for the presence of an idealized, reassuring figure. As a result, he was unable to sustain confidence in the face of routine experiences of doubt and confusion that had always been a part of his creative process.

Over time, Rob struggled with each instance of uncertainty as if it represented his ultimate unworthiness. His fragile capacity to sustain or recover self-experience led to extreme states of self-crisis, rather than to a sense of challenge and opportunity. Gradually, through his growing awareness of the sources of his vulnerability in his relationship with his father, and by virtue of his experience of my availability and confidence in him, he was able to come to terms with the meaning of his success and to move on with his career.

Here I would like to add a few words regarding the creative artist's challenge to conventions – something that is frequently seen, at least in modern Western art. It would seem from a cursory look at the lives of many modern artists that they exhibit what appears to be a driving need to challenge and provoke. Creativity has become synonymous with the different and the new, and the image of the artist as an outsider and rebel has become a common cultural stereotype. At least superficially, artists are more interested in disruption and conflict than in cohesion, continuity, and vitality.

If this view of the artist is valid, how can it be reconciled with the notion of the artist's search for selfobject experience? Rotenberg (1992) addressed this question in claiming that the creative artist is fundamentally driven by a desire to challenge conventional forms of thinking. He developed a set of terms for this trait – *optimal, operative,* and *perversity* – with the following definitions:

> *Perversity* is the expression of the artist who consistently, and with technical means, contradicts a previously held principle of organization [p. 171]. . . . The

introduction of elements that are original or new results in perception whose implications have not yet been assimilated into the order-making structures of the self [p. 172]. . . . *Optimal* refers to the quality and degree of unusualness that also achieves integration with the rest of the pictorial field of which it is a part [p. 177]. . . . *Operative* refers to the enacted quality of the artwork and to the technical skill that makes it possible. [p. 179]

Rotenberg believed that artists are driven to produce work with an unusual organization of meaning and form, which also achieves new levels of aesthetic integration. Once again, I believe that the desire to challenge convention is principally based on the artist's desire to truly express self-experience. The ability of conventional or traditional forms of art to express the subjective experience of artists over time is limited. The artist seeks to challenge conventions in the process of discovering new, more powerful means to express self-experience. It would be useless for an artist to adopt another artist's style unless he or she believed that use of that style or technique could convey his or her own experience. In addition, in recalling the artist's search for selfobject experience, we might view the revolutionary artist's underlying desire as the wish to be responded to as a unique and special person.

The bottom line is that the challenge of modern art is the desire to more completely, accurately, and vividly convey the experience of living in the modern world. Jackson Pollock said that new times require new art forms, and this is true; but in addition, new people who require new forms of self-expression populate new times. The old forms rarely suffice, unless the artist can find new potentials or new facets in them that can be made relevant to current experience.

For example, one of the most influential revolutionary movements in the history of modern art was abstract expressionism. These artists were viewed by many of the time as wild radicals seeking only to undermine and damage artistic traditions. Jackson Pollock, a prominent abstract expressionist, was once referred to in print as "Jack the Dripper," due to his use of dripped or poured paint. It is certainly true that these artists sought to create a new, radical vision of art. However, when one looks closely at their statements and writings, it appears that their primary motive was not only to disrupt, but also to create new ways of expressing their self-experiences. Not content with conflict, virtually all of them longed for professional and social recognition of their work.

In fact, it is interesting to note that for many of these artists, the failure to receive the requisite mirroring in response to their work, or the anticipation of selfobject failure, led to disastrous and even suicidal results. Once again, behind the revolutionary movement of abstract expressionism was a desire to express subjectivity more accurately, vividly, and powerfully. For these artists, the experience of the modern self required a new, more dramatic form of expression. Through the development of new approaches to technique and form, each abstract expressionist sought to create a sense of aesthetic resonance that would capture his or her sense of lived experience as accurately as possible.

Such a process is challenging and often stressful. Carol Press, in *The Dancing Self* (2002), emphasized the creative artist's need for strength, both from within and outside the self:

> The artist must possess enough psychological strength to destabilize, without overwhelming fragmentation, to venture into new realms and discoveries. The need for functioning selfobjects is paramount. The ability to find sustaining selfobject experiences is a sign of health. Artists must have the capacity to shore up their selves and find fulfillment from their selfobject needs as they progress through the significant and challenging phases of creativity.
>
> (p. 100)

Note

1 See also Rose (1992, p. 8).

Chapter 6

The Sense of Beauty

At several points in previous chapters, we have touched on the issue of beauty in aesthetic experience, idealization, and creativity, but we have not yet considered this important topic in any depth. This chapter will discuss the history of the psychoanalytic understanding of beauty and offer an integrative model that reflects not only much traditional thinking, but also the contemporary approach to aesthetics that is the major focus of this book.

Beauty has been a concern of Western thinkers for the past three thousand years. Plato argued that beautiful form was an inherent property of certain things. What people felt in their enjoyment of beauty was not as important as determining whether the object had the salient properties of beauty. Ultimately, the beauty of something should be clear and knowable; all one would have to do would be to strip away the blindfold of illusion and see what was there. What remained would reflect the ideal, and the object's beauty was simply a derivative, a shadow of the transcendent form's perfection.

Plato's theory (and that of the Western tradition that followed it for centuries) was a highly nonrelational one. In other words, the perceiver did not matter, nor did the community and culture of the perceiver; instead, what mattered was the proximity of the form of the thing to the eternal, higher reality of ideals.

This approach to beauty persisted for many centuries and remains a powerful influence on everyday thinking to the present time. However, in the eighteenth century, the Western conceptualization of aesthetics and beauty underwent a fundamental change. What came to be stressed was the personal experience of the perceiver. The efforts to quantify and classify beauty that had dominated European aesthetics were discarded. The source of beauty was no longer considered a quality of things; rather, for Hume and the Romantics, beauty was a matter of emotional response, and the pleasure of beauty was seen as a type of sense like sight and taste. Kant believed that the source of beauty was in a priori ideas embedded in the mind of man and manifest in his experience of things. Thus, the sense of beauty was relegated to the domain of taste, and no matter how hard philosophers tried to find a standard for taste, it was increasingly believed that beauty was just a matter of opinion.

DOI: 10.4324/9781003532484-6

In this way, beauty fell from grace, and with the elaboration of twentieth-century aesthetics, the concept of beauty was virtually abandoned. In reaction to traditional values that extolled beauty as the essence of aesthetic merit, modern artists have virtually defined themselves through opposition to communal standards of taste and critical judgment. Barnett Newman, the abstract expressionist, stated in 1948: "The impulse of modern art is the desire to destroy beauty" (p. 171). Building on the radical iconoclasm of Dadaists such as Duchamp, modern art discarded the preoccupation with beauty and instead emphasized political action, iconoclasm, and social critique.

However, there has been a growing recognition that beauty may be more central to human experience – and to art especially – than we "moderns" had thought. New thinkers do not argue for a return to old notions of classical beauty, but advocate a more diverse and complex model in which beauty is restored to an important position. I cannot discuss the range of arguments in favor of beauty without referring the reader to *Uncontrollable Beauty: Toward a New Aesthetics* (1998), edited by B. Beckley and D. Shapiro; *Regarding Beauty* (1998), edited by N. Benzara and O. Viso; *The Invisible Dragon* (1993), by Dave Hickey (1995); *Beauty* (1999), by James Kirwan; and *On Beauty* (1999), by Elizabeth Scarry. Most of these authors' works are not directly relevant to this chapter, but I would like to touch on one recent contribution.

An intriguing attempt to reconsider traditional notions of beauty was made by the philosopher and art critic Arthur Danto (1964). Danto agreed that the classical view of beauty as appearance is bankrupt and must be replaced with an approach that emphasizes the relation between form and meaning, between the subject and the means of expression, between the world and subjectivity. He stated: "It is required that artistic beauty be part of the meaning of the work, internally connected with its truth. I speak of the internal as against external beauty, which is indeed but skin-deep" (p. 195).

The notion of internal beauty describes something deeply subjective and richly related to experience, something interpenetrative and intersubjective. Danto's approach to the sense of beauty emphasized the restorative and even redemptive function of beauty. In the phrase "giving beauty for ashes," he evocatively captures beauty's role in transcending tragedy and even death. Danto's work appears to me to be consistent with a psychoanalytic perspective. It is in this spirit that I think psychoanalysis can offer a valuable contribution to the current debate.

I selected the title of this chapter, "The Sense of Beauty," for two reasons. One is to echo the title of one of the great essays on beauty, George Santayana's "The Sense of Beauty," published in 1896. The other reason is that the word *sense* has multiple nuances. It conveys sensory experience (through the five *senses*), the quality of awareness ("I *sense* what is going on"), intuitive ability to estimate or judge (a *sense* of direction), recognition or perception (a *sense* of guilt), something sound or reasonable (that makes *sense*), as well as the meaning of something (the *sense* of the word). The richness of the term and the ambiguity of its meanings reflect qualities of beauty to be discussed here.

In using the term *beauty*, I do not intend to give the impression that beauty is a thing, an objective entity or quality existing apart from experience. On the contrary, fundamental to a psychoanalytic perspective is the idea of beauty as a special type of subjective experience that exists at the borderline between self and world. Therefore, when I use the term *beauty*, I do so only to abbreviate the longer phrase. I will also at times use the word *enjoyer* to represent the person who is sensing beauty. Despite the quaintness of the term, I feel that it conveys the positive affective nature of the experience. It is also the term used by Rank in his work *Art and Artist*, and thus there is a solid precedent.

Starting with Freud, psychoanalysts have acknowledged the importance of a sense of beauty and have tried to integrate the concept into analytic thinking. This chapter is a first attempt to offer a comprehensive review of the problem. In the following sections, I will review the psychoanalytic literature regarding beauty. Then, despite the variety of theoretical approaches, I will offer an integrative model that I think will be useful to a broad array of analysts and others interested in art and beauty in general. I will then conclude with a brief comment on Freud's reverence for beauty.

I offer the following definition of the sense of beauty: Beauty is an aspect of the experience of idealization in which an object(s), sound(s), or concept(s) is (or are) believed to possess qualities of formal perfection. Normally, the sense of beauty is "pleasing" and may encompass a range of affect states, from a gentle sense of disinterested pleasure to awe and excited fascination. There is almost invariably a tendency to view beauty as a quality of objects (something they possess). The observer believes that the object in and of itself is beautiful. Beauty may seem so indubitable that it is as intrinsic to the object as color or shape. But it is the subjectivity of beauty that interests me here, and thus I include the terms experience and believed in the definition I use.

What is beautiful is felt to be perfect, exquisite, the finest, and the most harmonious; there is always a quality of the ideal with beauty. It is the object's form that is felt to determine the object's beauty, meaning not just its shape or structure, but its essence, the mode in which a thing exists, acts, or manifests itself. However, perfection of form is a necessary but not sufficient condition for beauty; the content of beauty is also important and may relate to anything from overt sexuality to raw aggression. Beauty is human subjectivity expressed in ideal form.

The Contribution of Psychoanalysis to Our Understanding of Beauty

In *Civilization and Its Discontents* (1930), Freud argued that the valuing of beauty is one of the primary characteristics of a civilized society. Nonetheless, he wrote very little about the sense of beauty; but from what he did write (Freud, 1905), it appears that he believed that the enjoyment of beauty was a sublimation of sexual attraction: "All that seems certain is its derivation from the field of sexual feeling" (1905, p. 156). He pointed out that, despite their arousing nature, the genitals are

never considered beautiful. Rather, it is always the secondary sexual characteristics –
face, hair, and figure – that are granted the status of beauty.

From the perspective of drive theory, the sense of beauty is the result of displacement and sublimation in which libido is transferred to nonsexual objects, and
sexual excitement becomes desexualized as aesthetic pleasure. However, despite
his claim of the sexual foundation of the sense of beauty, Freud (1930) admitted,
"psychoanalysis, unfortunately, has scarcely anything to say about beauty" (p. 83).

An important aspect of Freud's approach is that he saw beauty not as a thing,
as a quality of objects, but as a subjective process in which our experience of the
world is idealized. In other words, beauty is concretized through externalization.
The object is felt to be beautiful not because it *is* beautiful, but rather because it
has been made the secondary object of erotic longings. By its nature, the sense of
beauty lends itself to sublimation through its symbolic content. But the quality
of perfection embodied in the formal structure of the beautiful object is harder to
explain as the result of sublimation. Perhaps from a classical perspective, we might
extend the defensive function of beauty to the reparation or denial of castration
fantasies. (See Francette Pacteau's monograph, *The Symptom of Beauty* [1994], for
a provocative application of the classical model of beauty to the defensive idealization of the female image in our society.)

In *On Transience*, Freud argued that the ideal quality of beauty could function
to transcend feelings of loss and vulnerability. This notion of the transcendental
and/or reparative function of beauty played a central role in later psychoanalytic
approaches. Unfortunately, it is impossible to know what Freud ultimately believed
about beauty, given the brevity of his discussion of the subject. Regarding his claim
that psychoanalysis had nothing useful to say about beauty, perhaps he found the
subject so impenetrable because of its developmental link to early maternal/child
interaction, an area to which he paid scant attention (Spitz, 1985, p. 138).

The psychoanalysts whom I will now discuss expanded the understanding of
beauty beyond a specific defense mechanism such as sublimation and gave it a
function affecting the state of the entire human psyche. They argued that the sense
of beauty is a means of objectification of fantasy in which the anxieties and divi-
sions of the internal world are transcended, and a state of harmony, cohesion, and
well-being is achieved.

In *Art and Artist* (1932), Otto Rank wrote that beauty involved the idealized
objectification of the deepest, most important spiritual/psychological essence of
personality – the soul. In the creation of artworks, the artist gives an ideal, objective
form to his or her own soul (or self) and makes it available to "enjoyers" for their
own experience of transcendence. In the sense of beauty, there is a feeling of wholeness, pleasure, a lessening of anxiety, and the experience of merger with the object
that is felt to be perfect and ideal. The effect of beauty psychologically is to produce
an optimum emotional condition in which the self shares in an ideal subjective state.

Once more we find art expressing the same thing as the abstract-soul concept,
only in an objectified form, which we call beautiful precisely in so far as it is

unreal, "more than earthly." For this very essence of a man, his soul, which the artist puts into his work, and which is represented by it, is found again in the work by the enjoyer. Thus, the will-to-form of the artist gives objective expression, in his work, to the soul's tendency to self-externalization, while the aesthetic pleasure of the enjoyer is enabled, by high oneness with it, to participate in this objectification of immortality. But both, in the simultaneous dissolution of their individuality in a greater whole, enjoy, as high pleasure, the personal enrichment of that individuality through this feeling of oneness. They have yielded up their mortal ego for a moment, fearlessly and even joyfully, to receive it back in the next, the richer for this universal feeling.

(Rank, 1932, p. 110)

Despite the feeling of oneness, Rank stressed that the "enjoyer" does not lose his or her awareness of individuality in the appreciation of beauty. Nonetheless, the sense of beauty involves an experience in which the individual feels intimately related to an ideal other, and as a result feels whole, vital, and enriched by the experience.

Hans Sachs, in *The Creative Unconscious* (1942), argued that the sense of beauty involved a process of resolution of psychic conflict. The ubiquitous structural tensions between the ego, id, and superego are calmed when the conflicting drives of libido and aggression are amalgamated in the formal perfection of beauty. Anxiety is gone, the normally fragmented self is brought together, and a sense of transcendence predominates.

A thing of beauty – or anything as far as it has beauty – represents and brings home a precise nuance of an emotional situation. In a quite unusual way, by the stimulating perception of the senses, the possession of an Id-content is conferred on the Ego. The effect of this activity is what we called earlier "the healing of the cleft." A split in the personality has, at least for the moment, maybe permanently, ceased to exist, or the personality has been made more coherent and continuous. The Superego, sharing the triumphant feeling, participates also in the activity that leads towards it.

(p. 151)

This understanding of beauty has broader implications beyond structural conflict. Sachs saw beauty as one of the highest forms of human experience, embodying some of the most fundamental aspects of human life. Beauty is the expression of the internal forces of death and life.

We see that life and death both must be present for the creation of beauty. When we turn to the great, the pure beauty, we find them united by the strictest interdependence. Pure beauty holds life and death, not as toys serving for a moment's relaxation, but flaring up to their highest intensity. The creative activity of the mind, in reacting to beauty, in producing beauty, represents the highest form

of psychic life, in which all its parts – the Id, the Ego, and the Superego are
coordinated.

(p. 168)

For Sachs, beauty has a metaphysical function. The life and death instincts are
not just drives, but internal manifestations of fundamental forces of nature. The
most central problem of human existence, the conflict between life and death, is
resolved in the sense of beauty. Echoing Rank, Sachs believed in the transcendent
integrative function of beauty. Both authors emphasized the impact of the sense of
beauty on self-experience. The "enjoyer" of beauty is deeply affected psychologically and experiences a state of merger with the beautiful object as self-experience
becomes more cohesive, vital, and continuous.

John Rickman, in his paper entitled "Ugliness and the Creative Impulse" (1940),
argued that at the heart of the creation and appreciation of beauty is the urge for
reparation:

> Our need for beauty springs from the gloom and pain which we experience from
> our destructive impulses toward our good and loved objects; our wish is to find
> in art evidence of the triumph of life over death; we recognize the power of
> death when we say a thing is ugly.
>
> (p. 121)

Rickman saw the human experience as fraught with fear, pain, loss, and death.
Destruction is not just an impulse or a drive, but part of the very nature of living
and of loving. Rickman argued that the sense of beauty involves the search for a
new world built on the ruins of the old. In beauty, we find the expression of the
good object that, once thought destroyed, is now whole and alive again. We call
something *beautiful* because that is what we feel about life when we expect death;
"that is what we think when we see the signs of triumph over death" (p. 117).

> One of the characteristics of beauty is its power to convey the feeling that strug-
> gle is over, that peace has come at last. Though we may go into the depth of pain
> and depression again and again, we carry with us the assurance that through all
> violence and evil there has remained this marvelous witness to the endurance of
> life over death. Once deathless is deathless evermore!
>
> (p. 117)

Rickman's view of beauty as reparation for the destructiveness of our aggressive
fantasies is fundamental to the object relations theory of Melanie Klein and Hanna
Segal. According to Klein, healthy development depends on a progression from
the anxiety and fragmentation of the paranoid-schizoid position to the progressive
integration and affective stability of the depressive position. Rickman's notion of
beauty to bring about feelings of wholeness and vitality in the face of destructiveness was an elaboration of Segal's (1952, 1991) model of creativity and beauty.

Segal believed that the beautiful work of art conveys a sense of wholeness, completeness, and rhythmicity that contains within it the expression of the artist's (and the audience's) authentic experience, meaning the recognition and perhaps even celebration of mortality, aggression, and ugliness. Thus, for her, beauty becomes a characteristic of reparative processes of the depressive position, and the sense of beauty (especially the aesthetic) possesses the affective impact of self-experience, which resolves primitive fragmentation, reduces anxiety, and stimulates hope and perhaps even joy.

Adrian Stokes, a colleague of Segal, added that the mature experience of beauty must include:

> Two imagoes or prototypical experiences: first the feeling of one-ness with the breast and so, with the world: secondly, the keen recognition of a separate object, originally the mother's whole person whose loss was mourned in the infantile depressive position.
>
> (1957, p. 414)

For Stokes, the sense of beauty is a developmental achievement that comes with the resolution of the depressive position.

H. B. Lee wrote a series of papers on esthetic experience (1947, 1948, 1950) that represents the most sustained analysis of the sense of beauty in the psychoanalytic literature. Lee argued that the sense of beauty arises from the inner need of the individual – beauty is subjective. Specifically, he claimed that people seek to create or to find experiences of beauty to cope with psychological crises associated with dangerous aggressive fantasies and fragmentation:

> The rage that initiates the esthetic activity is directed towards some person who has thwarted either excessive self-regard demands or his excessive demands for a maternal kind of love and approval.
>
> (1947, p. 288)

This aggression is unconsciously experienced as directed toward the internalized representation of the mother. Through artistic activity and aesthetic appreciation, the damaged object is restored and perfected to satisfy the ideals of the mother. The experience of beauty stems from the artist's identification with the perfection of the restored object and being found "loveworthy" (i.e., loved by conscience and muse [mother]). Lee (1948) wrote: "The inner sense of beauty results from this magical regeneration of the object and the union with it" (p. 520).

The appreciator of the art product will "intuit" in the characteristics of the work "the same allegiance to ideal intentions as he is seeking to renew in himself" (Lee, 1948, p. 512). The pleasure of beauty derives from having satisfied these inner needs. The mere restoration of the object is not enough; Lee added that the object must also be elevated to a "unique organic unity; and the ego intends the object not only to live again, but to be animated with an unusual sense of aliveness" (p. 520).

The sense of beauty involves the experience of "wholeness, perfection, aliveness, and lovability" (p. 521) – not only of the object, but most important, of oneself.

Lee (1950) added that unconscious guilt is experienced as psychical disorder due to the disharmony within the mind. Another function of the sense of beauty is to identify with the perfect organization of the object and thus restore mental unity and harmony. The sense of beauty not only functions to alleviate guilt, but also to relieve the accompanying sense of "disorderliness" and "messiness" (p. 239). This experience is not simply passive and receptive; rather, the appreciation of beauty is a "passionate interaction with an object in whose esthetic content we can express recreative and loving intentions" (p. 267).

Finally, Lee (1950) claimed that two kinds of emotions are embodied in the beautiful object. One is the aesthetic emotion of the artist that lies latent in the emotional elements of the design and that contains moments of spiritual harmony and perfection. The other emotions are the non-aesthetic ones (such as aggression, fear, desire, and so on), expressed through the object's imagery.

In other words, Lee believed that the sense of beauty lies not in what the object appears to represent, but in what is latent, embodied within the formal structure or design of the object. In this way, something can be experienced as beautiful and thus restorative and transcendent, even though its content may be frightful, violent, or lustful. In fact, this is the most important trait of beauty in Lee's model; self-experience can be restored if the anxiety-producing fantasies are given concrete expression through integrated and perfected forms.

Although Heinz Kohut never addressed the problem of beauty directly, the concept is implicit in the experience of idealization that characterizes selfobject experience. What is idealized is felt to be perfect, and what is perfect is usually beautiful. The self psychologist Charles Kligerman (1980), in his discussion of the psychology of the artist, directly linked idealization and beauty as he described how the artist's experience of loss of perfection leads to the development of his or her lifelong efforts to recapture beauty.

One of the important qualities of idealization is the sense of "formal" perfection and value known as beauty. The idealized object or the grandiose self is experienced as possessing in its essence a perfection of form and mode of being that is beautiful. Therefore, the sense of beauty is an aspect of the experience of idealization. In his formulation, Kligerman speculated that the prototypical artist is someone who experienced consistent mirroring of his or her grandiosity in childhood. Inevitably, this archaic selfobject experience fails, and the artist-to-be is cast out from this state of perfection.

Central to Kligerman's psychology of the artist is the notion that archaic idealization involves the experience of the object's beauty. The sense of beauty throughout life recaptures the original beauty and perfection of our earliest archaic selfobject ties, which have inevitably and appropriately succumbed to disillusionment and, perhaps, failure. Thus, the mature sense of beauty is an effort to recover some aspects of an archaic state in which self-experience is linked to a beautiful, ideal selfobject. (See, in addition, Sheldon Bach's paper, "On the Narcissistic State of Consciousness" [1977], in which he discusses, from a related point of view, the struggle against diminishment of the self and its fantasized omnipotence.)

The Psychoanalytic Understanding of the Sense of Beauty: An Integration

> The sense of beauty is the harmony between our nature and our experience. When our senses and imagination find what they crave, when the world so shapes itself or so molds the mind that the correspondence between them is perfect, then perception is pleasure, and existence needs no apology.
>
> (Santayana, 1896, p. 269)

In the remaining sections of this chapter, I would like to present an integrative psychoanalytic understanding of beauty. This is not as difficult as it might seem, given that the writings I have just discussed, despite their differences in theory, describe beauty in remarkably similar ways. The most important contribution that psychoanalysis has made to the discourse has been to expand our understanding of the nature, sources, and functions of the subjective experience of beauty. Following are some of the most important of these findings.

Beauty as Sublimation

Freud conceived of beauty as a sublimation of sexual desire, in which libido is redirected and expressed in a socially appropriate manner. Several analysts have questioned the metapsychological explanation of beauty as sublimation (Boesky, 1986). However, given the association of beauty with such qualities as sensuousness and strong affect, as well as the frequent occurrence of drive-related content in beautiful things, I believe sublimation remains a useful way of thinking about beauty. The problem is the drive-based nature of the original metapsychological model of sublimation and the significant limitations to its applicability when used in that narrow sense. Toward remedying this situation, let us review Hans Loewald's (1988) reconsideration of sublimation from the vantage point of Freud's second theory of narcissism, also discussed in chapter three.

Loewald examined the role of sublimation in the internal homeostasis of narcissistic and object libido and, by extension, the reconciliation of the relation between self and world. I think this approach is very helpful in explaining the transitional quality of the sense of beauty, especially the way in which beauty seems to intertwine the enjoyer's sense of internal and external reality.

From this perspective, beauty as a form of sublimation functions to reconcile the separation and polarization between self and world that inevitably arise because of development. This is like Winnicott's (1971) notion of the area of cultural experience, the potential space that exists between subjective experience and objective reality. However, Loewald believed that subjectivity and objectivity are undifferentiated in the young infant, and that the transitional experience is of the gradually emerging differentiation between the two realities. Santayana (1896) described this regarding beauty in the following passage:

> There is the expression of a curious but well-known psychological phenomenon, viz., the transformation of an element of sensation into the quality of a thing. If we say that other men should see the beauties that we see, it is because we think those beauties *are in the object*, like its color, proportion, or size. Our judgment appears to us merely the perception and discovery of an external existence, of the real excellence that is without.
>
> (p. 29, italics in the original)

Santayana refers to this as *objectification*. More recently, psychoanalysts have called this process *concretization*, but both these terms imply that a sharp distinction between subjectivity and objectivity is possible. Loewald might have said that in the sense of beauty, the original relationship between inner and outer reality is restored. Subjectivity is granted the quality of an object as if it were an independent, external phenomenon, a thing; and the object is granted the quality of fantasy and affect. Clinically, the intense emotional response and sense of identification with the beautiful object belie its powerful link with the subjective realm. Beauty is never experienced as fully external or internal; we feel aroused, drawn in, fascinated by the beautiful – inner and outer experiences are unified.

For Loewald, the experience of sublimation continued to function throughout life as an area of unity. The "celebration" that characterizes the sublimation of creative work is at the heart of beauty. The "mania" that frequently characterizes the affective component of the sense of beauty arises from this sense of affirmation of unity as inner life and outer realities are linked. I think that many of the analytic thinkers whom we have discussed would find a lot to agree with in this point of view.

Loewald also argued that, even though sublimation usually results in desexualization and/or deaggressivation, the force of the instinctual energy can remain strong even as it is channeled and organized by the ego organization. Here Loewald distinguished between *true sublimation*, in which the "vital power of passion shines through," and *false sublimation*, in which there is a repression or gross sexualization of behavior. These points are relevant to our discussion, given the variation in degree of passion involved in the sense of beauty.

Idealization and Beauty

Idealization is a mental process in which an object's qualities and value are elevated to the point of perfection. One of the characteristics of idealization is beauty. Classical psychoanalysis emphasized idealization's role in the formation and elaboration of the individual's ego ideal; later, self psychologists argued that the internalization of the functions of the idealized parent imago was one of the poles of self-structure. On the other hand, object relations theorists viewed idealization as an aspect of the paranoid-schizoid defense.

I would argue that the lifelong love of beauty is an indication of the persisting importance of idealization during all phases of development. In this regard, it is not primarily defensive. The sense of beauty satisfies a fundamental, healthy human need to be in relation to something or someone that is felt to be ideal. I have coined the term *aesthetic resonance* for the way in which this self-experience and experience of the object interact in a manner like a dialectic. In this sense, beauty results from this dialectic between an inner readiness for idealization and the encounter with an object that is "worthy" of the projection. By "worthy," I mean that the object resonates with unconscious, archaic sources, fantasies (memories?) of paradise. But the powerful idealization that is beauty is also fragile, often transitory, and can never be possessed. "Beauty involves a holding fast to what exists only in the slipping away" (Kirwan, 1999, p. 49). The yearning that we experience before beauty is for an experience that is ultimately unattainable, which is already lost, perhaps forever. This is what makes beauty at times unbearable: the simultaneous sense of the ideal as both recovered and lost. Fulfillment and failure, presence and absence, are intertwined. Allen Wheelis, in his memoir *The Listener* (1999), describes how an encounter with beauty can result in an excruciating experience of vulnerability:

> Great beauty inflicts a wound. Private and somehow shameful. It can neither be acknowledged nor complained about. A deep burning pain. It will not go away. The pain is the longing; the wound is knowing that the longing can never be fulfilled, that, like hell, it will go on forever, always there inside. Beauty calls it forth as from a dark cavern, from some forlorn hidden place in me, and I know then that this longing is my essence. Once or twice in a lifetime, if I am lucky, I might venture to show it to someone I love.
>
> (p. 16)

Beauty as an Interactive Process

Wheelis (1999) describes his almost compulsive search for beautiful women, to whom he ascribes "a quality of heaven, a gift of redemption, a love that would enable me to become what I am not, will never be" (p. 15). For Wheelis, beauty is not just something to be admired; rather, it is through active engagement with beauty that we are granted release from the prison of self through a transcendent fusion with another. Given the archaic relational sources of beauty, I think it is also important to note that the sense of beauty is not passive. An individual does not simply submit to an experience of beauty that happens to him or her. The sense of beauty is interactive and intersubjective. There is a vital feeling of engagement with the object. In fact, some experiences of beauty involve active cognitive and affective processes before the beautiful experience crystallizes. There is often a give-and-take, an engagement with the complex meanings of the experience. This is true of both the created artwork and the found object.

Beauty is always an act of creation for the viewer and the creator. We engage with the object in a dialectic, from which the sense of beauty is an outcome. But this dialectic implies loss and frustration as much as it does fulfillment. Our yearning for the ideal encounters an object that fits the "specs," but that object, no matter how we cajole and manipulate the experience, can never fulfill our fantasies of a lost paradise. After all, the sense of beauty is not in the object, but in the space between, the potential space about which Winnicott (1971) spoke, "the area of yearning" in which we attempt to conjure up the sense of an ideal world and an ideal self. Over time, this creative engagement between self and world may deepen the experience of beauty as we learn more about the object or as we change in response to it.

The Aesthetic and Nonaesthetic Emotions

One of the rarely explored aspects of idealization is the intense affective response that accompanies the process. Commonly, in this context, analysts have described awe, wonder, excitement, and vitalization. The sense of beauty is accompanied by a similar intensification of certain affects and self-states; these are the *aesthetic emotions* that are experienced in response to the formal design of the beautiful object, the qualities that are felt to give it symmetry, harmony, and completeness. The aesthetic emotion involves both an affective response to the experience of the object and a related self-experience that mirrors the emotion felt toward the object. The sense of beauty may include feelings of awe, joy, excitement, optimism, and contentment. The *nonaesthetic emotions* are associated with and experienced regarding the content of the object. Emotions such as anger, sexual excitement, and fear are expressed within the formal structure of beauty, while the anxiety associated with these affects and fantasies is reduced or eliminated by the holding and containing provided by the sense of formal perfection.

Ultimately, the sense of beauty is an amalgamation of the aesthetic and nonaesthetic emotions. Some of the most brutal or violent fantasies, when given perfect form, are felt to be beautiful and evoke both joy and terror in a single sensation. Segal and Lee differentiate the content, which may in fact be ugly, from the form of the object, which is the expression of aesthetic emotion. In the following quotation, Rodin described how beauty could transform ugliness:

> We call ugly that which is formless, unhealthy, which suggests illness, suffering and destruction, which are contrary to regularity – the sign of health. We also call ugly the immoral, the vicious, the criminal and all abnormality that brings evil – the soul of the parricide, the traitor, and the self-seeker. But let a great artist get hold of this ugliness, immediately he transfigures it – with a touch of his magic wand he makes it into beauty.
>
> (Rodin as quoted by Segal, 1957, p. 401)

Surrendering to Beauty

The encounter with beauty lifts us out of everyday life and provides us with an occasion for transcendence. We do not have to be in any type of distress to find beauty invigorating and transformative. Our self-experience is intensified as we share in the state of perfection. We seek out and even cultivate such experiences, and some of us become experts at producing beauty and at explaining its effects. The intensity of beauty can vary greatly. Loewald's (1988) notion of *passionate sublimation* indicates that sublimations such as beauty can exhibit at one extreme a driveline, instinctual charge, and, at the other, quiet, satisfied contentment.

At the heart of beauty lies what Emmanuel Ghent (1990) referred to as the experience of surrender, the yielding of oneself to an object, allowing oneself to be seen, found, and ultimately used by the other. Our yearning for beauty is at least in part a desire to give ourselves over to the control of something external as we succumb to aesthetic rapture. Ghent believes that it is through this experience of surrender that we break out of the confines of our false selves and allow ourselves to be known, found, penetrated, and recognized – it is a vital, natural force toward psychological and spiritual growth.

However, there can be different degrees of surrender, and, as previously noted, varying intensities to the sense of beauty. On the one hand, beauty can be a pleasant and stimulating sense of admiration; on the other, it can be a wholehearted surrender to passionate enthrallment. I refer to these differing forms of beauty as *tame beauty* and *wild beauty* and see them as opposite ends of the normal range of the sense of beauty. Those people who either fear the experience of surrender or, for whatever reason, prefer just a taste of it may allow themselves only a sense of admiration for *tame beauty,* meaning that which is agreed upon and certified as beautiful. This form of beauty does not involve risk or disruption to self and world. Tame beauty is easily integrated, sensible, and consistent with the meanings that structure the viewer's reality – it confirms one's life world. Much of what we conventionally think of as beauty is tame in this sense.

On the other hand, *wild beauty* demands radical surrender and total commitment from the viewer, who becomes more like a lover and supplicant: fierce, slightly panicked by the excitement, even as he or she is ready to do anything for the beautiful one. This form of beauty disrupts and provokes. One is changed by wild beauty. It is uncontrollable and may even be wicked. The surrender to wild beauty may be experienced as an act of sedition and betrayal (and may quite literally be so, as we saw in several twentieth-century revolutionary artistic movements, such as Dadaism and Futurism). One is not safe before the wildly beautiful, but safety is irrelevant. When one surrenders to wild beauty, one is freed from the confines of safety and mortality. The essence of wild beauty is very different from the admiration that characterizes tame beauty; wild beauty is rapturous, and one experiences oneself as transported, overcome by ecstasy. This is the form of beauty that Rilke described when he wrote, "For Beauty's nothing but the beginning of Terror we're still not able to bear, and why we adore it so is because it serenely disdains to destroy us" (Rilke as quoted in Segal, 1957, p. 403).

Beauty, like many other psychological phenomena, can also help in coping with psychological disorder. I will conclude my discussion of beauty by briefly review-ing some of the ways in which the sense of beauty functions to alleviate psychic distress.

Beauty's Restorative Function

In the depressive position, good objects are believed to be either damaged, threat-ened, or destroyed by aggressive wishes. This notion of anxiety as related to fan-tasies of aggression directed toward internal objects has become widely accepted in psychoanalysis. Hence, the preservation or restoration of the relationship to the good object is of utmost importance. This is one of the major functions of the sense of beauty, according to Lee and Segal. Primarily the restorative function of beauty is tied to the relationship between expressive content (which may reflect aggres-sive or sexual wishes) and the perfection of form (by which the content is given organization, balance, and, most important, wholeness).

In addition, recently, the concept of internal beauty has included the idea of the harmony of internal meaning and the coherence of the idea of the object. Thus, beauty does not have to be conventionally beautiful if the meaning of the work is what lends it harmony, balance, and wholeness. In any case, whatever the source of beauty's effect, one of its principal functions is to repair the feared fragmentation or damage done to internal objects by aggressive wishes.

The Self-Integrative Function of Beauty

The sense of beauty can also function to reconcile and integrate self-states of frag-mentation and depletion. In many instances in which a person experiences a disor-der in self-experience, such as depression, fragmentation, or depletion, beauty may function to mitigate the disorder or to restore self-cohesion or vitality. True to the transitional nature of beauty, self-experience is powerfully linked to the experience of the object. The organization and wholeness that are felt to be of the object are shared by the self, and the individual feels a change in self-experience. "The self you lose to beauty is not gone. It returns refreshed" (Schjeldahl, 1999, p. 58).

Beauty as a Defense

In psychopathology, beauty can function defensively for the expression of uncon-scious impulses and fantasies, or as protection against self-crisis. We have empha-sized the developmentally appropriate nature of the sense of beauty; however, like many other subjective phenomena, the sense of beauty can function as a defense or a compensation for deficits. This is particularly appropriate given the way in which beauty involves powerful feelings of reparation and self-healing. Recognizing the complexity of this area, I would like to briefly touch on the writings of several authors concerned with the pathology of beauty.

Janine Chasseguet-Smirgel (1984) provides an example of the defensive function of beauty in her discussion of the psychodynamics of perversion. She notes that the pervert, to maintain the illusion that his infantile genitals are equal to those of the father and satisfactory to the mother, idealizes his pregenital erotogenic zones and part objects. In this way, he maintains the fantasy that pregenital sexuality is equal if not superior to genitality. This leads to a compulsion to idealize and to become preoccupied with beauty. According to Chasseguet-Smirgel:

> This accounts for the pervert's obvious affinity for art and beauty; the pervert is often an aesthete. The pregenital libido – which, if diverted may be sublimated – is not always available to the pervert since it is directly released in the perverse act. Moreover, because he has not projected his Ego ideal onto his father and genitality, he has not introjected his father's genital attributes. The resulting identification gaps constitute a major obstacle to a real sublimation process. Idealization tends more toward aestheticism than creation, and when creation nevertheless develops, it often bears the stamp of aestheticism. Thus, art is reduced to its decorative function.
>
> (p. 88)

In this way, for these individuals, anal fantasies, anal products, and aggressive wishes are "covered over," if you will, with a veneer of beautiful illusion by which "shit is spun into gold." The sense of beauty that results is brittle and easily disrupted. The constant risk is that the anal inadequacy will be revealed, with devastating results to self-experience. In this regard, Stephen Rittenberg (1987) discussed the psychological dangers associated with the individual's enthrallment with "charm," a frequent quality of the experience of beauty:

> The pleasures of charm, to which we happily succumb, can pose dangers. Good, blank, untroubled sleep may give way to bad sleep, destruction and death. Regression can occur in the service of the ego, but it can open the way to ego dissolution. The charmer, inheritor of mother's omnipotence, can restore and destroy.
>
> (p. 391)

Beauty is thus a way to organize pregenital fantasies, to express them in gilded form and to cling to the illusion of power and self-sufficiency. In this defensive organization, the sense of beauty usually does not allow for the depth of experience and the recognition of the reality of the other. In *The Symptom of Beauty* (1944), Francette Pacteau describes a similar process that occurs in men in our culture as they seek to defend against the recognition of infantile helplessness and loss. The image of the beautiful woman demolishes the experience of separateness and allows the man to retain an illusion of presence and possession (see also Wheelis, 1999).

Thus, for Chassequet-Smirgel's pervert as for Pacteau's male, beauty bestows the illusion of wholeness and power, while requiring that the stark reality of the object world and the separate subjectivity of the other be denied.

Beauty and Mortality

The sense of beauty can in some instances alleviate anxiety regarding death and feelings of vulnerability associated with mortality. (From Freud's *On Transience* [1915], we learn that beauty can increase these anxieties in some people, while others experience transcendence and hope.) Rank (1934) argued that beauty is such an affectively powerful and ideal experience that, for a moment, death and loss are overcome. In the pure and exquisite expression of the subjective, the intangible and fragile are given substance, formal perfection, and perhaps even immortality. In beauty, we the creators and viewers undergo a transcendent experience in which we become part of an eternal, transcendent truth. Once again, this feeling of transcendence is due to the transitional and idealized nature of the experience of beauty.

In closing my discussion of beauty, I would like to offer a new understanding of the quotation from *Civilization and Its Discontents* with which I began this chapter. Perhaps one of the reasons why Freud claimed reverence for beauty as a required trait of civilization was because beauty elevates human subjectivity and human values to a transcendent level. The sense of beauty in its reparative and preservative function asserts love over aggression, life over death, and harmony over disintegration. It may even be one of the ways that we reconcile our relationship with the world. Our sense of beauty may not always be certain or consistent with high aesthetic standards. We may challenge cultural assumptions about the beautiful, or we may even rebel against beauty. But beauty, like sex and aggression, has been a reality of human life in all cultures throughout history. As we view the sense of beauty through the psychoanalytic lens, we see in it man's search for perfection, transcendence, and hope. Beauty is not illusory, nor does it stand in for or cover up something else. Beauty may be one of the most exquisite forms of human meaning that exists. A civilization that does not value beauty would be one that cannot hope and that cannot assert life over the inevitable and ubiquitous forces of entropy and death.

Chapter 7

On Ugliness

The aesthetic valuation of our self and world is a fundamental human capacity. The feeling that life is pleasing, formally ordered and refined, perhaps even beautiful is important to our psychological well-being. Aesthetic experience has been the subject of several psychoanalytic contributions, especially in the object relations school (Segal, 1957; Winnicott, 1971). I have joined the exploration of psychoanalytic aesthetics with particular attention to the sense of beauty (see chapter six, as well as Hagman, 2002). However, beauty's shadow, ugliness, has rarely been discussed. While we cultivate beauty, we avoid ugliness, except in instances of psychological disorder, when we may feel trapped and tortured by it. The depressive person may continually lament the ugliness of self and world. The anorexic may struggle to mold his or her body from an ugly form into a pleasing one. Such a person may live in dread of the memories of harrowing, ugly experiences of abuse or violence.

More benignly (but no less significantly), the artist often works to convert ugliness into artistic knowledge and beautiful form. In fact, ugliness and concern about ugliness are common to all societies, but we do not want to look. For psychoanalysts, any psychological phenomenon that is as ubiquitous, affectively powerful, and behaviorally motivating as ugliness is of interest. In addition, I think that looking at ugliness can help us understand the relationship between the conscious organization of experience and unconscious fantasy. Specifically, ugliness is a dramatic symptom associated with the breakdown of sublimation and the eruption into consciousness of disruptive fantasy. However, what makes ugliness special is not simply the return of the repressed (which can take many forms, even the aesthetically pleasing); rather, it is the unique way in which there is a combination of expectation – even, perhaps, of need – for order, balance, and perfection (which serves defensive, expressive, and self-ordering functions) and an unexpected shattering of the desired aesthetic organization by threatening fantasy and anxiety.

Webster's Unabridged Dictionary (1996) defines the word *ugly* as "offensive to the sight; contrary to beauty; being of disagreeable or loathsome aspect; unsightly; repulsive; deformed" Wordnet (1997) defines ugly as "(1) Displeasing to the sense and morally revolting; (2) deficient in beauty; (3) inclined to anger or bad feelings with overtones of menace; (4) morally reprehensible; (5) threatening

DOI: 10.4324/9781003532484-7

or foreshadowing evil or tragic developments; (6) provoking horror." The word is derived from the Icelandic term *uglier,* which means fearful and includes the suffix *ligr,* indicating something that is like something else; therefore, *ugly* is derived from terms meaning "like fear." Experiencing something or someone as ugly is a powerful aesthetic response that is accompanied by intense negative affect (fear, horror, disgust, and/or loathing), moral condemnation (reprehensibility), and behavioral reactions (being repelled, looking away, fleeing).[1] It is important to note that from a psychoanalytic perspective, ugliness is not a quality of things; rather, it is a psychological experience that is felt to be external to the self, although its source lies primarily in fantasy and psychological conflict. Certain things and images that we encounter in life become occasions for a powerful experience, the perception of ugliness. It is undeniable that at the very least, some qualities of the image catalyze our reaction, but it is the disruption of the formal/aesthetic dimension of our subjectivity that forms the core of ugliness.

In the following section, I will review psychoanalytic writings that either directly or by implication address the problem of ugliness. I will then offer a psychoanalytic model of ugliness. During the chapter, various aspects of my arguments are illustrated with clinical vignettes. Finally, I will close with a discussion of how people – especially artists and psychoanalysts – are drawn to ugliness, to master the experience and to transform it into beauty – or at least into common homeliness.

The Problem of Ugliness

The problem of ugliness has troubled psychologists and philosophers for several thousand years. In the beginning, Plato and Aristotle took ugliness to be simply the painful opposite of the pleasure of beauty. Ugliness was essentially the aesthetic equivalent of evil in the ethical domain. But ugliness ended up being more complex and ambiguous than evil. In his discussion of tragedy, Aristotle pointed out that a positive aesthetic experience in theater may result from the observation of ugly and distressing events. Tragedy was even morally uplifting, despite its often "ugly" content. Aristotle extended the problem to other arts as well, noting that ugliness in art often has significant value and frequently accompanies pleasurable experiences.

Searching to find a basis for ugliness beyond the experiential, later philosophers postulated an *anti-aesthetic.* In other words, an ugly object lacked the characteristics of the aesthetic – specifically, the absence of form. Hypothetically, ugliness was formless. But many pointed out that existence implied the presence of form; the absence of form was not conceivable. In fact, common experience confirms that, although the formal traits of an ugly experience appear to possess bad form, nonetheless, ugliness can always be said to possess *some* form.

Still other philosophers and writers, such as Augustine, argued that ugliness does not exist, given the nature of the world as a reflection of God's goodness; the very notion of ugliness is inconceivable. Things may appear to lack beauty, but in the end, true knowledge leads to the discovery of the object's beauty as God's creation. Of course, this approach left us nowhere, since no one could argue that ugliness was not a frequent human experience, and that some ugly things resist our most urgent efforts to discover beauty in them.

After the Renaissance, writers developed a formal system of aesthetic standards to categorize beauty and ugliness. Specific criteria were established, and it became relatively simple to say that something was ugly based on certain of its traits. This approach bypassed the entire issue of ugliness as a meaningful human experience. One did not have to think too much about the problem; an object was ugly just because aesthetic standards said it was.

In the eighteenth century, the notion of aesthetic standards was rejected in favor of a more personal, psychological model of aesthetic experience. But this new approach did not help much in the understanding of ugliness. The old idea of ugliness as distressing and unpleasurable was contradicted by the recognition of the terrors and chaos of the sublime. In fact, the Romantic artists and writers often glorified ugliness and created beauty from it.

Of course, even the most refined, experienced, and educated person often finds things ugly – perhaps even more frequently than less discriminating people. So I feel that ugliness cannot be described merely as the absence of understanding or some failure of vision; rather, the experience of ugliness is more dynamic and personal. It arises not strictly from a lack of capacities, but rather from vulnerabilities in the aesthetic realm. As we shall see, ugliness is experienced more as a disruption than an absence, a form of aesthetic trauma in which the psychological conflicts of the spectator lead to a sense of acute disorder in the ongoing continuity of self-experience and self-in-relation. The aesthetic fabric out of which we have woven the meanings and reassuring formal structures of our lives is rent, and out of that tear emerge unwelcome fantasies of a frightening and often horrible nature.

The Problem of Ugliness and Psychoanalytic Theory

There is only one paper on ugliness in the psychoanalytic literature (Rickman, 1940), and I will consider it in turn. Primarily, I will draw on several psychoanalysts' writings in extrapolating the implications of their ideas for our understanding of ugliness, and I will suggest ways in which they might have considered the problem.

Freud never discussed ugliness. There is only one reference to it in the index of his complete works, and that refers to his argument (contra Adler) that personal ugliness does not cause neurosis. I would like to suggest that from the perspective of Freud's early theory, ugliness may be associated with two important visual traumas: the observation of the primal scene and the sight of the female genitals. According to Freud, both experiences result in the stimulation and projection of fantasies that are so disturbing that the visual image itself becomes inseparable from frightening and repulsive affect states.

Freud (1905, p. 196) defined the primal scene as the unexpected and unwanted witnessing of sexual intercourse between the parents. Along with the familiar traumatic effects, intense sexual stimulation, anxiety and defense, there is also what I would suggest is an aesthetic dimension that is experienced by the child as ugliness. From what is this ugliness derived? I infer that, from a classical Freudian perspective, ugliness derives from: (1) the misapprehension that the father is assaulting the mother, (2) the seemingly castrated nature of the mother's genitalia, and (3) the fear of punishment for Oedipal desires. The content of the experience is important, but it is also crucial to note the disruption of normal assumptions about relatedness and self-security. The observation of violent penetration and apparent disfigurement, as well as the possibility of mutilation, throws the child's psychological and aesthetic world into complete disorder. Panic ensues and emergency measures are mobilized to protect the self. The child represses the memory of the primal scene and fends off its reemergence through psychological defense. Just the idea, let alone the image, of parental sex becomes repugnant – an ugly thought.

Castration anxiety, an important part of the child's response to the primal scene, is present in many psychological conflicts. For example, Freud (1930) noted its occurrence upon sight of the female genitals. He believed that castration anxiety affects a person's aesthetic appreciation of the genitals – deflecting their beauty onto secondary sexual characteristics (the face, breasts, ankles, and so on). Based on this, the female genitals are felt to be ugly because the sight of them evokes fear of castration. Freud viewed this as the bedrock of many neuroses, an invariable and ubiquitous aesthetic reality.

In summary, then, ugliness is the frightening and repulsive nature of the visual image of sexual acts (parental coitus) and sexual body parts (genitals), which during childhood stimulated fantasies and fears pertaining to forbidden desire (incest) and punishing disfigurement (castration). However, Fleiss (1961), a drive psychologist, disputed the universality of the idea that the female genital is ugly. In fact, Fleiss argued that Freud's claim that the genitals were never considered beautiful was distorted by his own neurosis. For Fleiss, healthy sexual desire undisturbed by Oedipal conflict was possible and achievable, and he provided numerous clinical examples in support of this. Once freed from neurotic conflict, the normal adult can experience the genitals (female and male) as beautiful, and can gaze upon them with a sense of mingled aesthetic and erotic pleasure. Fleiss basically agreed with Freud that primal scene anxiety and castration fears interfere with the experience of genital beauty, but rather than concretizing and universalizing these neurotic responses, Fleiss noted that appreciation of the beauty of the genitals is not only possible but can also be a normal aspect of healthy sex.[2]

Klein (1929) saw all psychological life as a struggle between aggressive and loving impulses directed at important internal objects. Initially, during the paranoid-schizoid position, these objects are kept psychologically far apart. Later, normal psychological development demands that the individual bring these split objects together and find a way to safely integrate the impulse for destruction with the desire to love. For Klein, the process of reparation for harmful fantasies lay at the heart of the creative process, and beauty represents the most perfect accomplishment of love over the inner forces of the death drive.

Rickman (1940) agreed with Klein that the desire to make reparations is probably an integral part of creative activity. Reparation involves the assertion of continuity, the establishment of formal structure, and the successful articulation of ideals. For Rickman, ugliness is the utter failure of reparation, with disruption, disorder, and degradation prevailing. The fear and horror of the ugly and the desire to change it "thrusts us into constructive work in art, in science and even the humble tasks in our daily rounds" (p. 82). The need for beauty stems from our destructive impulses toward our good and loved objects. When we regard something as ugly, we recognize the power of death. We seek the triumph of life over death in art.

H. B. Lee (1947, 1948, 1950) wrote that people need to feel that there is an aesthetic organization, a sense of formal order and vitality to their lives. Lee felt that it was the emergence into consciousness of aggressive wishes that disrupted the orderliness and beauty of subjective life. Guilt associated with destructive fantasies results in general feelings of messiness and disorder. Significant amounts of guilt lead to depression and the activation in creative people of an urge to make reparation and to reconstruct an ideal, formal order by means of their art, to restore psychological well-being.

Although Lee never directly discussed ugliness, it can be extrapolated from his writing that ugliness results from the severe disruption of a person's sense of aesthetic organization, in which the value, order, and vitality of subjective life is violated and/or transgressed, to such an extent that, rather than experiencing merely a disturbing sense of messiness and disorder, the individual feels shocked at the perception of chaos, disfigurement, and horror. Ugliness leads to powerful affective reactions, psychological crises, and emergency attempts to restore aesthetic structure through avoidant, aversive, or creative behavior.

My assumption is that for Lee, the underlying source of ugliness is the emergence of powerful aggressive fantasies, well beyond those usually associated with normal levels of neurosis. But most significant for my purposes in this paper, it is understanding how these aggressive wishes impact the formal, aesthetic structure of experience that may offer the foundation for a psychoanalytic understanding of ugliness.

The psychoanalytic perspectives discussed so far view ugliness as a confrontation with something that evokes fantasies of a profoundly disruptive, even traumatic nature: i.e., the father's attack on the mother during sex, the castration represented by the female genitalia, and the resurgent destructiveness of the death drive. While these fantasies may involve other reactions and perceptions – fearful, overwhelming, brutal ones – it is the disruption of the formal, aesthetic dimension that is ugly. The ugliness of the primal scene is not just the result of observing violent sexuality between the parents; it is the appearance, the sight of parental intercourse, and the visual image that are felt to be ugly. In the same sense, the female genitalia are felt to be formally ugly, aesthetically displeasing, and to occasion castration fear.

Therefore, looking at it from another perspective, the primal scene and the sight of the female genitals are *aesthetically disruptive*. There is a focused, powerful disruption of the formal organization of experience. The person may not be clinically traumatized, but the ongoing quality of lived experience is upset to a greater or lesser degree. There is a range of degrees of ugliness: from an image that provokes mild discomfort (a signal affect) to one that elicits a grim loathing or horror (affective flooding). This varies according to the perception of the risk involved. In other words, the disruptive potential of any experience is determined by the extent to which fantasies and/or affects are felt to be threatening. The important point is that it is the formal qualities of the experience – the sounds, shapes, rhythms, and colors – that become the concrete manifestation of ugliness.

In the experience of ugliness, the expectation of beauty is radically disrupted. Instead of resonance, there is dissonance. The ideal is replaced by corruption and degradation. Harmony and wholeness are replaced by conflict and disintegration. For example, from a classical analytic perspective, it is not just the observation of the primal scene or the female genitals that evokes a sense of ugliness; rather, it is the expectation of one thing (loving affection between the parents and the presence of a penis, respectively) and the shock of encountering a form of violation of that expectation that results in anxiety, revulsion, and the sense of ugliness. In object relations terms, it is the expectation of unity and wholeness that is violated by the encounter with chaos and disintegration. In other words, the experience of ugliness is that aspect of an experience that leads to the disruption or shattering of the formal/aesthetic structure of experience.

Encountering Ugliness

> Once, when I was a boy on vacation with my family, we took a ferry ride across San Juan harbor. The experience was pleasant for me until I spied a strange boy sitting with a friend on a bench. He had wispy hair, a gray complexion, and a feral, bizarre face. I found him extremely ugly, and I immediately felt fear. I needed to look away, but I also found myself glancing back with terror and fascination. The entire atmosphere of the boat ride was infected with the horror I felt for this boy. I was amazed that his normal, even good-looking friend was laughing with him and seemed unconcerned by the strange boy's appearance. Even after we left the boat and were far away, I was preoccupied. The world seemed oddly dangerous, as if the boy's ugliness was still present and there remained a risk of his coming after me. In fact, I found myself scanning each new area we entered, as if he and I would become unexpectedly drawn together and I would be powerless to stop it. I continued to be afraid for several hours.

My experience just described dramatizes some of the most important qualities of the experience of ugliness. First, there is a pronounced, immediate, cognitive/affective reaction to the perception of something that in most cases is part of the external world, although it may occur regarding a thought or memory. The reaction is one of fear and repulsion; however, accompanying these responses, there is often, paradoxically, fascination and even attraction – although, as in my memory as described, this attraction is experienced as unwanted and ego-dystonic.

Second, the object provokes the eruption of powerful unconscious fantasies, commonly of a sexual or aggressive nature, but sometimes expressing a feared self-state. The specific content of these fantasies usually does not enter awareness; rather, the image of the external object is invested with the inordinate and bizarre significance we call ugliness. This ugliness is both disruptive and expressive. For example, in the example from my own childhood, the panic that accompanies ugliness was analyzed, revealing a complex set of fantasies and defenses.

The memory of the feral boy played a part in my first analysis. This was during a time when several issues related to my adolescent sexuality and emerging ambitions were being explored. In fact, the memory of the boy reemerged in association to a series of dreams in which I was struggling to protect myself from a maniac, a wild man on a rampage through my childhood hometown. The current wild-man dream was linked to the memory of the feral boy, both of whom were felt by me to be uncivilized, primitive, and threatening. The boy's image seemed to combine a number of elements: first, the experience of maturing sexuality, due to his animal appearance and my physical excitement (repulsion/fascination) in reaction to him; second, I experienced a sense of dangerous aggression in my fears of his doing me harm; and third, he embodied my self-experience at the time, especially distortions in my body image, since I was experiencing rapid physical changes. There were other unconscious determinants of my sense of the boy's ugliness, such as homosexual fantasies, aggressive wishes toward my family, incestuous desire toward my mother (the wispy hair on the boy's head being associated with genital hair). All these unconscious fantasies seemed to crystallize around my perception of the feral boy, over determining my reaction.

The stimulation of unconscious fantasy, even the most threatening, does not necessarily result in the experience of ugliness. Most neurotic symptoms are painful or upsetting, but not ugly. So there is a third quality to my experience that makes it different from most psychological symptoms, which is that *the provocation and projection of these unconscious fantasies alter the sense of aesthetic experience in such a way that the formal qualities of the experience, the shape, texture, and color, become what we experience as the sources of our most disturbing and repulsive feelings.*

Gilbert Rose (1992) wrote: "We are in fluid interaction with our environment on various levels. Forms are configurations or levels of balance in these interactions. They create order where otherwise there would be chaos or void" (p. 25). According to Rose, human beings are not just passive recipients of experience, but are active creators of the reality they perceive. This view applies to both inner and outer worlds and the relations between them. Without this meaning making and formal organizing function, we would cease to be human. Thus, the creation and maintenance of form is central to human psychological life (see also Stokes, 1957).

The formal organization of experience can be viewed in terms of content and aesthetics. Regarding content, the primary constituent of self-experience is the inner world of fantasy and meaning that provides the psychological and emotional substance that defines who we are and how we live our lives (Kohut, 1971, 1977; Ulman and Brothers, 1988). These conscious and unconscious fantasies coexist in dynamic relation to each other, such that the conflicts and contradictions present within us are managed with an optimal degree of psychological continuity and stability. In recent explorations of the problem of trauma, some analysts have emphasized the impact of stressful events on the central organizing fantasies of the self. Ulman and Brothers (1988) argued that traumatic experience can shatter fantasies (such as omnipotence, for example), causing severe damage to self-organization. They noted that the traumatized person attempts to restore the self, but the repairs are sometimes faulty. Various types of psychopathology, such as post-traumatic stress disorder, may result. This model of trauma focuses on the contents of self-organization and, most important, fantasies of selfobject relationships.

However, self-experience has structure as well as content, and the *formal* quality of psychological structure is imbued with aesthetic meaning. This aesthetic dimension of self-experience plays an essential role in psychological continuity, vitality, and coherence. It manifests not in fantasy but in form, rhythm, tone, color, and structural configuration, which make up the aesthetics of both conscious and unconscious psychological life. This aesthetic dimension is crucial to our sense of well-being, self-continuity, and fittedness. It provides the *feeling* tone of our selves and our experience of self-in-world. Like the organizing fantasies of the self and the impact of traumatic events on them, this personal aesthetic can suffer a disruption, which may be experienced as a tear or discontinuity in the flow of being, the formal organization of self.

> My encounter with the feral boy occurred on a brilliant, sunny afternoon as we floated across a tropical bay, with a city in the distance. My sense of self and self-with-others had been undisturbed, pleasant, even idealized. The experience of the boy's ugliness was like an eruption, a tear in the general sense of aesthetic balance and continuity. Everything else remained the same, but suddenly the beautiful became precarious and ungrounded. My sense of internal and external order and the quality of self-experience and self-in-relation-to-world became unhinged, and psychological collapse suddenly seemed possible – unless I could escape. The boy's formal qualities attracted my attention. His thin hair, the color of his skin, and the shape of his face seemed equally to terrify me and to rivet my attention, being perceived as both an immediate danger and an inviting, undeniable seduction.

As illustrated by my experience, ugliness disrupts or shatters the formal structure of experience such that an image cannot be integrated into the meaning structures of the self. In fact, the individual may feel that the image must be destroyed or avoided due to the level of threat it poses. He or she may respond with fear, revulsion, repudiation, or flight. In the least serious instances, the image may be bracketed in moral or aesthetic condemnation to reduce or eliminate the potential for psychological distress.

The Failure of Sublimation

From the perspective of drive psychology, the source of the experience of ugliness lies in the return of repressed fantasies related to Oedipal desire and retribution. The primal scene and the female genitalia may both have been considered ugly by the child not because of any intrinsic qualities, but rather due to the activation of fantasies of sexual violence – specifically, castration, which became associated with the appearance of the primal scene and genitalia. In other words, ugliness may be associated with the disruptive emergence of sexual fantasy in which libido and aggression are expressed in a manner resulting in psychic conflict.

Several analysts have questioned the metapsychological explanation of subli- mation. However, given the association of ugliness with such qualities as sensuous- ness and strong affect, as well as the frequent occurrence of drive-related content in that which we consider ugly (just as in that which we find beautiful), I believe that sublimation remains a useful way of thinking about ugliness. To this end, I would like to discuss Loewald's (1988) reconsideration of sublimation from the vantage point of Freud's second theory of narcissism.

Loewald examined the role of sublimation in the internal homeostasis of narcis- sistic and object libido, and, by extension, the reconciliation of the relation between self and world. Even though Loewald did not address the problem of ugliness here, I think his approach is very helpful in explaining the transitional quality of the experience of ugliness, and especially the way in which ugliness seems to dis- rupt the balance between a person's sense of internal and external reality. Loewald (1988) wrote:

> The polarization that arises in the differentiation of primary narcissism into nar- cissistic and object libido is counterbalanced, modulated, tempered by sublima- tion. Relations with external objects change into internal "narcissistic" relations, and these desexualized libidinal bonds are instrumental in molding aims and relations with external objects, so that these themselves are likely to become desexualized. Freud said that the shadow of the object falls on the ego. Equally, the shadow of the altered ego falls on objects and object relations. Sublimation is a kind of reconciliation of the subject–object dichotomy – atonement for the polarization (the word atone derives from *at one)* and a narrowing of the gulf between object libido and narcissistic libido, between object world and self.
>
> (p. 20]

As a failure in sublimation, ugliness disrupts the normal reconciliation of the separation and polarization between self and world that inevitably arise because of development. Objects and/or other experiences become highly affectively charged, but rather than binding the world more closely to the self, the narcissistic charge imbues them with a bizarre, repulsive fascination indicative of the projection of anal or early genital fantasies – while, due to their threatening nature, they are repudiated as external or even alien to the self. This failure occurs in a psychic area like Winnicott's (1971) notion of the area of cultural experience, the potential space that exists between subjective experience and objective reality. In ugliness, potential space collapses and creative engagement may cease as the object is repudiated.[3]

Loewald believed that subjectivity and objectivity are undifferentiated in the young infant, and that differentiation between the two realities emerges only gradually. Sublimation, along with the safe discharge of the drives, leads to the balanced investment of narcissistic energy and a more fluid relationship between self and world. Further, Loewald believed that optimal psychological health allowed for the capacity for differentiation and de-differentiation of a reality sense, accompanied by the ability to unite. However, if sublimation fails, the emergence into consciousness of unmodulated, raw fantasy and sudden differentiation produces an experience of strangeness and horror. On the one hand, unity is felt to be threatening; on the other, separateness is a source of terror. The experience of ugliness becomes associated with the object. The *thing* is what is ugly – not something in ourselves.

During the moments prior to my sighting of the feral boy, my sense of relationship to external reality was quiescent; my wishes and fantasies were comfortably sublimated within my environment, which was sensual without being sexual; the motion of the ferry and the splashing of the water in our wake resonated with my inner state of balanced sublimation. In retrospect, I note that the sublimation of my inner life into my experience of my activity in the world was strikingly successful and complete. However, my vision of the boy disrupted my ability to sublimate. Unexpectedly, the investment of the image of the boy with primitive fantasy ruptured the continuity and formal organization of my experience. My relationship to the world, the enjoyable interpenetration of my inner world and outer experience, was violently cleaved apart, and suddenly, what was external became terrifying and noxious.

In the failure of sublimation, the relationship between inner and outer reality is radically alienated. Subjectivity is granted the quality of an object, as if it were an independent, external phenomenon, a thing; and the object is granted the quality of fantasy and affect. Clinically, the intense emotional response and sense of identification with the ugly object belie its powerful link to the subjective realm. Ugliness is never experienced as fully external or internal; instead, we feel aroused, drawn in, fascinated by the ugly – but it is also felt to be a bizarre intruder, an aesthetic poison. Inner and outer realities are thrown into disjunction.

For Loewald (1988), sublimation should continue to function throughout life as a source of unity:

> Sublimation then brings together what had become separate. It plays a decisive part in the "mastery of reality" (Hartmann, 1955) – mastery conceived not as domination but as coming to terms – as it brings external and material reality within the compass of psychic reality, and psychic reality within the sweep of external reality. In its most developed form in creative work, it culminates in celebration. This "manic" element is not a denial, or not only that, but an affirmation of unity as well.

(p. 22)

The failure of sublimation induces greater separation, but the unconscious tie still lingers, infected with fantasy and anxiety. Our ability to master reality is threatened. Confronted with ugliness, we feel that we cannot come to terms with it, and by association, neither with the world around us. The "celebration" that characterizes the successful sublimation of creative living is transformed into repugnance and horror. The "mania" that frequently characterizes the affective component of the sense of beauty is absent; rather, depression and fear dominate while an alien and malevolent reality confronts us.

On the other hand, the following quotation from Loewald (1988) highlights the unity found in successful sublimation:

> In genuine sublimation, this alienating differentiation is being reversed in such a way that a fresh unit is created by an act of uniting. In this reversal – a restoration of unity – there comes into being a *differentiated unity* (a manifold) that captures separateness in the act of uniting, and unity in the act of separating.
>
> (p. 24, italics in the original)

The failure of sublimation in the experience of ugliness results in an accentuation of the differentiation between inner and outer realities. Rather than a fresh unity, there is a bizarre and disturbing juxtaposition of fearful self and horrible object. Rather than restoration, there is failure and collapse. Rather than union with an ideal, there is an experience of repulsion that is undeniable and disorienting.

The Collapse of Idealization

The developmental elaboration of archaic forms of idealization is essential to the experiences of well-being and of the formal goodness of the external world (Kohut, 1971, 1977). The mutual cathexis of parent and child and the intensification of that cathexis through pleasurable, joyful interaction result in a relatively sustained sense of idealization, both object and self. This idealization becomes an essential aspect of the child's relationship with the parent, gradually promoting the development of a core self-structure, the child's sense of self. The world, morally neutral, becomes invested with value that over a lifetime is articulated, elaborated, and refined. Initially, this valuation centers on the parent/child relationship, but over time, if not traumatically disillusioned, the child (in cooperation with the parents and other loving people) extends the parental idealization to other persons, objects, goals, and even complex images of the self. This process gives the world value.

Normally, an adult feels that the relationship between the mental and physical domains is aesthetically balanced, and this contributes to a sense of quality and fittedness, despite the moment-to-moment disruptions that may require active efforts to restore equilibrium (Hartmann, 1958). We come to expect that our experience of the world fits into a certain range of aesthetic standards, and individuals and society spend quite a bit of effort and money creating objects and environments that maintain this basic level of aesthetic equilibrium. The value assigned to fine arts and skilled crafts is the most obvious example of the importance of the presence of the ideal and the perfect in our environment, but even in more mundane areas, we seek to heighten the quality (a gradient aspect of the ideal) of our inner and outer lives. In the encounter with ugliness, which seems like a form of antibeauty, the ideal is expelled, challenging our assumptions about the formal goodness of our world, to a greater or lesser degree.

The following brief vignette is illustrative of these points:

Brad, a musician whom I saw in psychoanalytic therapy, came to a session in distress. He had given a performance the previous night that did not go well.

"I was more and more tense. My mouth, my breath. It felt so lifeless – so ugly. I felt ugly, but there was nothing to do but keep playing."

As a young man, Brad had endured the endless and often violent arguments of his parents. His father, self-centered and cruel, would lure Brad into competitive games expressly to defeat him. As a teenager, Brad discovered a remarkable talent for music, and despite his father's criticism, chose it as a career. Music came to be the only truly enriching experience in his life; he would become animated and articulate as he spoke of performing and of the beauty of music. However, he was also riddled with conflict about his ambition. A good part of the analysis focused on working through his anxiety about performing, particularly his fears of failure. In his "ugly" performance, he experienced the startling collapse of his idealization.

"It's like the music is still out there, but I can't get close to it," he explained. "I myself am stopping it, and the ugliness takes over."

In this instance, Brad felt ugly when he failed to embody in his performance the ideal beauty of the composition. Our analytic work revealed many conflicts about his competition with and defiance of his father, as well as a fantasy of seducing his mother (who preferred him to his father, he felt). In the experience of ugliness, he both protected against the real danger of success (self-destruction or defeat of his father) and the possession of beauty (his mother). Interestingly, the immediate precipitant of the failure to perform was physical tension associated with aggressive wishes; rather than relaxing and allowing his body to just play, he became rigid and focused on "doing it right." The image of the longed-for ideal became corrupted by aggressive wishes and fantasies of retribution.

Ugliness and Interaction

Ugliness has a power over us; we cannot treat it with indifference. It rouses our deep-set emotions, and its horror lingers in the memory. . . . It is something that stirs fantasies so profoundly that our minds cannot let the object alone.

(Rickman, 1940, p. 118)

We may feel as if ugliness forces itself upon us, compelling us to respond affectively and sometimes physically. Unlike interaction with the beautiful, in which attunement and resonance predominate, that with the ugly is dissonant and uncomfortable. The experience is of struggle and negativity. There is a break in our relationship with at least this aspect of the world, and we may even feel a general disequilibrium and anxiety regarding other aspects of experience.

Thomas Mann (1911), in his great novella *Death in Venice*, described an ugly experience endured by the main character. Gustave von Aschenbach is taking a boat ride from Trieste to Venice while on holiday. Already in a state of psychological crisis, he stands on the deck watching a group of rowdy young men. One of these, a straw-hatted man, very gay and boisterous, Aschenbach discovers to be an old man like himself, made up as a dandy, but clearly and grotesquely a pretender to youth. Aschenbach is overwhelmed with disgust for the old man's ugliness. He:

> was shocked to see that the apparent youth was no youth at all. He was an old man, beyond a doubt, with wrinkles and crow's-feet round eye and mouth; the neck was shrunken and sinewy, his turned-up mustaches and small imperial were dyed, and the unbroken double row of yellow teeth that showed when he laughed were but too obviously a cheapish false set. Aschenbach was moved to shudder as he watched the creature and his association with the rest of the group. Could they not see he was old, that he had no right to wear the clothes they wore and present to be one of them? Aschenbach put his hand to his brow and covered his eyes. He felt quite canny, as though the world were suffering a break-like distortion of perspective that he might arrest by shutting it out for a few minutes.
>
> (p. 390)

Had some horrible distorting mirror been held up to Aschenbach? It was as though he foresaw his own impending psychological deterioration in the ugliness of the old dandy. In fact, a motif throughout the novel is the shadowing of Aschenbach by a series of ugly and menacing male figures whose appearances mark each stage of his descent into madness and eventual death.

For Aschenbach as Mann depicts him, and for me, the perception of the aged dandy and the feral boy, respectively, represented the unexpected (and unwanted) emergence into consciousness of frightening fantasies of ourselves. We were not disinterested, somewhat displeased onlookers; we were powerfully and tellingly provoked and engaged by the images before us. The ugly other were both alien and got under our skins. Both of us were fascinated and repulsed, physically aroused as if in the presence of danger. In these two examples, the interactive nature of ugliness is vividly portrayed.

Ugliness and Affect

The experience of ugliness involves strong negative affects. Disgust, fear, anxiety, terror, repulsion, and dread, as well as desire and fascination, all contribute to a range of powerful affective states that characterize our response to ugliness. Clearly, these affects can be partially explained by the fact that ugliness embodies fantasies of a disturbing nature, linked to aggressive wishes, sexual desire, and developmental disturbances. But in addition, the disruption of our relationship to reality, the sense of disjunction and alienation between self and world, can account for at least part of the horror and other fears, as well as the desire for and fascination with a reality that seems so close but ineluctably alien. Most important, ugliness triggers the anxiety of disorientation, the collapse of ideals, and the eruption of frightening fantasies, the rending of the aesthetic fabric of one's inner and outer experience. Like Aschenbach, we, too, may close our eyes in distress, hoping for things to be made whole again.

Ugliness in Psychopathology

Normally, the experience of ugliness is a transitory and relatively infrequent experience. However, in some forms of psychopathology, ugliness plays a central part in symptomatology. I believe that, in these patients, the concern with ugliness indicates an inner state of crisis, part of which involves an experience of rupture or distortion in aesthetic sensibility, in the formal organization of the individual's psychological life. I will illustrate this through discussions of anorexia nervosa, in which the patient's sense of his or her own body as ugly is common, and of depression, in which self and world are transformed into ugly, loathsome versions of the normal.

The Sense of Ugliness in Anorexic Patients

The self of the anorexic exists in a state of persistent crisis that may have several sources. The inner world is so at risk of annihilation or collapse that there is a defensive organization of experience around the physical perception of the anorectic's body. The psychological self is no longer the problem; rather, the body becomes the object of preoccupation. Specifically, the person finds his or her normal body to be ugly. Usually, this is associated with fat, but other body distortions can also be objects of concern. Most important, the patient believes him- or herself to be ugly and begins to take action to improve his or her appearance; this belief underlies the characteristic obsession with losing weight to repair the perceived deficit.

Many possible reasons have been given for this phenomenon – most commonly, conflict about sexuality. But as for the defensive function of ugliness, it is commonly the case that the underlying problem – whatever that may be – is transferred from an inner disturbance to one concretely linked to the external body. The anorexic believes that if he or she can change the form of the ugly body and beautify the self, the problem will be solved. In the worst of cases, the ultimate beauty is the disappearance of the self entirely.

In her autobiography, Lucy Daniels (2002) described her struggle with anorexia during her adolescent and young adult years. In the following quotation, she describes the physical horror she experienced as she gazed at her changing body in the mirror. At first, from a relative distance, she found the image reassuring:

> The reflection usually soothed those concerns about breasts and pubic hair by making what was there looks [sic] less than my fingers felt. In the mirror, my bony chest appeared full but not knobby, and the pubic hair wasn't visible at all unless I got right up next to the glass. But disgust would well up in me again whenever I did that: I felt dizziness and nausea, as well as a sudden cold tingling at the roots of my hair, on my arms and legs as well as scalp. My body changing made me feel as though an alien force was taking over against my will, turning me into a gross and hateful monster.
>
> (p. 73)

Daniels's experience of the formal alteration of her body led to preoccupation with her appearance and to meticulous and relentless efforts to sculpt her physical shape through controlled caloric intake. Later, psychoanalysis helped her to understand the unconscious determinants of her illness: a tortured identification with her mother, combined with internalization of her father's ambivalence about her sexuality and ambition. But fundamentally, it was ugliness that shadowed her, day and night.

The Sense of Ugliness in Depressive Patients

An experience of ugliness may also be a symptom of depression. Struggles with self-depletion, guilt, and fragmentation are spread out over the depressive person's experience of his or her entire reality. Inner horror becomes outer ugliness. In Kleinian terms, there is a projection of aggression onto a world that can be engaged and controlled. But the depression reflects dread that aggression will prevail nonetheless and that all will be lost, so the world becomes repulsive and aesthetically grotesque. Formal order collapses or becomes bizarre and alien. Ugliness presses itself upon the depressive patient, who becomes increasingly unable to resist. Suicide becomes necessary when the ugliness of the world reaches even the core of the self. Self-destruction and a fantasized union with a beautiful afterlife become the only way out. Whatever the cause of depression, the depressed person experiences ugliness as a concretization of self-crisis. Invariably, one of the defining traits of clinical improvement is a reduction of this sense of ugliness and the resurgence of a more benignly aesthetic experience of living.

Clinical Illustration

Jim was a 30-year-old man who began psychoanalytic treatment due to problems with work performance and a general sense of dysthymia. His initial response to his male analyst was distrust and angry expressions of discontent. The analyst could do nothing right. Jim would often accuse him of being distracted or asleep during sessions.

Six months into treatment, the analyst went on a one-week vacation. Upon his return, Jim reported a remarkable experience: "The night you went away, I went to a party and met this incredible girl. She was exquisitely beautiful, and I fell in love immediately. It was such a surprise. I just saw her and suddenly I was in love. I couldn't stop looking at her." Jim reported that he spent quite a bit of time with her during the week, but since she was involved with someone else, the relationship came to an end just prior to the analyst's return.

"Do you think your falling in love may have been connected to my being away?" the analyst asked.

"I don't know. I don't think so."

"What do you associate to my question?"

"Well . . ." Jim paused. "There *is* one thing. It doesn't make sense, but I see in my mind a crooked old branch that used to hang over the lake near our summer house. It's all twisted and black, an ugly, frightening thing, like in a haunted house or something. The image makes my skin crawl."

"Where was the branch?"

"At our summer house, upstate. But what does this have to do with anything?" Jim was quite anxious.

"The house where you used to go when your father was sick." (Jim's father had died of a long illness when he was a teenager.)

"Yeah, but there was another place. Another branch. In the backyard of my old girlfriend's house. We would sit out there during visits. Her father was writing a book, and he would ask me questions . . . about homosexuality."

The analyst and Jim then discussed the way in which falling in love with the beautiful girl may have been Jim's response to the analyst's absence. The unexpected longings associated with the loss of the patient's father and an intensification of homosexual fantasies were triggered by intimacy with the analyst.

In terms of our subject here, ugliness, the patient's image of the branch was most striking. Interestingly, his first level of defense was the discovery of the beautiful woman. This enthrallment, more aesthetic than erotic, disguised threatening fantasies associated with the analyst. Jim's feelings toward the girl were not simply sexual; it was her strikingly youthful look and beauty that captivated him. (The analyst was middle-aged and not beautiful.) In the analytic session, the image of the twisted branch became the focus of an experience of intense ugliness. The lovely aesthetic experience was shattered, and a dead withered object replaced it. This ugliness was directly associated with several things: the dead father who had wasted away during his illness; the analyst, who had a mild physical handicap; and the branch under which Jim discussed homosexuality with a paternal figure. A shriveled penis was still another, later association, indicative of Jim's anxiety about sexual performance.

The key factor here was the pronounced way in which Jim's experiences of beauty and ugliness were juxtaposed in dynamic relation with each other, with the former acting as a reparative, protective defense, and the latter representing the presence of disruptive, disorienting longings and fantasies associated with sexuality, dependence, and death.

Conclusion

The question has sometimes been asked: Can ugliness become so profound that it acquires a beauty of its own? To answer this question, I think it is important to reiterate that beauty and ugliness are not qualities of external phenomena, but instead are psychological in nature. Therefore, it is not that ugliness acquires beauty; rather, the person experiences as beautiful that which was once considered ugly. I suggest that many experiences of ugliness lead to a process of working through in which the sense of disruption and disorder is subject to integration into familiar modes of understanding and aesthetic order. Although ugliness can be especially challenging in this regard, it is a common enough occurrence that a person confronted by an ugly experience can eventually integrate the unique form of the object into a special category of idealization. For this to occur, the internal dangers cannot be too severe nor the aesthetic disruptions too radical – for example, a car can be so ugly that it is beautiful.

Another factor in this type of idealization is the capacity to empathize or to comfortably project nonthreatening fantasies onto the object. In the experience of ugliness, as noted earlier, there is a rupture between internal and external reality, and the ugly object is felt to be both disturbingly similar and utterly foreign – an untenable psychological state. The comfortable intermingling of fantasy and reality breaks down, and fear and repulsion dominate. When we gradually begin to find what was ugly to be beautiful, we feel able to engage the object in an interplay of fantasy, projection, and identification; and the object, once alien, is now recognized as having an odd but special status in our experience of the world.

Another interesting question is whether something can be simultaneously experienced as both ugly and beautiful. I do not think this is possible, since the perceptions, feelings, and behaviors of the two experiences are antithetical. However, it is nonetheless true that in the conversion to beauty, the once-ugly thing has not changed its appearance; it still looks the same. So the formal qualities that had been perceived as ugly remain, but they no longer evoke anxiety, nor do they disrupt the observer's aesthetic sensibility; they simply cease to cause revulsion. They may still seem unique and even odd, but they are no longer ugly.

For the artist, ugliness can be an opportunity – he or she confronts ugliness, and through the creative process, brings form and perfection to bear on disintegration and disorder. In a similar way, analysts and their patients engage in a structured dialogue in which ugly memories, experiences, and fantasies are given form and meaning, and ultimately, through the special aesthetic organization of the analytic process, the power of ugliness to harm is eliminated. In fact, it can be said that both the artist and the analyst are drawn to ugliness. Both professionals seek to immerse themselves in the tragic and disordered side of life. They study and come to understand their own humanity, and one of the most human experiences is of ugliness. Whether through art or understanding, ugliness can become a valuable part of a meaningful life world. The struggle to understand and empathize with what is at first considered ugly can result in an expansion of the psychological and relational horizon that defines one's life. In this way, ugliness succumbs to beauty.

Notes

1 In this paper, I am not concerned with the more colloquial and watered-down use of the term *ugly* that we often use in everyday speech for things that displease us.
2 For a reconsideration of the primal scene in this context, see Esman (1973). Esman argued persuasively against the idea that the primal scene is invariably traumatic to the child. He did not explicitly address the aesthetic dimension, as Fleiss did, but by implication, Esman might have been arguing that the observation of parental coitus is not necessarily ugly to the child either.
3 Later in this chapter, I will consider an important exception to this phenomenon in the attitude of the artist.

Chapter 8

The Sublime

In addition to beauty and ugliness, an important concern of Western aesthetic philosophy and psychology has been the problem of the *sublime*. The sublime is the general term for a form of aesthetic experience that is characterized by extreme affective states such as awe, astonishment, rapture, fear, and enthrallment; these feelings are stimulated in response to an object, event, and/or idea that is perceived to possess immensity, power, obscurity, formlessness, and other terrible aspects, where human comprehension and emotionality are pushed to (and perhaps beyond) their limits. Throughout history, people have sought out and cultivated the sublime, from Homer's depiction of the battle of the gods, to Dante's evocation of hell, to Milton's fallen angels, to Frederick Church's cataract of Niagara, to Jackson Pollock's swirling masses of thrown pigments, to Tolkien's creation of Middle Earth.

However, strangely, the sublime has rarely been mentioned in the psychoanalytic literature. Freud never referred to it, and later psychoanalysts, despite interest in other aesthetic issues, have discussed the subject only in the context of other issues. This is remarkable, especially since the sublime was of major interest to philosophers such as Kant and Hegel, as well as to important literary figures, such as Schiller, and to musicians like Wagner and Mahler.

This chapter presents a perspective on the sublime that reflects contemporary psychoanalytic aesthetic thinking. My goals here are: (1) given the lack of attention to the subject in psychoanalysis, I will discuss the history of the concept of the sublime, so that the reader feels grounded in the historical and philosophical roots of the concept; (2) I will review the psychoanalytic literature (brief as it is) regarding the sublime; (3) I will propose a psychoanalytic model of sublime experience that links the concept to other aesthetic ideas, such as beauty, in addition to noting its foundation in developmental experience – specifically, in the emergence of the paternal aesthetic in early childhood; and (4) I will conclude with a discussion of the function of sublime experience in psychological life.

A Brief History of the Sublime

The concept of the sublime has had a long history, but it did not develop into a central focus of Western aesthetics until the eighteenth century. The classical Greeks distinguished three styles of rhetoric: high, middle, and low. These were technical

DOI: 10.4324/9781003532484-8

distinctions, however. The first philosopher to relate the idea of "high" style to the phenomenological concept of the sublime, beyond the technical, was Longinus, who authored a treatise entitled "On the Sublime" in the first century CE. For Longinus, "sublimity is the echo of greatness of the spirit" (1991, p. 4). In fact, finding it more than an echo, Longinus argued that the sublime was like a thunderclap, suddenly leaping in between author and reader to create a powerful perception of greatness.

Most remarkable about Longinus's perspective was his emphasis on the psy- chological domain, the realm of profound experience and emotion, beyond the formal and technical approach. However, Longinus had almost no effect on classical Greek and Roman thought, and it was not until the Boileau translation appeared in 1672 that the philosophy of the sublime became a prominent part of aesthetic thinking.

In the 1680s, Thomas Burnett published *Sacred Theory of the Earth*, a physi- cotheological treatise in which he argued that God, in creating mountains and riv- erbeds as enduring signs of his judgment and power, had permanently scarred the once pure and smooth earth. Paradoxically, Burnett wrote that he was both awed by and attracted to the earth's tormented landscape. This had nothing to do with beauty, he argued; rather, it was the vast awfulness of nature's grandeur that ren- dered him so "rapt" and "ravished." Burnett's work touched on many of the central themes of what would become the aesthetics of the sublime: the rapture before enormous power, immensity, violence, formlessness, and the infinite. (Burnett's argument that sublime experience was a response to the manifestation of God's power in the tortured surface of the earth was an influential idea that emphasized the paternal source of the sublime.)

The problem of the sublime became central to Western aesthetic thought dur- ing the eighteenth century, with numerous thinkers struggling with the concept (Ashfield and De Bolla, 1996). In 1757, Edmund Burke wrote one of the first great philosophical works on the sublime. Significantly, Burke argued that the experi- ence of the sublime was grounded in states of extreme emotionality and, specifi- cally, that of terror. He stated:

Whatever is fitted in any sort to excite the ideas of pain, and danger whatever is in any sort terrible, or is conversant about terrible objects, or operates in a man- ner analogous to terror, is a source of the Sublime, that is, it is productive of the strongest emotion that the mind is capable of feeling.
(Burke as quoted in Ashfield and De Bolla, 1996, p. 86)

But Burke argued that simple fear is not sublime. The emotional state provoked by the sublime, however, is more of a state of shock or astonishment. He wrote:

The passion caused by the great and sublime in nature, when those causes oper- ate most powerfully, is astonishment; and astonishment is that state of the soul, in which all its motions are suspended, with some degree of horror. In this case the mind is so entirely filled neither with its object, that it cannot entertain any other, nor by consequence reason on that object which employs it. Hence arises the great power of the sublime, that far from being produced by them, it antici-pates our reasoning, and hurries us on by an irresistible force. Astonishment, as I have said, is the effect of the sublime in the highest degree; the inferior effects are admiration, reverence, and respect.

(Burke as quoted in Ashfield and De Bolla, 1996, p. 101]

Paradoxically, the pain, shock, and terror of the sublime are always accom-panied by a "relative pleasure," according to Burke, "a sort of delightful horror, which is the most genuine effect, and the truest test of the sublime" (p. 115). He distinguished between the positive pleasures found in the satisfaction of needs, on the one hand, and the delight experienced because of cessation of pain, on the other. He argued that the sublime always comprises both the experience of terror and a sense of safety; in fact, if danger or pain "pressed too dearly," the experience would be simply terrible, not sublime. The sublime involves an encounter with the terrible from a position (a psychological or moral one) of safety. This sense of "delightful horror" became a central part of all subsequent models of the sublime.

In 1790, Immanuel Kant published *Critique of Aesthetic Judgment*, in which he presented his model of the "Analytic of the Sublime." He moved away from Burke's emphasis on the emotional basis of sublime experience, proposing instead an approach based on judgment and reason:

The proper unchangeable fundamental measure of nature is its absolute whole, which, regarding nature as a phenomenon, would be infinity comprehended. But since this fundamental measure is a self-contradictory concept (on account of the impossibility of the absolute totality of an endless progress), that magnitude of a natural object on which the imagination fruitlessly spends its whole faculty of comprehension must carry our concept of nature to a supersensible substrate (which lies at its basis and at the basis of our faculty of thought). As this, how-ever, is great beyond all standards of sense, it makes us judge as *sublime,* not so much the object, as our own state of mind in the estimation of it.

(Kant as quoted in Ashfield and De Bolla, 1996, p. 198)

Human reason is thus confronted by its own limits, even as it comprehends those limits by recognizing the existence of an unimaginable infinity. In sublimity, the imagination is free from all internal bounds. Kant saw this as encompassing the simultaneous feeling of pain at the contradiction between aesthetic estimation and reason, and pleasure at the mind's ability to grasp the true limits of the senses and human thought itself. Fear, awe, respect, and even veneration accompany this sublime experience, but ultimately, in the truly sublime experience, all terror sub-sides; there is a cessation of uneasiness, replaced by a state of joy. The safety in the sublime experience is internal; it comes from the full recognition of the futility of human resistance before the immensity and ultimate power of nature. We not only intuit infinite space and power – we also resign ourselves to that knowledge, and thus the mind is no longer subject to the tyranny of nature; it is free. Kant's contemporary, Friedrich Schiller (1793, 1801) wrote several influential papers elaborating on Kant's model of the sublime from a more literary and romantic perspective.

A major focus in the study of the sublime is its difference from beauty. Although some thinkers have conflated the concepts, making the sublime a subgrouping of the beautiful, most models of the sublime have argued for a sharp distinction. For one thing, the phenomenologies of the two are seen as quite different: the sublime is vast in size, while beauty is of a human scale; the sublime is powerful and beauty is gentle; the sublime is terrible, with beauty being peaceful and calming; the sublime is formless, while beauty is clear and defined, and the sublime is incomprehensible, in contrast to beauty's meaningfulness.

The affective experience of the subject is also different: before the sublime, the individual trembles, and joy is mingled with terror; before the beautiful, the subject is pleased and reassured, and there is a sense of comfort and peace. However, both the sublime and beauty are considered aesthetic experiences in which idealization plays a central part, whether it is the perfect balance and grace of a beautiful summer day, or the terrible grandeur of a thunderstorm in the mountains. I believe that the distinction between beauty and the sublime is real and important; later in this chapter, that distinction will help us formulate a psychoanalytic approach to the topic.

The aesthetic of the sublime has had a major influence on Western culture for the past four hundred years. Prominent examples are numerous: the music of Beethoven, Wagner, and the early Stravinsky, as well as the paintings of J. M. W. Turner in England, and Thomas Cole, Edwin Church, and Albert Bierstadt in the United States. Even into the mid-twentieth century, the sublime continued to manifest in the works of the abstract expressionists (Newman, 1948). For example, in the work of Jackson Pollock, the formlessness, power, and terror of the sublime became associated with the natural forces within the self. When Pollack was asked why he did not paint from nature, he answered, "I *am* nature." Interestingly, the artist Barnett Newman reasserted the traditional distinction between beauty and the sublime when he argued that the primary goal of modern art was to destroy beauty and to pursue the sublime.

Our culture's interest in the sublime continues to the present day, with the popular success of such movies as *Lord of the Rings* and *Star Wars*, both of which rely extensively on the cultivation of the sublime in narrative, music, and imagery. In addition, the sublime continues to interest art criticism and philosophy – for example, in Bill Beckley's collection of essays titled *Sticky Sublime* (2001).

In the next section, I will discuss the psychoanalytic literature of the sublime, but before we begin, let me propose a definition that we can employ to develop a psychoanalytic approach. My definition is consistent with the classical view of the sublime, that of Burke and Kant, largely because I believe that their definition was the most precise and psychologically grounded. More modern approaches have tended to be too varied, often vague and academic. In addition, my definition captures a form of aesthetic experience that many of us recognize from our own experience, both outside and inside the world of art and artists (being an aspect of general psychology, rather than just the psychology of art). Thus, even though the sublime may have several definitions, the following one seems most appropriate for psychoanalytic exploration.

The sublime is a form of experience of the world, most often a landscape, natural event, or weather, but it may also be a human activity, such as war, or an artistic creation (for example, a symphony or a painting) that is perceived to possess qualities that are transcendent, powerful, spatially large, exceedingly complex, and/or extraordinarily beautiful. The sublime experience is sudden, sensually powerful, and affectively moving. It can provoke horror, awe, wonder, or rapture, but most important, it provokes astonishment.

The sublime is also felt to be vast, myriad, and complex, according to my definition, and the individual's capacity to understand, organize, and give meaning to the experience is pushed to the limit, perhaps resulting in the failure to cognitively grasp it. Paradoxically, the sublime experience involves feelings of pain at the encounter with the limits of thought, and delight or joy at the recognition of our freedom from restriction and threat.

Psychoanalytic Contributions to the Concept of the Sublime

Earlier, I noted the lack of psychoanalytic discussion of the sublime. However, several important analytic thinkers have addressed the topic indirectly or by implication. I would like to discuss some of the ideas of Kris, Greenacre, and Kohut that I think may offer a jumping-off point for our discussion of a more elaborate psychoanalytic model.

Ernst Kris, in *Psychoanalytic Explorations in Art* (1952), links the sublime with the experience of ecstasy in his discussion of the Freudian theory of the comic. Here there is a sudden and unexpected, pleasurable reduction in psychic tensions associated with the resolution of a potential conflict between drive and superego demands. In other words, after an increase in excitation and conflict, there is a gratifying reduction in psychic expenditure. On the other hand, in mania, the ego triumphs over the superego (which renounces its power), and the resolution of conflict is achieved through a one-sided, extreme state of pleasure, unmodulated by conscience. Kris (1952) added regarding the sublime:

If mania is to be regarded as the pathological correlate of the comic, we must look to the Sublime for the experience that corresponds to the normal life of ecstasy. But we know that the Sublime is a "psychic greatness." And if the comic effects a reduction of mental energy, the Sublime calls for a surplus expenditure of this.

(p. 187)

In the sublime experience, a surplus of cathexis is projected by means of fantasies that are of an exalted and aggrandized manner. For example, there is an experience of a storm, a sunset, a mountain, or perhaps simply of a profound idea – one that is felt to have extraordinary traits or supernatural powers. These are aspects of the superego that are externalized, thereby becoming a source of awe and dread. However, in the sublime, there is also an identification with the externalized superego, in which the ego is neither overwhelmed nor triumphant, but rather, there is an experience of unity between the ego and the sublime object.

The conflict that characterizes the comic and the triumph of the ego in mania is avoided in the sublime through the experience of unity of ego and superego, where both remain intact in a stable and balanced relationship. This accounts for the unique combination of intense pleasure and fear, as well as the positive effect that the sublime experience has on the ego. In addition, part of the power of the sublime is the successful and sanctioned discharge of desexualized libido. This results from the ecstatic expenditure of surplus mental energy to which Kris referred.

Phyllis Greenacre (1953, 1956) discussed the experience of awe in childhood. She defined awe as "solemn and reverential wonder, tinged with latent fear, inspired by what is *sublime and majestic in nature*" or "dread mingled with veneration, as of the Divine Being" (1956, p. 31, emphasis in the original). Greenacre argued that the experience of the sublime arises in childhood because of observation of the father's penis. However, she pointed out that, before the child can respond to the phallus, he or she must first have begun the process of differentiation from the mother, so that there is some understanding of separateness – variations in body configuration and size combined with an increase in genital feelings. The encounter with the penis (especially if it is erect) is felt as a shock, and the child experiences a combination of fear, fascination, and admiration. However, the awesome nature of the father's penis is based not just on its relative size, but also on the stimulation of sexual fantasies that blend desire with fears of harmful, even violent penetration (heterosexual in the girl, homosexual in the boy). This accounts for the highly charged, internal state of "delightful horror" associated with the sight of the penis.

In her 1956 paper on awe in childhood, Greenacre extended the source of the sublime from the father's penis to the child's experience of the father as a whole: "experiences involving masculine strength, power, glory, virility, or the phallus itself" (p. 79). Greenacre's idea of the origin of the experience of the sublime in the encounter with the masculinity of the father (concretely represented in its purest form in the erect phallus) has important implications for the notion of a paternal aesthetic, which I will take up in the next section.

Heinz Kohut, although not directly discussing the sublime, linked experiences of awe – and by implication, the sublime – to aspects of the experience of the idealized parental imago. Although in *The Analysis of the Self* (1971), he described awe as a part of the symptom picture of narcissistic character disorder, I believe it is safe to say that the feeling of awe and the experience of the sublime may form parts of experiences of idealization that occur not just in mental disorders (where Kohut notes that the awe is often vague, fragmentary, and not associated with a whole object), but also in states of mental health (where the sense of awe would be clear, encompassing, and associated with a distinct object or sensation).

However, I would argue that the experience of awe and the sublime would be most clearly associated with the experience of the archaic, idealized paternal imago, in which there is also some disintegration associated with empathic failure. This would account for the balance between admiration and fear that is part of the sublime. But the failure in empathy and the resulting self-crisis and disintegration would not be severe enough to lead to a neurotic or psychotic reaction; rather, in the sublime, the capacity to idealize remains intact, and the paternal imago retains a high degree of idealization, but the emergence of aggression invests the idealization with a malevolent taint, and hence a unique combination of terror and admiration results.

I believe that Kris, Greenacre, and Kohut offer a solid foundation for the theory of a psychoanalytic sublime. First, it is a normal state in which the ego and an idealized object are experienced as powerfully linked, if not at times merged; second, the experience of the sublime originates in middle childhood, when the differentiation from the mother is being accomplished and awareness of the father is beginning; third, the sublime is linked to the child's experience of the father's unique characteristics: power, size, importance, the phallus; and fourth, the sublime blends qualities of idealization with aggression and is an outgrowth of normal levels of empathic failure associated with the child's relationship with the father.

In the next section, I will integrate these concepts into a model of the paternal aesthetic in which the child's response to formal aspects of the relationship with the father results in the experience that we know as the sublime. This model includes the following: (1) establishment of a link between the sublime experience and developmental processes, (2) clarification of the sources of aesthetic sensibility in the infant's relationship with his or her parents, (3) differentiation between the maternal aesthetic (beauty) and the paternal aesthetic (the sublime), (4) elaboration of specific characteristics of the sublime in terms of the paternal aesthetic, and (5) illustration of the psychological function of sublime experience.

The Psychoanalytic Sublime

The model of psychoanalytic aesthetics discussed in this book takes as its object of study the *form* of the individual's internal and external experience: how it is shaped, colored, given texture and rhythm. For example, we are interested in the psychological sources of the formal experience of the sublime – e.g., size (immense), shape (formless, without boundary), color (either extraordinarily pure or intricately multiple), light (of obliterating intensity, or resulting in deep shadow), rhythm (rough, jagged, choppy), and clarity of detail (obscure). An individual's aesthetic sense has its origin in early development, during which formal aspects of experiences are shaped, made meaningful, and granted affective significance. We examine how these experiences are psychologically structured and elaborated over time. Toward this end, I will discuss the vicissitudes of maternal aesthetics (beauty) and paternal aesthetics (the sublime). I am using the terms *maternal* and *paternal* not to identify persons of a particular gender or social/familial role, but rather as orientations toward self and self-in-the-world that are fundamental to the evolution of human aesthetic sensibility.

The Maternal Aesthetic: The Matrix of Beauty

From a developmental point of view, the earliest aesthetic-like experiences (what Ellen Dissanayake (2000] called *protoaesthetic experience*) occur primarily between mother and infant. The maternal aesthetic crystallizes out of the complex and dynamic experiences of rhythm, flow, texture, sound, warmth, shape, and tonality that characterize the qualities of interrelatedness and self-experience within the mother/infant dyad (Beebe and Lachmann, 2002). These formal qualities, as opposed to the contents of interaction (*what* is said, *what* is fed and eaten, *what* is provided), are internalized procedurally; that is, they are prereflective and nonverbal forms of knowing. Over time, this aesthetic sensibility is extended beyond the dyad and becomes a template for the child's formal organization of self and world. Another important part of the child's developing aesthetic orientation involves the idealization of the mother and mother/child dyad itself (as well as aspects of self-experience linked to the mother). Specifically, this idealization occurs through the exchange of *value affects*.

Every infant is hard-wired to recognize his or her mother as a special object and to engage with her through affect. Of course, the normal mother is also oriented toward her infant and motivated to engage him or her affectively. From the start, an important component of the mother/infant interaction is the sharing of affects that communicate mutual valuation. Affect, which Kohut refers to as "the gleam in the mother's eye" – communicating her excitement, joy, and pride in her child – is shared with the infant, who responds with pleasure, excitement, and joy. The infant's affective response has a positive and reinforcing impact on the mother, whose value affect intensifies, leading to an amplification of the value affect exchange. In other words, there is a positive feedback loop that becomes an established, positively reinforcing pattern of affective interaction. This pattern colors internalization of the value experience in terms of the infant's representation of both the mother and self-experience.

Thus, the normal tendency to experience the mother as special becomes elaborated and structuralized as idealization: the mother is idealized, the self-in-relation to the mother is idealized, and the relationship is idealized. In addition, the formal aspects of such idealization (the mother's touch; the sound of her voice; the rhythms of her words and her soothing rocking; the colors of her skin, hair, and eyes; the configuration of lines and forms in her smiling face; the tastes and smells of her body) become the highly valued sensations that coalesce and crystallize into an aesthetic sensibility, which is gradually articulated and elaborated into mature forms of aesthetic experience, such as the sense of beauty (see chapter six).

The Paternal Aesthetic: The Source of the Sublime

Another form of aesthetic experience is associated with the paternal imago – this, as we shall see, is the source of the sublime. (In fact, if we examine Burnett's writings, we find that the origin of the sublime in nature is literally the disruption and scarring of the beautifully round and pure earth via God's aggressive acts. Over time, this notion became more abstract, but never lost its source in the power and immensity of the father.)

During normal development, the father enters or touches upon the aesthetic space that the mother and infant have created and cultivated. Traditionally, this is viewed as occurring later than the infant's analogous experience of the mother, but it is probably more accurate to say that the father's aesthetic orientation is simultaneous with the mother's, and only partially differentiated from hers. These experiences of the father become the stimulus for the internalization of complex object and self-with-object representations that make up the paternal imago.

The paternal imago is not singular or static but reflects dynamic and multiple sets of representations that are organized around the child's experience of the relationship with the father. The *form* of these representations – gestures, shapes, colors, sounds, and textures – makes up the paternal aesthetic, and its elements are important components of what becomes for the child a distinct aesthetic sensibility. This imago is derived from actual and fantasized experiences of the father in the context of other familial relationships – most significantly, that with the mother.

Thus, the paternal imago is over-determined and can reflect the child's response to maternal traits as well as realistic experiences of the father. It is also important to note that there are tremendous variations in the paternal aesthetic; the approach that I am taking here is for heuristic purposes and should not be mistaken for a varied and multifaceted reality. That said, the father/child aesthetic is quite different from the mother/infant aesthetic. From the child's perspective, it is characterized by immense size, extraordinary power, obscurity, formlessness, intense affects (such as fear), and even danger – all characteristics of sublime experience.

Like the mother, the father is also a special object that becomes idealized by the child. This process involves the exchange and augmentation of value affects that invest the representations of the father, self, and relationship with a high degree of value. The types of value affects are different in the father/child relationship compared to the mother/infant dyad. Father and child are more inclined toward noisy and/or expansive expressions of affect having to do with enthusiastic reactions ("Wow, that was great!"), playful aggressiveness (roughhousing), and scary pretending ("I'll get you!"). These affects, which are shared through facial expressions, verbal exchange, and action, infuse the relationship with an intense form of value.

Optimally, both father and child experience a heightened sense of well-being, enhanced self-esteem, vitality, and joy at being together. At the same time, many of these affects also involve intense excitement, fear (even panic), expansiveness, and awe. Paternal idealizations that crystallize out of these affective exchanges acquire a different tone from the maternal idealization, and this will largely determine the unique combination of affective responses that compose the paternal aesthetic experience. The father is experienced as loved but feared, intimate but expansive, familiar but complex, accessible but immense – in other words, an entire range of often contradictory experiences that lend a remarkable intensity to the paternal aesthetic sensibility.

Another important factor of the paternal imago is its function in the psychological separation process, in which the child's internal and external worlds become increasingly individuated. The father's function in this process is to create additional opportunities for self-development and to offer the child new types of interpersonal experiences. Regarding aesthetics, as noted, the father offers distinctly different ways of structuring and giving form to interactions. This alternative aesthetic creates experiences of newness and stimulates the child's excitement and creativity. Joseph Addison (1712) discussed these feelings in sublime experience:

> He has annexed a secret pleasure to the ideas of anything that is new, or uncommon, that he might encourage us in the pursuit after knowledge, and engage us to search into the wonders of creation; for every new idea brings such a pleasure along with it, as rewards any pains we have taken in its acquisition, and consequently serves as a motive to put us upon fresh discoveries.
>
> (Addison as quoted in Ashfield and De Bolla, 1996, p. 64)

In other words, the paternal aesthetic found in sublime experience both gratifies the desire and motivation to seek out the new and different and creates opportunities for us to investigate and discover the world. Our sense of vigor and curiosity intensifies, and the inherent drive to separate and individuate becomes inseparable from our curiosity about the world around us. For the young child who encounters an entire universe of new experience, we can only guess at the awe, wonder, and astonishment that are evoked. New forms, shapes, the ever-expanding and open-ended line, and rich new colors mesmerize the child and draw him or her outward into a reality both fearsome and exhilarating.

During development, the child's experience of the paternal aesthetic is structuralized and extended beyond the relationship with the father through the pull toward cognitive/affective states that we know as the sublime. To illustrate this, I will discuss several different characteristics of sublime experience that can be directly linked to features of the paternal aesthetic.

Imagination

The sublime evokes entire realms of fantasy that invest the imagery of the natural world or the subject of an artwork with powerful and elaborate unconscious meaning. In fact, some critics, such as Ruskin, advise young painters to use dark colors and images of shadow to stimulate the imagination of the viewer toward the fearful and fantastic. Similarly, the maternal aesthetic creates a transitional zone in which the capacity to imagine and fantasize is stimulated and elaborated. Within the enclosed, safe, and attuned reality of the maternal dyad, the child dreams and strengthens the capacity to externalize the internal world and to enter a dialectic with what lies outside. Imagination is elaborated within the familiar container of the mother/infant dyad.

Winnicott noted that it is within this transitional space that the world is created and found, the infant's subjectivity merging indistinguishably with his or her environment. Over time, the repeated encounters with proof of the object's independent existence result in a growing recognition of the world apart from the child's own omnipotence. This is the dialectic between fantasy and reality, out of which meaning and knowledge emerge. The paternal aesthetic challenges the limits of the child's imagination; rather than experiencing the world as "created and found," the child encounters a dramatic and new external world that does not fit the familiar maternal mold. The father's power and size, the endless complexity of his world, the formless flux and flow of sensation, the excitement and fear that the child experiences as she is taken into this sublime universe – all these contribute to the dramatic quality of the paternal aesthetic, stimulating fantasy that is unconstrained, vivid, and therefore delightfully frightening.

Delight and Horror

Almost all theorists have noted the distinctive amalgamation of the affects of delight and horror in the sublime. From a psychoanalytic perspective, the intensity and the complex nature of emotional experience associated with the sublime suggest a source in the vicissitudes of fantasies and drives, and especially the possibility of some type of distortion in the mechanisms of sublimation. Failure of sublimation typically results in the emergence into consciousness of undisguised drive fantasies that cause intense anxiety and even horror. On the other hand, the sublime experience mixes anxiety with joy in almost equal measure, thereby appearing to contradict traditional psychoanalytic models that negate the simultaneous experience of pain and pleasure (except in perversion).

Normally, sublimation is the healthy and socially approved way in which forbidden desires and fantasies can be expressed and/or discharged in transformed but socially acceptable ways. The failure of sublimation does not result just in the internal experience of threatening desires and fantasies, but also in the inability to transform fantasies into forms that are compatible with the defensive strategies of the ego. The result is a disruption in the reconciliation between internal and external worlds. The externalization of fantasies occurs – fantasies that are then felt to be bizarre, alien, and threatening to self-organization. Horror is the most common affective response to the ugliness that we then encounter when our own more threatening wishes come to life and confront us with that which we most fear about ourselves (see chapter seven).

The father stimulates intense drive and affect states that were not part of the original maternal/infant dyad. He introduces the child to new levels of aggressiveness, physical discharge, and body excitation that push the limit of the young child's capacity to sublimate. The idealization of the father and the activities that the father engages in to contain and manage the child's excitement help to channel these drives and reduce anxiety. However, anxiety and the stimulation of fantasy and affect continue to be a part of the child's experience of the father. These lead to a form of sublimation that, rather than fully repressing and displacing fantasy, allows for the partial discharge of fantasy, within an experience in which enactment is both explicit and disguised. The result is that, in the paternal aesthetic experience, there is a blend of raw drive expression (the high mountains, torrents of water, tumbling clouds) and idealization (these passionate images and the feelings that they stir are felt to possess a type of formal perfection and high moral value). This form of sublimation thus allows both expression and protection. The result is that the child with the father, and the adult with the sublime object, experience a combination of horror and awe at the affective/drive intensity experienced in the presence of the other, and the delight that is felt in the expression/discharge of passions is embodied in an ideal being that has been separated from threatening fantasy content.

Immensity

The most common feature of the sublime is enormous size. Most authors have noted that sublimity is pronounced in the experience of mountains, vast empty spaces, the ocean, or immense storms. This characteristic is clearly seen in the work of American landscapists such as Bierstadt, who created images of mountains in which jagged pinnacles of rock soar beyond measure.

In contrast, the space of the maternal aesthetic is enclosed. The mother molds her body to match that of her child, curving inward, constructing a shared space in which two bodies (two persons) define together a human-sized, discreet environment, creating for the infant a sense of the mother as an object within the infant's range of size and limited perspective. She also creates and manages structures and spaces within which the child lives, which are compatible in size with the infant's self-experience. This results in an aesthetic of maternal space, which conforms comfortably to the infant's scale. Within the containing space of the dyad, the child's capacity to engage in and manage fantasy develops. Aesthetic experiences, associated with forms, sounds, and rhythms that define the dyadic space, are internalized, and over time, these experiences evolve into templates for the organization of beauty.

Conversely, the sublime is expansive and extraordinarily large. The father takes the child out of the specially structured environment and offers an experience of immensity. The father's body is the child's first encounter with immense size, not only based on its physical bulk, but also due to the opening outward of the father's body – a body that, rather than enfolding and circling back like the mother's, moves beyond, gesturing toward the wide world.

In this way, the father explodes the interpersonal space, leading and accompanying the child into a vastly enlarged new universe. The size of the world into which the child is taken is experienced as immense, and this underlies the experience of the sublime. As the father lifts the child high into the air, that immensity spreads out endlessly, as from the peak of a high mountain. The experience is complex: the child is in the arms of the idealized father, and even while feeling held safely, is excited by the expansion of space and the experience of the world beyond the maternal/infant dyadic environment.

Incomprehensibility

The sublime is ultimately unknowable. There is a sense of such vastness, complexity, or obscurity that the limits of the ability of human thought to grasp the nature of the sublime object are surpassed. In fact, Burke and Kant both argued that it is the recognition of the limits of thought that results in psychical pain – but also, paradoxically, in pleasure at the recognition of one's limitations in confronting the universe. The incomprehensible sublime both terrifies and thrills us; it compels us to confront our limitations even as it makes clear the futility of thought in the face of eternal mysteries.

The maternal aesthetic is elaborated through communication. The beauty found in this aesthetic makes sense and brings meaning to experience. The infant gradually comes to know the mother and to understand the feelings and interactions that the two of them share. In addition, it is through the mother's responsiveness that the child comes to organize and know his or her internal world, developing a capacity to articulate meaningful affect in the relationship. The sublime begins with meaningful reality, but then evokes the disturbing sense that the most compelling aspects of the experience are unintelligible. The father and child enter a large, expanded world that is no longer centered around the child's capacity to communicate and learn, but exists outside on its own. Meaning is no longer centered within the maternal/infant dyad; it now becomes external and, ultimately, never fully knowable, especially given the child's limited experience and ability. As the child struggles to make sense of the experience, he or she becomes aware of the incapacity to do so.

In this sense, then, part of the paternal aesthetic is the experience of the organizing capacity of the mind pushed to its limit. Potential forms, colors, rhythms, and sounds cover an endless range, and the child's amplified experience results in a cascade of new stimuli with strange and powerful aesthetics. The paternal aesthetic experience (the sublime) is beyond the ability of the mind to structure or give meaning to it. In fact, I would say that part of the pleasure of the sublime is the way that it exercises the mind's capacity for meaning making, but in the end, the most stirring truth that the mind recognizes is its own limitations (a factor Kant took pleasure in). There is pleasure in the act of engaging an ultimately unsolvable problem within the context of the idealized father's power and immensity.

Power

The sublime is about the sensation of power. The coming storms, the angry waves, the jagged and rocky tower – all are part of an experience of stupendous energy and might. This power is both frightening and thrilling, and, once again, such power is experienced as inherent to the sublime object, which is safely located yet vividly present.

The power found in the mother's aesthetic is strong but attuned to the child's own capacity. She matches her grip, her touch, the rhythms of her rocking, and the intensity of her voice to the child's own level of power. For the child, there is a balance between his or her own feelings of self-efficacy and the mother's responsiveness. The infant gains confidence in its own power to affect and create the world.

On the other hand, the paternal aesthetic involves the experience of power that is extraordinary and potentially overwhelming for the child. The child experiences the father's power as externally centered and oriented, rather than attuned to and linked with the child's sense of self-efficacy. The child feels lifted and transported by the father's power; his power is experienced as not controllable, and the child learns that this sublime power is both terrifyingly effective and associated with an idealized object that is a source of security and protection. These contradictory elements account for our combined sense of threat and terror before the overwhelming and the sense of joy and safety that we experience as we give ourselves over to the force of the sublime.

Obscurity

Although our awareness of the presence of the sublime is vivid, the exact nature of it is obscure. The sublime is frequently depicted in darkness or as veiled by clouds or mist. The setting sun, its light diffuse and powerful, blinds the viewer's eye to the details of the landscape that appears to extend endlessly into the distance. Even though the normal human desire is to understand what one is dealing with, the sublime eludes all efforts at comprehension. In fact, that is one of its essences: we experience a compelling need to know, but we are forever blocked from that knowledge. In fact, the powerful and terrifying nature of the sublime makes observation and knowledge crucial even as our ability to know it is continually thwarted.

The maternal aesthetic is known. Beauty is often distinguished for its clarity. The mother creates a world for the infant in which everything has a place, where behaviors are basically predictable and reliable, and where both internal and external needs are structured and addressed in ways that the child can cognitively grasp and process. The optimal world of the maternal aesthetic is characterized by formal structures and configurations, which the child knows well, values highly, enjoys, and depends upon.

The paternal aesthetic is a new formal organization that is structured not according to the child's world, but by the immensity and complexity of the real world that the father introduces to the child. New places, new objects, new sensations are no longer limited to the infant's sphere of being but incorporate the infinite variety of objects and experiences in the outside world. The boundaries of experience, of the knowable world, are expanded exponentially. The child realizes that the infant world reflects the infant's self, structured by the mother to meet his or her needs; but the new world is vast, unknowable, and profoundly obscure. There are no boundaries in the paternal aesthetic: the colors, shapes, and contours endlessly expand, and the limits of what is observed spread beyond the child's vision into infinity. New aesthetic dimensions are introduced, as the child experiences the father's guidance and knowledge as a comfort and a source of gradually accruing meanings.

Formlessness

In the sublime experience, the observer is unable to fully perceive or articulate the formal structure of the object – an immense black cloud mass, a churning ocean, a climactic confluence of music and voices, a swirling web of paint drippings so complex that it seems to become an amorphous cloud of color. Once again, this quality of the sublime assaults our capacity to grasp reality, yet from our position of safety, we experience astonishment and awe at this wondrous experience.

The maternal aesthetic gives shape to experience. At a very basic level, the nursing mother creates and sustains an environment of shape, texture, temperature, and rhythm in which the infant can feel safe and contained. She provides the child with activities and playthings that are clearly defined and that facilitate the child's developing capacity to recognize and give form to experience. The paternal aesthetic lifts the child out of the aesthetic context that has thus far been organized around the child's subjective experience. This new aesthetic is initially experienced as without comprehensible form, a new series of worlds without the predictability and accessibility of the maternal environment. In fact, the continually unfolding and expanding reality of the paternal aesthetic introduces the child to the ultimate formlessness of the universe, itself having a form that will forever be unclear. This is not to say that the paternal aesthetic lacks form, but its form is ultimately uncontainable, and the possibilities for configurations and relationships are endless. The final impact on the child's experience is an extraordinarily complex and excessive, formal arrangement of color, shape, and line, to the extent that the overall impression is inchoateness and formlessness.

Complexity

The sublime is rarely simple. Many images of the sublime are loaded with additional inner images, suggesting an infinitely complex system of relationships and interactions that approaches the chaotic. The clear night sky is one example of this, as are many of the canvases of Turner, which seem to reel with a profusion of people, boats, and buildings, all surging with an uncontrolled intensity. We are made aware of an infinite reality outside our self-centered world, and we are at the same time both overwhelmed and liberated.

The maternal aesthetic is clear, and its elements and their relations can be grasped without struggle. The child and mother find patterns and routines to structure and manage their relationship. The mother's touch, her smell, the rhythms of movement and vocalizations all come together into a graspable, enjoyable, and reassuring aesthetic experience. The paternal aesthetic disrupts this aesthetic organization. The child's experience of the world with the father expands to include new sensations and perceptions, sounds, modes of touching and vocalizing. The newness and complexity of the father/child world is thrilling and exhausting. There are scary things and wondrous things. The child's world begins to expand, and the varieties of things, textures, sounds, rhythms, colors, and spaces proliferate into a tremendous, exciting confusion.

The sublime represents the experience of the fantastically complex world beyond the dyad; the child is astonished at this complexity, and fearful as well. The relationship to the idealized father and the ongoing communication with him and the mother about this new world allows the child to recognize the possibility of further knowledge, while at the same time experiencing a shared sense of awe at the infinite variety of the world and the universe.

Now that we have discussed the origins of the sublime in the child's experience of the paternal aesthetic, the next area to consider is the psychological function of the sublime in adult life.

The Psychological Function of the Sublime

People seek out the beautiful and the sublime because these experiences, to a greater or lesser degree, reproduce aspects of the original relationships to maternal and paternal figures. In adulthood, these developmentally early forms of aesthetic experiences are manifest and are articulated by means of highly sophisticated and refined cultural institutions that derive and gain their aesthetic significance from ties to these unconscious, archaic relational experiences. The specific function of the sublime is to provide an opportunity to reproduce in mature, derivative forms the paternal aesthetic. Both the immediate, positive sensations of the paternal aesthetic and the powerful way in which the father functioned to challenge and expand the constraints of self and reality, are part of the experience. We seek through the sublime to experience and confront normally frightening states of vulnerability, horror, smallness, confusion, and powerlessness in a context of safety in which our affective state becomes a blend of opposites: we feel small but excited by our closeness to the large; we feel horror and delight; we see how vulnerable we are and we feel protected; we acknowledge our essential weakness and we rejoice at the object's power. Thus, we simultaneously confront and undo some of our greatest fears by means of the sublime experience.

Through the sublime, the individual can confront both internal fears and external threats, while at the same time greatly reducing feelings of impending danger. The most obvious example of this is horror contemplated from a position of security, a characteristic of the sublime that has been noted by many. But, in addition, the sublime is an experience in which familiar and acceptable ways of organizing and giving meaning to self-experience and self-in-relation are pleasantly disrupted; this is desirable because it frees up self-organization, along with the constraints and limitations imposed on us, and offers an expanded, passionate, and highly idealized experience of self and world.

The sublime provides the sensation of the externalization of extreme affective states. However, in sublime experience, aggressive imagery must not directly threaten the welfare of the individual, nor should it stimulate significant internal reactions, such as fear and terror. Rather, the imagery must convey power and aggression, but the sense of imminence and risk is attenuated; preconsciously, the threat is real, while consciously, the individual feels safe. Rationally, the subject knows that he or she is secure; irrationally, danger or horror looms.

Unlike projective identification, where the projected fantasy (usually aggressive) remains a threat against which the individual continues to feel the need for defense, in the sublime experience, the externalized aggressive affect is not experienced as dangerous. This is true even though there is usually a strong sense of the object's power and terrifying nature. This, I believe, is an important function of the sublime: to allow the projection of threatening mental contents in which those contents can be experienced fully, vividly, and safely. It is easy to see how this experience might be derived from the father's role in both enacting and eliciting aggression, while simultaneously maintaining a sense of safety and containment. Friedrich Schiller (1793) wrote of this experience of transcendent safety:

> When something sublime is represented or entertained, we become conscious not of *material* security in a single instance, but rather of an *ideal* security extending over all possible instances.
> (Schiller in Ashfield and De Bolla, 1996, p. 35, emphasis in the original)

From a psychoanalytic perspective, what Schiller wrote implies that the demands of the superego and the constraints of character are temporarily overcome in sublime experience. But, unlike the situation in mania or intoxication, the influence of the superego is not eliminated; rather, it is merged with the protective and idealizing functions of the ego ideal. The powerful and aggressive paternal imago and its benevolent counterpart coexist within an experience that combines threat and beauty. The result is a state of astonishment in which there is an internal experience of subjection to the father's power, even as we exalt at being in his presence.

In addition, self-experience is affected in the sublime. Even while a sense of security is maintained, the normal confines of the self are fantastically expanded, and psychological boundaries disappear. We are temporarily and nontraumatically overwhelmed, and there is a feeling of selflessness accompanied by a pleasurable anxiety. Unlike the oceanic feeling, this is not comforting, but disruptive; the self is carried away in the rough water – over the falls, so to speak – captured by the current. This amalgamation of anxiety and pleasure is a special feature of the sublime. It serves to reproduce the child's experience of awe and joy at the father's presence.

In the sublime experience, we feel small and vulnerable; this feeling is combined with wonder at the immensity and power of the sublime object. Despite our vulnerability, we are not truly afraid; rather, our joy and excitement increase. We feel joy at our ability to enter a relationship with and be close to such an extraordinary presence. Thus, the normal anxiety regarding our awareness of vulnerability and mortality is attenuated in sublimity; in fact, we are acutely aware of our small-ness as a cause for celebration, rather than simply an occasion for fear. There is a link between this self-state and our early encounters with paternal power and immensity, in which – rather than panic – we felt a thrilling fear, a sense of wonder and excitement about our smallness in the arms of such a great person.

As we saw in the last chapter, unlike beauty and the sublime, ugliness disrupts and threatens our aesthetic self-organization; idealization collapses, and the secu-rity found in the forms and rhythms of the world is shaken. However, the sublime can make use of the imagery of ugliness for the purpose of provoking and repair-ing aesthetic traumas. Ugliness functions within the sublime to create a pleasant and liberating trauma in which the normality and complacency of the child's self-experience and aesthetic sensibility are challenged, and the self is thereby enlarged and enriched. The resulting anxiety becomes an occasion for self-expansion, and there is an opening up of the person's relation to both internal and external worlds. Ugliness is transformed into beauty; beauty is pushed beyond the domestic and feminine into a muscular, masculine realm.

In conclusion, the sublime functions to bring several different terrors within a containable, ordered universe. It is the powerful discharge of desire and aggression without catastrophe; it can portray the results of discharge without the destruc-tion of self or loved one. Death, sexuality, aggression, loss of self, vulnerability, and isolation are embraced and overcome (yet not by being negated or denied). Paradoxically, the experience of these terrors in the sublime is vitalizing and self-confirming, not disorganizing. There is an emotional state of arousal/tranquility. What is internally threatening is safely put outside the self. There is an externaliza-tion of fantasy, desire, and fear.

The experience of the sublime would not be possible without a sense of security; one must know that, ultimately, one is safe. Otherwise, terror, trauma, and self-fragmentation would result, and the sublime would be horrible, unbearable. But on the other hand, the sublime would not be possible if one were too secure. The sublime is the experience of vulnerability from a position of safety. It begins with the father observed from the arms of the mother and continues with the world sur-veyed from within his firm grasp. It is the rawness of affect, the passion of fantasy, and the shock of the new that are contained and expressed within a formal structure experienced as astonishing and ultimately transcendent.

Chapter 9

Art and Self

So far in this book we have not addressed the problem of art and the artist. This chapter presents a new psychoanalytic understanding of art and the psychology of the artist. It includes recent advances in psychoanalytic thinking and self psychology, especially an appreciation of the relational context of aesthetic experience and the role of relatedness and intersubjectivity in the creative process. Several of the most important points of this new aesthetic perspective are highlighted, specifically: (1) that the source and enduring core of aesthetic experience is found in early childhood, (2) that the creative process is self-dialectical, and (3) that the sense of beauty is an aesthetically organized selfobject experience. I will propose how the evocation of the sense of beauty is the goal of artistic creativity when the inner vision and artwork intertwine in dialogue with the form of an ideal, a creation possessing perfection.

I will start with brief review of the issues of intersubjectivity and self-experience in the psychoanalytic literature on art and creativity. We will then discuss the work of Gilbert Rose, Daniel Stern, and Ellen Dissanayake that links art and creativity to the intimacy of parent and child. This idea will be extended to recent self psychological ideas about creativity, the function of artwork, and the sense of beauty in human psychodynamics.

Psychoanalysts have studied art, aesthetic experience and the dynamics of the creative process for generations. Initially creativity and art were viewed as sublimations, defending against forbidden sexual wishes (Freud, 1908, 1910, 1925a, 1925b). Hence Freud's approach to the study of art was interpretive, in which the symbolic forms of artistic expression were unmasked, revealing hidden fantasies and wishes. This view of the psychology of art and creativity as a type of dreamwork or defensive operation has been the center of classical psychoanalytic aesthetics. Later analysts viewed art more progressively with the ego harnessing the resources of the unconscious for the purpose of self-expression (Kris, 1952). This ego psychological perspective continued to emphasize symbolism, but now saw regression as being at the "service of the ego" rather than the other way around. Eventually analysts such as Gilbert Rose and Jerome Oremland would elevate creativity to the status of a complex developmental accomplishment resulting in a higher level of human experience. In keeping with the classical analytic perspective on the mind as a self-regulating system, most analysts have approached the

DOI: 10.4324/9781003532484-9

psychology of art and the artist from a primarily intrapsychic viewpoint, only tangentially related to other people (for example, the potential audience). This is consistent with contemporary culture's myth of the artist as a solitary rebel who defies convention and critical judgment. However, some recent thinkers have argued that the artist is a far more social being than has generally been admitted to. I believe that the major limitation of the analytic approach has been the limitation of focus to the intrapsychic dynamic of the individual artist's mind. This has become increasingly obvious given the recent revolution in psychoanalytic thinking, which views human psychology as more relational and intersubjective than previously thought.

Since Freud saw art as a compromise formation between conflicting parts of the mental apparatus, the issue of the relational and developmental sources of art was not relevant to him. For Freud, art was just one of the many manifestations of the defense mechanism of sublimation and while taking on the trappings of culture, was, at heart, an intrapsychic phenomenon. The ego psychologist Ernst Kris viewed art as resulting from regression in the service of the ego whereby earlier forms of mentation and instinctual life are temporarily allowed access to consciousness, permitting aesthetic expression for the purpose of mastery. However, once again the source of art lay in the functions of the ego, which made use of infantile modes of thinking, but these early forms of mentation did not constitute aesthetic experience itself. Ultimately the notion of the elaboration of the products of regression during the later phase of the creative process placed the heart of successful creativity in the mature emotional and mental capacities of the artist.

Gilbert Rose in his monograph *The Power of Form* (1980) argued that artists seek through their art to recover lost ego states, specifically early experiences of fusion with the ego ideal as well as the archaic mother. Rose believed that artists, as part of their normal capacities, have a greater ability to merge with reality and then to disengage. They immerse themselves in an unconscious psychological process in which there are rhythmical disintegrative and integrative states. Unlike Kris, Rose viewed these regressive processes as capacities that, rather than just being at the service of the ego, have progressive, creative potential in and of themselves. He wrote regarding the artist's creative process:

> Later in life, a person's ego may scan back over unconscious memory traces of early fusion states. Unconsciously reliving these memories of dissolving and reforming early ego boundaries is an attempt at mastering the potential traumas of the original situation. It is often accompanied by unconscious birth fantasies. They signify the re-establishment (rebirth) of ego boundaries from the fusion of primary narcissism. The reemergence from narcissistic fusion and the re-establishment of ego boundaries carry the possibility of altered, perhaps even innovative, arrangements of the building blocks of reality.
>
> (Rose, 1980, p. 70)

Rose describes this scanning back as an *autonomous capacity of the ego* to which some aspects of reality are readily available as "malleable or plastic material to be adaptively reintegrated in the light of more customary aspects of reality" (p. 77). Creative imagination restructures reality and deepens and expands our understanding of the world. The production of art is according to Rose essentially an enhancement of normal capacities and processes by which all people test and master reality, "relating inner and outer in repeated fusion and separations" (p, 78). Ultimately the goal is an externalization of the early ego ideal that the artist has endowed with all the perfection of the parents. "By creating it and loving it and being loved by the world for making it the artist is **rematriated**" (p. 64).

Through this notion of rematriation Rose began to move towards a more relational view of creativity in which the core of aesthetic experience could be said to contain an intensely interactive component, the mutual engagement of artist with artwork and audience resulting in the emergence of an archaic state of self-experience associated with the early bond with the mother.

Daniel Stern, the psychoanalyst and infant researcher, supported the notion that mature creativity involves the activation of archaic affective states and cross-modal perception. In the following quote, Stern emphasized the emergent organization of the infant's subjective world as a template for aesthetic creation:

Infants are not lost at sea awash of abstractable qualities of experience. They are gradually and systematically ordering these elements of experience . . . to identify self-invariant and other-invariant constellations. This global domain of human subjectivity is the ultimate reservoir that can be dipped into for all creative experience. That domain alone is concerned with the coming-into-being of organization that is at the heart of creating and learning.

(p. 67)

Stern supported Rose's argument that early regressive ego states and experiences play a part in creativity but additionally he stresses that it is the progressive organizational capacities of the infant, not just regression, that underlies the creative processes in later life. Surprisingly Stern did not emphasis the relational context of these archaic processes. However, one would assume that these organizational capacities emerge and are elaborated within an interpersonal context. Mature forms of creativity involve the type of rematriation discussed by Rose, but additionally the self-experience-in-relation-to-other which Stern's research highlighted.

From a self psychological perspective, Charles Kligerman (1980) explored this area in his discussion of the motivation of the artist to recapture the experience of an archaic selfobject tie. In his formulation, Kligerman speculated that the prototypical artist is someone who experienced consistent mirroring of his or her grandiosity in childhood. Eventually this selfobject experience fails and the artist-to-be is cast out from this state of perfection. He wrote how the artist, confronted with selfobject failure, possesses:

The need to regain a lost paradise – the original bliss of perfection – to overcome the empty feeling of self-depletion and to recover self-esteem. In the metapsychology of the self this would amount to healing the threatened fragmentation and restoring firm self-cohesion through a merger with the selfobject – the work of art – and a bid for mirroring approval of the world. We can also add a fourth current to the creative drive – the need to regain perfection by merging with the ideals of the powerful selfobjects, first the parents, then later revered models who represent the highest standards of some great artistic tradition.

(Kligerman, 1980, pp. 387–388)

For Kligerman, art is linked to the recreation of early experiences of relationship with important caregivers and involves the expression and embodiment of psychological processes of idealization and merger associated with selfobject experience. This self psychological perspective while clarifying the psychological function of art and creativity in self-experience does not capture what we now know to be the intensely relational nature of infantile experience. Considering recent insights in infant research and the intersubjective nature of human psychological experience, some authors have started to consider how the fundamental drive for and experience of mutuality and intimacy play a part in aesthetic experience and the creative process.

In her book *Art and Intimacy,* the anthropologist Ellen Dissanayake argued that the source of art lies in the intimate mutuality of mother and child, specifically in the affective and behavioral attunement between the members of the dyad. Referring to the burgeoning field of infant research that has elucidated the complex interpersonal relatedness of the human infant, Dissanayake highlighted the affective interplay that characterizes the infant/parent dyad. She argued that the internalization of these rhythms and modes becomes the bedrock of the aesthetic forms, values, and experiences that eventually develops among people in a culture. In fact, Dissanayake believed that one can find the intimate aesthetics of mother and child in the rituals and art forms of larger cultures, which seek to increase connection and mutuality among members through the evocation of developmentally early experiences of attunement. Dissanayake wrote:

It is in the inborn capacity and need for (1) mutuality between mother and infant (the prototype for intimacy and love) that four other essential capacities and psychological imperatives are enfolded and embedded and gradually, in their time emerge. Mother–infant mutuality contains and influences the capacity for (2) belonging to (and acceptance by) a social group, (3) finding and making meaning, (4) acquiring a sense of competence through handling and making, and (5) elaborating these meanings and competencies as a way of expressing or acknowledging their vital importance.

(p. 8)

Dissanayake argued that the creation and valuing of art is one of the most important imperatives in the human need for relatedness and self-experience. She believed that communities create artistic culture as a means of enhancing mutuality and thus group survival, and that individuals work within the given artistic culture to achieve experiences of meaning and personal competence. But her idea of *elaborating* emphasized how meaning is not just in terms of everyday realities; rather the artist seeks to create works that possess special power, authority, and beauty so that the importance of the work in the experience of the community is made manifest. Dissanayake argued that underlying even the most idiosyncratic creative efforts is the elaboration of these archaic experiences of self with other.

Creativity: Context and Process

Art and creativity serve different functions when you approach them from the vantage point of culture, relationships, and individual subjective life. The social function of art in the preservation and enhancement of group relations within a particular society is quite different from the psychological function of art in the affirmation and enhancement of the self-experience of the individual working artist. Yet a complete analytic aesthetic theory must acknowledge the relationship between these different domains. Although in this chapter we will emphasize the creative process, as it is manifest in the individual artist's experience, the creative act is intelligible only from within the culture and social milieu out of which it arises.

Art and artists are embedded in culture. Art cannot be conceived of outside a cultural milieu in which not only the forms and methods of art are promulgated but the general standards that define quality as well. This is true of even the most personal aspects of art. The artist in her studio relies on the tools, maps, and measuring instruments of outside culture, and though she might challenge her culture, she cannot escape it. We take our artistic language from culture that becomes the personal aesthetic idiom through which aesthetic experience and creativity is possible and intelligible.

Artists are also embedded in a network of relationships within which their aesthetics develops and is perfected. Many have noted the frequent occurrence of artistic dyads in which an artist or artists rely on dialogue with a valued other person who functions for them as a muse. It is out of this intersubjective matrix that many revolutionary aesthetic movements are spawned and sustained. These groupings of artists take from the metasubjective horizon of culture those themes: styles, values, and art forms that are best suited to express their special intersubjective vision. They then, through dialogue, create the unique aesthetic of their generation. It is the cultural and relational contexts that compose the working ground of individual artistic effort.

In the end neither culture nor relationships have the adaptability and resourcefulness of the individual artist's creative process. This is why, though there are grand cultures and great movements in art, it is in the individual struggle of the single artist that these larger processes emerge. The artist working within, taking from and acting against the culture and relationships, within which she lives, creates something new. It is this domain of aesthetics that is the primary concern of this paper. Therefore, I will emphasize the way in which self-experience (which includes the experience of self-in-relationship) is expressed in the formal structure of the artwork. However, it is crucial that I be clear that the individual intrapsychic experience of the artist crystallizes out of and is constituted by relational and cultural meanings, which are also the artist's motive, form, and subject. In fact, artists may be more profoundly engaged with their environment and social milieu than others may. In 1966 Heinz Kohut made this claim:

> The creative individual is less separated from his surroundings than non-creative one; the "I–You" barrier is not as clearly defined. The creative individual is keenly aware of these aspects of his surroundings that are of significance to his work, and he invests them with narcissistically idealizing libido.
>
> (p. 112)

Although Kohut in 1966 utilized a classical model of intrapsychic mental life, the artist he described is intensely relational. The normal boundaries between self and other are fluid; the artist engages dynamically with the world. He or she is not introspectively ruminating in his or her own world; to the contrary, the artist's self-experience is powerfully linked to the world of objects and others who are also in paradoxical creations of the artist. In fact, extending Kohut's thinking, I would argue that *aesthetics* is fundamentally intersubjective in this sense. It involves both the externalization of self-experience intertwined with the discovery of the world. This is the process Dissanayake emphasized in which the rhythms and modes of archaic attunement become the templates for our aesthetic engagement with culture. It is like the concept of projective identification and Winnicott's transitional experience, but includes the notion of action, in which the person does something to effect the object to express subjectivity. Once an action is taken, altering the object in some way, it can be said that subjectivity is externalized, and the artist enters a relationship with an object that is now invested with qualities of the artist's own subjective experience. I am not proposing a solipsistic model of aesthetics; rather the qualities of the external object are essential (as in the maternal/infant dialogue). In fact, the action taken upon the object *must* include the qualities of the object (its color, plasticity, etc.), as well as the changing relationship between the internal and external aspects of subjectivity.

However, once an action is taken and an aspect of subjectivity can be said to be expressed in the work, this externalized subjectivity becomes to a greater or lesser degree disjunctive with self-experience (either because of the object on the form of self-expression or the rapid unfolding of the self-experience of the artist). The artist then acts upon the subjective objects as both internal and external to self-experience. There is a unique dialectic that is established between the internal and external aspects of subjectivity. Because of this dialectic, further actions are taken, and the artwork develops towards perfection. Carl Rotenberg described this process in his 1988 paper *Selfobject Theory and the Artistic Process*:

> The area of interaction between the artist and his own work, he puts his own puzzles and mental ambiguities outside himself and then reacts to them as if

they were other than his. In a sense, once the artist begins a work, he surrenders to it as though the work were dominating him, demanding a solution of its own ambiguities, and requiring completion. The artist experiences selfobject functioning of the artwork as alive, active, interpretive and eventually having transformative capabilities, to the extent that inner puzzles of the artist are worked through this externalization.

(p. 209)

Rotenberg described a unique form of intersubjectivity in which the artist engages with an "other," which was in fact once part of self-experience, but is now external, possessing through concretization in media or language a separate subjectivity. That which has been made external, in other words has been "expressed" is the artist's self-experience.

Self-expression in aesthetic experience is not limited to emotion, affect, or even specific ideas or impressions (although it may contain all of these). The form of self-expression contained in artistic creation is best captured in the idea of being, of conveying in the work aspects of how it feels to be the living person – who one is. However, art is not simply a mirror, a representation of ourselves, it is a new creation that evokes self-experience and embodies the self-in-relation through aesthetic perfection. This allows us to include within the idea of art the cosmic tapestry of the Sistine Chapel and the stark simplicity of a Rothko painting. As different as they may be, both can be said to contain within them some perfect expression of human experience.

The unfolding dialectic between artist and artwork is accompanied by the fluctuation of states of emotional tension and self-experience. The sense of resonance between the external and internal aspects of subjectivity is self-confirming and pleasurable. Dissonance leads to varying levels of self-crisis. *Aesthetic resonance* is the degree in which internal aspects of subjectivity and the external aspects of subjectivity, concretized in the artwork, are conjunctive one to the other. The way in which the relationships between the colors and forms of a painting express the organization of the artist's internal world. Fundamental to this idea is that the artwork and the artist's subjectivity are a single intersubjective field in which inner and outer are from a certain point of view irrelevant because, due to the experience of *aesthetic resonance*, the artist feels vitalized, more cohesive, directed, and alive. If the artist is successful in developing the work towards greater perfection, this inner state can be quite powerful, and the artist's self-experience is idealized.

Self psychologists use the term *selfobject experience* to capture this psychological state. This is a psychological experience in which a person enters a relationship to an object that is felt to have ideal qualities (an idealized selfobject) and/or when one experiences the object as reflecting the ideal qualities of oneself (the grandiose self). In most cases successful creativity involves both an idealized and grandiose selfobject experience. The artist feels in the presence of an ideal object that reflects an experience of the ideal self.

However, selfobject experience tends to be precarious or fragile. The person inevitably experiences *selfobject failure* in which the object for whatever reason is no longer experienced as ideal or reflective of one's grandiose self. An example of this disjunction is when an artist begins work in the morning and finds a confusing jumble where the night prior, he had left a "masterpiece." In such a case, external-ized aspects of subjectivity are no longer in conjunction with self-experience, and they are experienced as something other – at times as something far removed from what is imagined or desired. This leads to a state of self-crisis that can result in a permanent rupture of the relation to the artwork, or optimally to further effort to restore the selfobject tie through work. It is important to remember that it is not solely the qualities of the object that determine resonance and dissonance but the relation between the internal subjective world and its externalization in the object. From the point of view of a third party, the object may be beautiful, but the artist may nonetheless experience a sense of disappointment or even failure.

Successful art involves the artist's creation of an opportunity for selfobject expe-rience. He or she does this by externalizing some aspect of subjectivity by means of an action upon some aspect of the external world. She then enters a dialectical relationship with these externalized aspects of her won subjectivity. The intent of this dialectic is to take further action to alter the artwork towards a goal of greater expressive perfection. On the other hand, the artist is affected by the artwork, his inner working model of the work and emotional state responsive to the object being created. Optimally the artwork not only resonates with inner experience, but also externalizes subjectivity in an increasingly ideal form. The relationship with the ideal artwork that reflects the perfection of the artist is at the heart of the *aesthetic selfobject experience*. Heinz Kohut saw this as being at the heart of the creative drive. He wrote:

> Creative artists may be attached to their work with the intensity of an addiction, and they try to control and shape it with forces and for purposes that belong to narcissistically experienced world. They are attempting to re-create a perfection that formerly was directly an attribute of their own.
>
> (Kohut, 1985, p. 115)

Art and Gesture

Art is a psychological process in which an artist improves the articulation of his or her subjectivity through the creation and perfection of an artwork. During the initial phase of the creative process, the artist invests something in the world with subjectivity – he does this by means of a particular type of gesture (e.g., a swipe of paint on a canvas, a written phrase, a series of notes, etc.). This new element, the artist's externalized subjectivity, what Winnicott calls "the subjective object," becomes the focus of the artist's creative attention and work. This process becomes art when the artist engages the new or altered object in a dialectic during which inner and outer subjective elements interact and change each other – gesture follows and builds on gesture – the artwork gradually crystallizing as a framework or network of gestures. The driving force that orients the direction of change in the artwork is the artist's search for perfection, to make something "special." Thus, in the creation of art the artist's subjectivity is expressed, elaborated, and refined.

Human activity always involves some degree and type of projection by which we give order and meaning to the world. In other words, we are not passive recipients; rather, we actively construct our experience according to templates and organizing principles based on our past experiences combined with neurological readiness to experience the world in certain ways. In art, these subjective meanings become expressed and made real. In this way, part of the world becomes humanized, an artwork. It is this subjective object; the human element of our experience that becomes the focus of the artist as he or she attempts to perfect the articulation of subjectivity.

When we talk about the expression or objectification of subjectivity, what do we mean? Gilbert Rose argued that self-experience becomes real and sustains itself by means of objective patterns of behavior. In this light I suggest that one way to view subjectivity in art is through the concept of gesture – that artists use a series of related gestures to create any form of art, and that it is the residue of those gestures that composes the artwork.

By the word *gesture* we mean a movement or position of the hand, body, head, or face that is expressive of an idea, opinion, emotion, etc. or the use of such movements to express thought, emotion. However, gesture can is a dimension of all forms of human expression. In fact, there is no way to conceive of the expression of subjectivity except as a gesture of some type. Of course, the first and most fundamental forms of gesture are physical, having to do with the body – limbs, face, head movements. All sensory modalities may play a part since it is through the senses that subjectivity engages the world. The earliest form of communication – gesture –occurs, and it remains the substrate (and subtext) of all forms of human gesture. Thus, it is through gesture that subjectivity is expressed and made real. For our purposes, I believe that the expressive dimension of art is gesture. Once again, the most familiar, restrictive form of gesture is bodily action, but I believe that gesture also includes any activity in which the environment is given form through expressive action (use of words, other symbols, touch, sight, sounds, etc.). Thus, it is not the content of an expression that is gesture, but the content as expressed through movement, sensation, and action. In other words, meaning is inseparable from gesture. However, gesture requires a medium. Whether that medium is as basic and personal as a limb, or a tube of florescent light, or the evocation of an idea through the display of a found object, in each case subjectivity requires a *means* of expression. The artist makes use of a medium to express subjectivity, and this making use of the medium is manifest as *gesture*. Once this is understood, we can go a step further to say that subjectivity is perfected through the refinement of the expressive qualities of gesture.

Gesture is important to the experience of the self. We come to know ourselves though our sense of our own gestures, most importantly our gestures in relation to other people and their responsive gestures in turn. Our bodies, words, behaviors, ever changing and loaded with emotion and intension, are observed and linked to who we are, and most importantly who we are in the minds of others. In other words, gestures are fundamentally implicit, procedural forms of self-experience, and hence we may not be conscious of the meanings of our gestures, given that gestures are linked to emergent and preconscious expressions of self-in-the-world. Most importantly it is gesture in vocalizations, body movement, and facial expressions that is how we communicate self-states and influence each other's internal representational worlds. D. W. Winnicott spoke of "the spontaneous gesture" as an action involving a feeling of authenticity. He believed that this authentic response, originating in an untrammeled (yet uninhibited) part of the self, is the source of creativity and the sensation of being real. The mother's response to the infant's spontaneous gestures facilitates the infant's creativity and sense of selfhood (and prevents the necessity for the development of restrictive, protective self-organization) – this spontaneous gesture, however, is simultaneously simple and complex.

In other words, we come to know ourselves, especially our internal emotional lives, through interactions with others when they respond to our emotional expressions with their own emotional responses. Our sense of self, our internal representational world, crystallizes through this interchange of gestures. In fact, thinking itself is given form through psychological structures or organizations of meaning that have form and gestural qualities. As a result, my thoughts "look and feel" different from yours. They have their own form and texture, rhythm, and tone; in this sense, thoughts also bear the signature of the self. They become a way I know and reflect on myself – and the gestural quality of thought is an important way that I am a self.

As we have noted, our earliest gestures occur within the context of intimate caretaking relationships. We act towards and with others, and the response of the other helps to invest meaning into our gestures. We gradually begin to be concerned with how others are experiencing and judging us. This interactional engagement is composed of gestures that are emergent, and that make real the sensations, feelings and thoughts between us. Hungry gestures, loving gestures, angry gestures, sexual gestures, are the meat and blood of our relationships. In other words, we live through gesture. We know ourselves, our relationships, and our worlds by means of the gestures out of which we ourselves crystallize and evolve. Normally we take gestures for granted. Artists make gesture the object of their creative efforts, the refined articulation of gesture becomes the means for the most powerful expressions of human meanings. However, although the artist's use of gesture has its roots in these fundamental intersubjective processes we have been describing, what the mature artist brings to his or her work with gesture is far more complex and advanced.

Throughout life the creative person, the artist, channels the spontaneous gesture within the disciplines, methods, and contexts of his professional training and practice. Through effort and devotion to craft, this gesture of self-expression and/or gesture of response to the world emerge, and the artist brings to that gesture a practice of recognition and selection built on a lifetime of experience. Once the gesture or impulse has caught his attention, he works on it through a disciplined creative process that only years of study and practice can attain. The deepest sources of gesture are in the spontaneous, physical processes and response to living; the sensory matrix of selfhood – as we mature and grow, becoming ourselves – we refine our gestures and hone our senses, they come to reflect who we are in body and mind, gestures are molded in the crucible of relationships, and in education gestures are further refined through knowledge, discipline, practice, criticism, and appreciation. For the artist, gesture is the vehicle of expressive meaning, fully integrated into craft and elaborated by creative effort. The artist "makes use" of his/her own gestural repertory (implicit and explicit). At the same time, he/she allows her/his body and mind to sense, to respond, to make mistakes, in other words to create the readiness for new, yet unseen, gestures. The artist uses what he knows and what is available, in other words what is "at hand," but he also creates the conditions for surprise out of this generative complexity.

When we say that art begins with the externalized subjectivity of the artist, we are not just talking about feeling or emotion. The artist's subjectivity is the personal experience of being. It is the sense of self both in terms of body but also being-in-the-world. In this sense the artist is just like us: all human actions have a subjective signature, the unique quality that each individual life possesses. The artist makes that subjective signature the focus of creative work, and by means of the creative process the artist's being is articulated and refined. In the best of cases, we experience the artwork as an exquisite and powerful aesthetic experience – the human being communicated with power and grace.

In closing this section, we want to fully answer the question as to What Art Is, then we must recognize that at its heart is the experience of community. As George Gadamer noted:

> We celebrate since we are gathered for something, and this is particularly clear in the case of the experience of art. It is not simply the fact that we are all in the same place, but rather the intention that unites us and prevents us as individuals from falling into private conversations and private, subjective experiences.
>
> (Gadamer, 1986, p. 40)

What Art Is

Anyone who offers a new model of the creative process and of art must qualify his or her argument with an admission of the truth that any model is more honored in the breach than the observance. Most artists worth their sale will recoil from any model that limits or reduces the uniquely personal nature of his or her own experience. Of course, most models are heuristic and help us to identify certain common traits and characteristics; they clarify a process that seems common to the things described, but artists (especially modern artists) play around with accepted norms, perhaps not simply to be rebellious, but just because that's where their instincts or interests take them. To say that art is subjectivity externalized and refined does not say anything about the infinite variability of people, the myriad ways that subjectivity can be expressed and concretized, or the vast array of criteria by which art can be said to be refined or perfected (from the cultural dictates of a powerful church to the highly personal taste of a painting from Wyoming), all of these components of our model, when applied, account for a phenomenon of vast complexity and variability. However, I would like to summarize the model of art that I have sketched out in the last several pages. As we will see in subsequent chapters, when you look at the lives and works of individual artists (as we will do) this model will prove both true and highly variable, let me just admit that and get on with the work.

As we have seen in prior sections of this paper, the creative artist makes changes in the object that involve the projection of his or her subjectivity. Thus, the object is the medium for an objectification of feeling, thought, and fantasy. Subjectivity is literally *trans-substantiated*; it remains grounded in the self but has also become another thing entirely. As a result of this process the artist's subjectivity is externalized – the artwork is a subjective object. The artist's subjectivity has a *real presence* in the artwork, but it is not a mirror of the inner experience of the artist. The artwork is a creation of the artist, based on his or her subjectivity, but not equivalent to it. The act of creation, as well as the movement of time, forces a disengagement between the inner experience of the artist and the artwork that now exists on its own terms. When the artist studies the artwork, he both recognizes it as his own (of his own flesh, if you will), but it is also *other,* apart from the self; thus it can be known both for what it shares with the artist's mind and how it is different. It contains parts of her or him, altered by the very act of creation. However, now the subjective object as artwork can be further transformed; thus, the artist engages in a creative process with externalized aspects of his own subjective life. This is what makes art distinct as a human activity: the artist works to refine and perfect the expression of his or her subjectivity as it is concretized in the artwork. Hence *art is a unique, evolving dialectical relationship between internal and external aspects of the artist's own subjectivity.* The result of any successful creative act is a synthesis, or an aesthetic integration, concretized as a new object (or a new elaboration of the artwork). Of course, this synthesis continues to be the target of the artist's creative attention until the artwork is finished. Optimally, with a skilled and experienced artist, this dialectic leads to an increasingly refined and perfected articulation of subjective experience – human life expressed at the most exquisite level. When this creative work is at its best and the artist's efforts are most successful, the result is a thing of beauty.

Does Art Heal?

Throughout the psychological literature on creativity and the psychology of the artist runs the assumption that there is something therapeutic about creating art. Of course, this is fundamental to the clinical foundations of art therapy as a profession, but in general, many have asserted that art itself heals. In part, this may be due to the similarities between artistic creation and traditional psychoanalytic practice regarding the expression and exploration of fantasy which has been seen as cura-tive. However, I would also argue that the idealization of art and the impact of art on positive self-states and emotions may also skew analysts towards a view of art as healing. In this section I would like to address this issue by considering a book that highlights just this issue.

Mended by the Muse: Creative Transformations of Trauma is a sustained, impassioned argument for the psychotherapeutic potential of the creative arts. The author, Sophia Richman (faculty, NYU Postdoctoral Program in Psychotherapy and Psychoanalysis), argues that art has an important role in the process of self-repair following trauma. Building on Winnicott's idea of transitional space, Rich-man describes how the artist plays with aspects of reality and fantasy, and in the process comes to articulate and give aesthetic form to aspects of self-experience that have been damaged and hidden, perhaps even from oneself.

Richman's book begins with a chapter in which she recounts her own family's experiences of trauma during and after the Holocaust. Pretending to be a Catholic widow and her daughter, Richman and her mother lived out the Second World War in plain sight, all the time fearing discovery of their Jewish identities. Her father, having escape from a concentration camp early in the war, was hidden in their attic where he eventually began to compose a memoir of his incarceration and escape. Richman describes how the process of writing for her father (and then later in life for her) served the purpose of providing "a sense of control and mastery over the humiliating experiences" they had endured. In addition, she notes how in her father's case the sharing of his writing with her mother helped them to reconnect. However, the failure to connect between herself and her father survived the years of hiding and continued throughout their later years. The story of family trauma and recovery through art is fundamental to Richman's thesis.

Richman goes on from her personal story to explore the psychoanalytic litera-ture on creativity. This chapter is an excellent review, and I recommend it to anyone interested in the diverse ways that analysts think about the creative arts and the psychology of artists. Following that is a chapter on dissociation. An adherent to recent models of dissociation such as Bromberg's, Richman argues that the creative arts provide an avenue to bring together radically dissociated aspects of memory, riven and sequestered by trauma. She states that, "when individuals are engaged in the creative process, whether they are regressing, progressing, to moving from one self-state to another, they enter a place where they have more access to internal problematical material and have an opportunity for working through the material towards self-continuity" (p. 73).

Richman believes in the therapeutic power of art. "It has long been known that artistic endeavors have the power to heal the artist" (p. 62). The power of creativity to overcome trauma and support self-healing is examined by Richman from many angles. In one chapter she discusses genocide, in another mortality, and the healing function of memoir. She uses examples from the lives of artists and other analysts to illustrate her thesis.

If you examine the unfolding of Richman's argument closely, there are in fact two sides to her thesis, the first and most important one being that the creative arts can heal the psychological damage of trauma, and second that the sharing of one's artistic products can lead to a healing reengagement with other people. These are two very different claims. Richman is far more persuasive regarding the latter dimension of her thesis than the former. Let me take each in turn.

Although it feels good to imagine that art making has some kind of healing role, it is much harder to find evidence of this. Clearly, when it goes well, art making can be joyous and satisfying, one of the most meaningful of human experiences. On the other hand, when it does not go well, a common complaint of all artists, it can be a debilitating torment. Taking the former, more positive perspective, Richman offers several examples from art history. While it is obviously true that artists often seem to be trying to articulate and make sense of trauma (often successfully), this does not mean that psychological repair follows. Unfortunately, in her biographical examples Richman fails to show convincing example of such healing. For example, the two examples that Richman gives of artists healed by their art, Frida Kahlo and Francis Bacon, are actually very poor examples of mental health. Both alcoholic and depressives despite artistic success over many years, neither showed any evidence of psychological healing. In fact, there is clear evidence of continued deterioration and self-destructiveness, even as they achieved some of their finest artistic work.

In considering Richman's thesis, I thought back on many of the great artists whom I have admired and with whose biographies I am familiar. Despite high levels of accomplishment (even the fulfillment of genius), most of these artists did not show any improvement in their psychological health. An obvious example is Van Gogh, but there are innumerable others. If art healed, then Hemingway would not have been a suicide, or Faulkner, Fitzgerald, Cheever, and Carver chronic alcoholics and depressives. I do not subscribe to the idea that mental illness is somehow essential to creativity, but the healing power of art is another matter. I am sure the reader can come up with numerous examples of productive and ascetically successful artists who failed to evidence psychological healing. In fact, the opposite has too often been true.

I am not saying that art may not be useful in recovering from trauma. In fact, this is where Richman succeeds in providing convincing evidence regarding the second part of her thesis. In this case, art can support healing in the context of a relationship with another with whom one shares the process and its results. In her report of analytic work with a patient named Marnie, Richman describes the way the therapeutic process is enhanced when the patient finds out about Richman's shared interest in writing. The patient deeply immersed in a memoir begins to bring her work into sessions. Richman writes: "the experiential space we shared became alive with energy. . . . Marnie's writing was something we could look at together and discuss[;] . . . we co-created a narrative" (p. 99). In other words it was not so much the art making as the art-sharing in the context of a positive and engaged therapeutic relationship which was therapeutic. In fact, Richman argues that "artistic expression in conjunction with psychoanalysis that makes for a most effective combination" (p, 96).

Richman's success in arguing for the relational nature of creativity and art appreciation underscores another major problem in the book. Richman's discussion of the creative process seems to rely on a model that emphasizes the solitary, even private nature of creativity. She notes many times the mysterious, solitary work of the individual artist. Given the fact that art throughout human history has been communal and interpersonal, the relatively recent myth of the solitary artist in his studio distorts the true nature of art in human life.

People can use art to heal. But this is not inherent to art itself but the way that the artist makes use of it. Most important is when artists engage with others, family, friends, mentors, etc. in a healing process in which art has a role, that healing and growth become possible.

As Richman's treatment of Marnie illustrates, art and art making can be used to provide added meaning and emotional resonance to the dialogue between patient and analyst. Whether we discuss a creative project in which the patient is involved, or a movie, television program, or play, the meanings of these art forms to the patient, perhaps a character they hate or love, a situation that evokes memories of childhood, or the dramatic depiction of a trauma, or loss that the patient has gone through or fears, all these can enrich the clinical dialogue.

As with the treatment of Marnie, when the patient and analyst share enthusiasm for art, this mutual idealization may increase the potential for clinical benefit for both therapist and patient so that the artwork vitalizes and provides cohesion to self-experience. In addition, the shared discussion of art in sessions can create diverse opportunities for the exploration and elaboration of fantasy.

Over time, the externalization of the patient's creative and fantasy life through artwork can be a rich means to continue the analytic dialogue and evaluate the evolving nature of the patient's psychological life and sense of self. Richman describes this process when she describes the writing of her memoir. Having terminated her treatment, she continues to elaborate memory and experience through her writing, once again with the enthusiastic encouragement and interest of her analyst, who remains in contact and urges her on in her writing.

Like anything else, the effective integration of art into the treatment must be based on an in-depth and sensitive attunement to patients' experiences, their vulnerabilities and needs. Artists can be highly vulnerable at the best of times, and the importance of the analyst's response should not be minimized. But the management of the patient's vulnerability is our stock and trade. In this regard Sophia Richman's *Mended by the Muse: Creative Transformations of Trauma* is testimony and guide to the importance of art in the clinical exchange as she demonstrates how we can leverage its special power to heighten meaning, communication, and positive outcomes.

Psychopathology and Creativity

Artistic creativity is a manner of thinking, of feeling, of being within a medium and symbolic language of forms. It is a dialectical process, in which the artist alters the medium, infuses objects with subjectivity, and engages the new, subjective object (both actively and psychically). Thus, artistic creativity is not just something the artist does, a pastime or occupation, it is a way of being in the world, and of experiencing one's inner and outer life. Like breath or sight, the creative act is inseparable from self, and over time and with effort, it becomes the artist's primary medium of self-experience, self-in-relation to the world, and as a part of the world with other people.

The fact that artistic creativity can provide an opportunity for autonomous, self-referential selfobject experiences explains why artistic creativity and an artistic career can be attractive to people with histories of insecure or traumatic attachment. A review of the lives of many great artists (especially in modern times) reveals that many of them had childhoods in which good enough parenting was absent. Some of these artists may in fact have disrupted or deficient aesthetic development, which may contribute to depression and self-dysregulation in adulthood. However, what if these people possess artistic talent? What if he or she discovers the possibility of using the talent to bring about positive aesthetic experiences – within the limited scope of creative work – and that work provides the opportunity for selfobject experiences that are otherwise unavailable until then – for this self-disordered person the creation of artwork may serve a powerful defensive or compensatory function – a longed-for realization of archaic selfobject needs. In the most successful instances, the artist may achieve an aesthetic experience of such perfection and emotional satisfaction that, at least temporarily, he or she feels restored, whole, and vital. This is the experience of having created something of aesthetic perfection, of beauty. I believe that this can explain the frequent phenomenon (especially within the community of modern artists) of the psychotic or character-disordered artist, who during a tormented and disrupted life, successfully organizes him- or herself around a productive and aesthetically successful career as an artist.

Self psychologist Charles Kligerman claimed that the artist idealizes beauty and that "by and large the artist is concerned with exhibiting a beauty that was originally his own (or that of the idealized maternal selfobject)" (p. 386). It is the experience of perfection that is at the heart of the sense of beauty. Beauty is an invariant characteristic of anything that is experienced as ideal. We all value and seek beauty as an opportunity for selfobject experience. When we are in the presence of something beautiful, we are enlivened, we feel whole and happy. Beauty is a special element in the aesthetic experience in which the investment of reality with subjectivity creates an experience of that reality as both ideal and harmonious with our inner life (see also Lee, 1947, 1948, 1950; Hagman, 2001). George Santayana described a similar experience:

> The sense of beauty is the harmony between our nature and our experience. When our senses and imagination find what they crave, when the world so

shapes itself or so molds the mind that the correspondence between them is perfect, then perception is pleasure, and existence needs no apology.

(Santayana, 1896, p. 269)

Santayana described what he believed characterized the general human experience of beauty that could occur spontaneously and without obvious effort. For the artist this experience is something that he or she seeks to bring about through his or her own creative efforts. While in general artists do not make the creation of beauty a conscious goal (Thomas Mann claimed that the artist was not at all interested in creating beauty, but in making his artwork), nonetheless a characteristic of all successful artistic efforts is that the result evokes the experience of beauty, which transcends the artist's intention. Given this it makes sense to say that beauty can never be produced (except by imitation) but only evoked because of the pursuit of perfection and the memory of a lost ideal. Jacques Martian in his monograph *Creative Intuition in Art and Poetry* stated: "Art engenders beauty, it does not produce beauty as an object, or a thing contained in a genus." In the same work Martian quotes the artist Robert Henri, "Things are not done beautifully. The beauty is an integral part of their being done." In a similar sense the artist does not make or produce a selfobject experience; he or she through the creative process brings about an opportunity for selfobject experience, and thus beauty; whether beauty is found in the external attributes of the object or in the interrelationship among the ideas that are concretized in the work.

The importance of beauty in human life is stressed in the following quote from Freud (1930):

We observe that this useless thing which we expect civilization to value is beauty. We require civilized man to reverence beauty wherever he sees it in nature and to create it in objects of his handiwork as far as he is able.

(Freud, 1930)

In closing, I would like to offer considering our discussion an understanding of the preceding quotation from *Civilization and Its Discontents*. Perhaps one of the reasons that Freud claimed reverence for beauty as a required trait of civilization was that beauty elevates human subjectivity and human values to a transcendent level. The sense of beauty in its reparative and preservative function asserts love over aggression, life over death, and harmony over disintegration. It may even be one of the ways that we reconcile our relationship with the world. Our sense of beauty may not always be certain, or consistent with high aesthetic standards. We may challenge cultural assumptions about the beautiful, or we may even rebel against beauty. But beauty like sex and aggression has been a reality of human life in all cultures, throughout history. Beauty is not illusory, nor does it stand in or cover up for something else. Beauty may be one of the most exquisite forms of human meaning that exists. As we view the sense of beauty through psychoanalytic lenses, we see in it man's search for perfection, transcendence, and hope.

Chapter 10

Art, Creativity, and the Clinical Process

In this chapter I discuss the aesthetic foundation of human experience and the way in which an aesthetic perspective can shed light on the psychoanalytic process (Hagman, 2006, 2010, 2015, 2016). I will begin with a discussion of the aesthetic dimension of early childhood experience, the emergence of aesthetic form and value from the child's experience of the relational field, and its elaboration into a mature, fully developed aesthetic sense. I will then show how aesthetics can inform our understanding of psychotherapeutic process in terms yet neglected. Finally, I will discuss creativity as it is manifest in psychotherapy through the construction of the *cotransference* (Orange, 1993), an aesthetically organized *subjective object*, which becomes the focus of analysis and creative change (Winnicott, 1971). I will close with a case example as an illustration of the structure and dynamics of a *creative analysis* (Hagman, 2015)

Aesthetic Experience in Life and Therapy

An unfolding series of feelings and forms woven together constitute the fabric of a human life. Embedded in that fabric are the words and concepts that we use to discriminate and order our experience, but, like unthreaded beads, these symbols would scatter into fragments if unsecured by the affective surround. For it is commonly noted that the full meaning of language cannot be understood out of its context, the vast, complex sense of the "form" of our experience as well as the specific instances for which language tools are utilized (Hagman, 2006, pp. 13–27). Words exist and matter because they are in a context of the meaningful, formal order or our being in the world. "I love you" is never said in a vacuum. No, it is said to another over a candlelight dinner, or while sitting on the edge of the bed, or while nursing, or saying goodbye at the airport, or while laughing, or when the gift is given and appreciated, or just as a reminder, a placeholder when we go off to work. "I love you" is always part of a story, and it is set in a scene which has a look, a feel, a narrative coherence which affects us – its sense is found in its context. We receive the message, being assured or reassured of our special connection, our love for each other. Traditionally this exchange is considered the finest manifestation of beauty, the ideal configuration of our aesthetic sense. (See Hagman [2006,

DOI: 10.4324/9781003532484-10

pp. 85–102] for a discussion of beauty as the formal organization of idealization.) When we idealize someone or something, as in the declaration of love just noted, that other is experienced as beautiful. But beauty is only one dimension of our aesthetic, the formal aspect of experience and the sense of quality that we feel it possesses. Where does our capacity and motivation for aesthetics come from, how does it develop within us and for what purpose, and, most importantly, how is it, on a very pragmatic level, the quality that defines us as human?

First, we must consider the question of form. Human experience would be incomprehensible and unmanageable without our inherent drive to give order, structure, and meaning to our perceptions and experiences. However, form is not a quality of reality, the world in and of itself can never be known directly, for in the process of coming to know, we create order out of the formlessness, which is the true reality. This formal ordering of our experience gives our "world" shape, color, texture, rhythm, pattern, and tone. These are products of our brains in interaction with whatever is "out there." The right hemisphere organizes experience according to gestalts and the feel of things. We give shape, rhythm, texture, and an overall sense of structure to our experience. The left hemisphere organizes the details, the unique traits, and specific qualities of experience. The left hemisphere seeks consistency and order. We are less concerned with the feeling; rather we look to be decisive, "pin things down," and come to some definitive meaning. We impose form on the "booming, buzzing" reality that we come up against and must somehow deal with, and we do this by bringing wild reality under the yoke of meaningful form. However, the form we construct out of our experiences is also used to negotiate and manage the world. So it cannot be an arbitrary formal order that we construct and use, but rather the form by which we give order to our world that needs to be "matched" to reality. Although the world is nothing like how we perceive it, our formal organization of experience must in some essential way fit what's out there, must be proven to be useful in bringing about the results we require from the world for our survival.

The formal organization of human experience is not simply some bland, practical matter. Human life is affect-laden, passionate, and embedded in the urges, desires, and needs of our bodies, and in the relationships between our bodies. This is why, as we construct the form of our worlds, we also imbue those forms with feeling, vitality, eroticism, and beauty. Thus, we create a human world, which expresses our relational reality, within which human beings' breathe, love, rage, compete, and care for each other. This formal essence of our human world is its aesthetics. As we will discuss later, aesthetics is the value we give to the form of our experience. It is the quality of the forms. And crucial to this experience of quality is the feel of things, the way in which the rich tapestry of our affects is interwoven with the ever evolving, unfolding structures of our lived lives. This is why aesthetics is so central to psychological well-being and mental health. At heart, aesthetics is how it feels for us to exist, and the quality of our felt existence, the overarching aesthetic form of our experience, makes the difference between torment and happiness, and all that falls between. Aesthetics is also essentially about relationships, which is why so much art is created and enjoyed together. We experience our world, our being together, aesthetically. Even from our earlier cries, yearnings, and hungers we cannot resist giving formal quality to our experience.

The capacity to organize experience according to aesthetic form is not a given but is acquired out of innumerable interactions with a dynamic and responsive world. In the case of a newborn infant lacking the maturity and neural capability needed to organize perceptions, his or her experience of the world must be wild and chaotic. All that intrauterine thumping, dim light, murmuring, and warmth (what I would call the primordial aesthetic, or protoaesthetic) gives way, after a rather unexpected ordeal, to harsh light, exploding colors, loudness, and big forms rising and swirling around – voices, no longer mumbling, but bright and shocking. Gradually the baby begins to recognize something, a voice, a smell, a touch, and he or she reaches out with hands, eyes, lips – for "her." It is this other, the mother, who will begin the process of guiding the child to make sense of the formlessness. As she is with her child, holding, feeding him, the baby begins to see shapes, hear tones, feel rhythms that are soothing, exciting, familiar. A curve of her arm, a gentle song, a soft rocking, a touch and shape of her face become the first, most important opportunities for aesthetic experience – the formal organization of the world infused with passion, feeling, longing – in short, the fundamental aesthetic organization of human connection (Hagman, 2006, pp. 29–40).

The Sense of Quality

In other words, when we talk about aesthetics, we must include the quality of the experience, such things as its beauty, sublimity, or ugliness (Hagman, 2006, pp. 85–142). As noted, aesthetic experience is molded and elaborated in intimate attachments, and we also must consider the experience of the quality of those interactions – most importantly the role of idealization. A mother and child are not only attached; they also invest each other with value, through the exchange of *value affects*. Mom is the most wonderful mom – "the **most beautiful mom**." I am her most darling and lovely boy – "the **most beautiful boy in the world**." Such idealizations involve a profound aesthetic experience of the other. And as we interact, loving each other, praising each other, the idealization is augmented ("value augmentation"; Hagman, 2006, p. 60) until there is a sustained and thrilling sense of the beautiful, which is shared and leads to an enhancement of self-experience and self with other.

Obviously, some of us lack such early experiences of mutual idealization (Hagman, 2015, p. 15). Unfortunately, many of our patients all too often experienced the opposite – neglect, denigration, and abuse. In these people the aesthetic sense may be distorted and precarious, with disorder and ugliness shadowing everyday life, their moods and relationships. But paradoxically, the drive to idealize, to give value to experience can remain active despite trauma and loss. For many, the search for beauty intensifies, creating a hunger for formal beauty in relationships, self-experience, and art (see Wheelis [1999] for a personal account of compulsive longing for beauty). Being beautiful, being close to the beautiful, and/or creating beauty becomes an intoxication, a hunger, which can thrill and destroy, because the connection to such aesthetic states is often precarious, uncertain, and prone to collapse. On the one hand the successful experience of getting one's aesthetic needs met contributes to the healthy elaboration of confident selfhood, with one's relation to beauty secured; on the other hand aesthetic failure leads to self-disorder and vulnerability, with an accompanying hunger for a state of beautiful connection, which is forever absent, denied, or precariously, tantalizingly fragile.

But in most instances the meeting of our aesthetic needs over time by a good enough context of love, responsiveness and reliability, encourages us to elaborate outwardly the formal structure of our self and world (Hagman, 2006). We imbue the objective world with a complex and variegated subjectivity in which a positive formal organization of experience is taken for granted, within which moments of exquisite perfection and beauty, along with the sublime and ugly, becomes possible. In optimal conditions because of this aesthetic drive, we find ourselves actively creating positive aesthetic organizations of ourselves and world within which we can live relatively healthy and happy lives. Unfortunately for persons who experienced trauma, significant illness or injury, this drive may be inhibited, derailed, or skewed resulting in a depleted or deranged aesthetic, characterized by a sense of blandness, rather than vibrancy, or ugliness rather than beauty. However, such people may experience a heightened aesthetic drive in which the hunger for beauty and even perfection predominates. Of course, this desperate need may also be a source of torment, especially when beauty proves elusive, or life perversely asserts its inclination for the ugly.

Given the importance of this aesthetic drive, we can assume that all human relationships have aesthetic dimensions, whether this is the mutual fittedness of the mother holding and playing with her baby, a presentation to the Board of Directors of an advertising agency, or the physical engagement of psychotherapist and patient. These interactions are shaped by formally encoded, procedural representations that are models for participation in later relationships (Beebe and Lachmann, 2002). This implicit, procedural memory organization possesses a particular set of aesthetic dimensions that capture and create the "feel" of life, of self, and of self-in-relation (Stern, 2010). As we will see later, the psychotherapeutic situation offers us an opportunity to experience and reflect on these aesthetic dimensions in a secure, structured, and, to an extent, controlled environment. We would say that the psychotherapy is replete with aesthetic qualities that are stimulated and intensified by the structured yet intimate nature of the relationship (Hagman, 2015, pp. 19–30).

What role do these aesthetic dimensions play in the psychotherapy process, and most importantly in therapeutic success? No one factor results in therapeutic change. Interpretation, once seen as the purest, most directly mutative component of techniques, is now viewed within the context of many factors: security, attachment style, and attunement to mention several. Currently the patient's experience of the psychotherapist's empathy is viewed as one of the most important factors in therapeutic effectiveness. A dimension of the psychotherapeutic interaction, which contributes to the crystallization and elaboration of empathy (e.g., the sense of the other's inner life), is the aesthetics of the psychotherapeutic exchange and situation. The psychotherapist feels his way into the patient's inner world not vicariously, but through intense and sustained engagement in an interaction that is experienced in terms of rhythms, tones, shapes, colors, sensations, and other qualitative aspects of formal organization (Press and Hagman in Hagman, 2015). From this point of view, empathy is not a type of imaginative work, but a "feeling into" the experience of the other, through attunement to their bodies, voice, visual appearance, even perhaps smell and feel. As with all other relationships, especially early attachments, this engagement stimulates mutual affects, fantasies, and meanings, which compose the intersubjective matrix of empathy.

In other words, over time both parties begin to develop a sense of "being" together. This occurs primarily on a physical and affective level. Our bodies respond to each other, and we begin to identify a familiar feel within the body of the other – this may involve sexual feelings in our skin and genitals, defensive tensions in the mouth, the tightness of fear in the chest, aggressive arousal manifest by a stiffening neck and shoulders, as well as less pronounced, implicit states of comfort or discomfort as the sessions progress. We also are linked affectively with a range of emotions being elicited from one another. Over time we begin to be familiar with certain forms and patterns of feeling and body sensations. These make up the aesthetic dance of the relationship, the primary means by which we experience connection, attunement, and empathy.

As discussed earlier, central to this aesthetic is the experience of its quality and value. In other words, when we experience the psychotherapeutic relationship aesthetically, we make a judgment about its quality. In another context we refer to this experience as *value affects* when love, excitement, pleasure, or anxiety is directly tied to a qualitative judgment about someone or something. Fundamentally, value affects are not moral, but aesthetic, not about goodness or badness but about beauty, or on the other hand ugliness – and all that lies in between (Hagman, 2006, pp. 85–142). There is, of course, no objective way to judge the quality of connection, but we know it when we feel it.

Once the psychotherapist becomes aware of this aesthetic dimension and begins to organize his/her experience of the aesthetics on a conscious level, she can move this recognition to the forefront of her experience of the interaction, and we believe this can heighten the visceral understanding of the relationship and even reveal previously unknown aspects of the clinical exchange. In fact, it is when the aesthetic dimension is linked to and elaborated along with other dimensions (verbal, affective, narrative) that these other dimensions can be more clearly and forcefully appreciated within the relational field of the therapy.

Creativity

However, to understand the dynamics of aesthetics in the clinical process we must also consider the problem of creativity and its importance to psychotherapy. For it is only when we can see the artfulness of therapy, and the central role of creativity in the process that we can understand how our aesthetic is manifest, worked on, and elaborated during treatment (Hagman, 2015, pp. 19–30).

Creativity is the process by which something new is made or happens (Hagman, 2006, pp. 61–83). Relationships can be creative as we struggle with each other and with the stubborn world we must live in and make do with. Creativity can move life forward. It is the drive to solve the problem, to heal the wound, to evoke that moment of joy again, and again whenever it fades. Creativity is essential to vital and satisfying living. If we give up, resign ourselves simply to what is, then we are stuck with the same old thing, which some of us can't tolerate (this is what drives us to therapy). But we can't approach creativity too directly – the best way is to not think about it at all, only solving the problem, but more specifically engaging that which is not us, which may have been us, but is now Other. Or maybe we cannot avoid it, so we are compelled (for the sake of our welfare, happiness, existence) to engage the Other (also sometimes Ourselves as Other), and from that struggle the unexpected happens. Something we didn't count on. Something surprising. But in some cases, we can't stop there. We can't stop until we get it right. (That is probably the hardest thing – to know when we have got what we want, to learn how to decide). Maybe we only know it when we feel it. "Does it feel right?" we ask ourselves. We live our lives day to day, trying to feel good about ourselves, maybe even to be happy. Perhaps that's what drives creativity forward, the feeling that guides us. We know the new thing, the thing we created, because we are pleased, satisfied with it, maybe it makes us feel alive, vital, immortal (the best illusion!). But more pragmatically, the challenge of creativity, begs the question of life – do you want to truly live, or cling to the familiar and safe. Creativity is a risk. After all there is nothing more miserable than a failing artist, ambitions stymied, stuck with old solutions, or none. Or the patient (failed artist of her life) repeating the same old patterns, the same painful feelings, without a way out, no way to move forward (Phillips, 1998). The desperate patient makes the call, shows up, and drops down into the chair – adrift, clueless, but hoping for something to happen. Frequently, there is that dim, almost formless sense, a hope or anticipation, that the longed for, special person or thing which we have never really had, will be there in the therapist's office – finally, after all these years – and we will be saved.

Whatever the particulars of these fantasies, longings, and fears, this is how the patient attempts to bring about the conditions for something new to happen (Hagman, 2015, pp. 61–71). The active patient attempts to provoke the psychotherapist into an enactment – the psychotherapeutic relationship. In this way the patient and psychotherapist give substance and form to their relationship by means of the construction of the cotransference. (I will be adopting this term from Donna Orange [1993] to designate what has been traditionally called transference and countertransference.) The cotransference is organized as the subjectivity of the participants is externalized by means of a sustained, relatively durable construction of actions, affects, words, narratives, rhythms, etc., which become a subjective object, a rich amalgam of fantasy, desire, and dread. This *subjective object* (Winnicott, 1971), the cotransference, ultimately becomes both the object and

driving force of the treatment (Orange, 1993). And it is the elaboration and perfection of the cotransference, which is the creative heart of psychotherapy. This
is what makes psychotherapy an art, not a science. The externalization of subjectivity in the form of a subjective object, the cotransference, which becomes the
object of understanding, elaboration, and perfection, and most importantly the
object of change. Like the artwork it is, the cotransference is made move vivid,
expressive, and vital and is transformed through the clinical interaction into something more whole and meaningful, reflecting the healthy desires and needs of the
psychotherapeutic couple.

Case Example: Paul

One of my patients, Paul, is a young man with strong professional ambitions while
at the same time struggling with a compulsion to accommodate others and neglect
his own needs. He would enter my office and after a thoughtful pause, as if col-
lecting his thoughts, would begin taking off from what he remembered about our
last session. He would discuss his frustration as a consultant, his inability to find
ways to express his personal vision and creative ambitions. He would tell me of
his relationship with his girlfriend. He described her as overly anxious, dependent,
and needy. His emotional life was focused continually on trying to calm her, if not
make her happy – his needs were on hold. He even claimed to have lost touch with
simple wishes of his own. He said he did not have any idea what he wanted.

In many ways Paul was an ideal patient, and he handled the technicalities of our
relationship well. He was reliable, arrived early, and paid on time. Invariably verbal, he was thoughtful and self-analytical. However, I was aware from the start, that
despite these positive qualities, something was off. It was more in the feel of being
with him, the quality of our interactions, physically, the changing relative positions
of our bodies, the mutual adjustments in tone, volume, and timber of voice, the
shape of our dialogue, as our imagery and constructed narrative were woven as if
on a loom of many gradually intertwining colored strands. But the mix was wrong,
the weave awkward and offline, the dialogue clumsy, our voices clashing, off beat,
and flat. Our aesthetic dance was out of sync.

For example, symptomatic of these derailments in self-development, in sessions, Paul was unable to articulate any personal desire, need, or wish, other than
that which was directed at others. He struggled to account for any hobbies or interests; nor was he able to say where he wanted to go on vacation, or even if he did.
He would sit across from me, his shoulders stooped, looking flustered, unable to
describe to me any interest or priority that he could call his own. His aesthetic
experience of his life was flat, colorless without vitality. In one session he told me:

> My girlfriend, Jill, and I are going on a vacation next week, to the islands.
> I am afraid that it won't be any good. I am sure it will be a wonderful place,
> but it's me. I am afraid that I will get that feeling again – like I am not sure it
> is right, not what is best for me. I don't know what that is, but it makes it hard

to choose, as if I choose what I want it won't be the right thing that I will have chosen incorrectly.

But you also say you don't have a clear idea what you would <u>want</u> to choose.

Right. It ends up being a matter of luck, but of course I expect to feel disappointment, not fulfillment.

Being unable to articulate what he wanted, he nonetheless felt that he had to choose the right thing. But his "feeling of being" in his life had low aesthetic value, and there was no way that he could judge what was right for him, or what he preferred. There was no way to know what choice to make – so he did nothing regarding his personal needs or wishes – he remained radically noncommittal, or rather unable to decide.

Around and around in his mind he reworked this impossible puzzle, longing to accomplish something satisfying in life, but unable to act – a type of aesthetic Hamlet – he would soliloquize in his sessions, drab and plain, unengaged and uninspired – not exactly depressed, but suppressed and uninspired. His experience of life was of a world without pizzazz or beauty, a plain, uninviting place. On the other hand, during these sessions I always felt restless, my legs ached, and I shifted uncomfortably in my chair. I experienced no position as relaxing as I maneuvered myself in the chair. I worried that this would upset him, since I obviously was uncomfortable and physically unresponsive to him.

However, he had had times in his life when this aesthetic wasteland had opened and revealed to him another way of being. He recalled that as a child he spent summers in Cape Cod. One summer (he is not sure which one) he felt unusually excited by the town and the ocean beach. He remembers wandering the town and the dunes, reveling in the sun and salty beach air. The old, gray-shingled beach houses seemed particularly charming to him. He played and wandered – a happy, lively, and playful young boy. The memories of that summer remained with him and were the source of both hope and despair. Hope that he was indeed capable of such feelings, and despair that he might not recover that sense of creativity and vitality.

Much more recently, he told me that he had been walking down a New York street on a sunny day. Lost in thought, feeling hopeless and at a loss as usual, he looked up at one of the nearby buildings, where a broadleaved tree stood against a red brick wall. At that moment the sun was shining on the wall, and above was a bright blue sky. Unexpectedly, shockingly, he experienced a surge of joy, fascination, and enthrallment. This familiar sight suddenly seemed transcendent. He felt alive, stirred by excitement at the beauty of the scene.

"I know I am capable of such a feeling, but I don't know how to hold onto it. I want too so bad. I want to feel about my life something like that moment, or the summer at the beach. But then afterward, I am back where I was unable to feel, unable to be able to feel any confidence about what I want, or even what I love."

When patients such as Paul enter treatment, we rarely evaluate the quality of his or her aesthetic life. Part of this is due to the patient's lack of awareness of their aesthetic sense. It is transparent to them, taken for granted, like the air. Another part lies with us, we also don't think about aesthetics, as we evaluate the patient's story, self-experience, and relationships, we rarely think of the sense of quality of formal experience, of the patient's relationship to beauty and ugliness. It is also a failure of theory and clinical training that have emphasized objectivity and content, over subjectivity and the phenomenology of aesthetic experience. But our patients' unhappiness is often embodied in their sense of the relative quality of their aesthetic world. For the depressive, the world is drab and even ugly. The narcissist is plagued by the distortions of a precarious and vulnerable connection to beauty, of self or other. The borderline patient is tormented by an erratic and overwrought aesthetic connection in which beauty can morph into ugliness in an instant, a plague of devils and angels, a world in which the aesthetic sense is caught up in a swirl of uncertainty. Perhaps we therapists see this aesthetic sense as peripheral – that it will take care of itself as we treat the patient's neurosis, addiction, or character disorder. But as I will argue, the aesthetic of the patient is an area of primary concern and can be treated directly if the therapist and patient "see it" and include the aesthetic dimension as an important part of the experience of transference.

In his memory of sun and sky, Paul was recalling a powerful moment of positive and enlivening aesthetic experiences, during which his engagement with the world became infused with the excitement of light, color, shape, rhythm, tone, and sensation. The quality of these aesthetic experiences was thrilling. The sky and the sunny building were beautiful and even sublime, things of high quality and formal perfection. He felt stirred within his deepest self, and alive like he had never felt before, or since. Kuspit (2006) has written about "aesthetic shock" in which all our expectations and assumptions are thrown over and a new and dazzling world is revealed to us. We feel as if we are confronted by a pure and basic reality, but at the same time it is beautiful, infused with vitality and hope. Having had a taste of such an aesthetic experience, Paul hungered for more – but despaired.

I learned that Paul was raised in a depressed and rather cruel family. His father, an academic, was often angry and did not offer Paul any opportunity for a sustained and involved relationship. Most importantly the father did not protect Paul from the mother, whom Paul described as depressed and extremely self-centered. Paul learned the hard way to walk gingerly around the mother who was easily perturbed. When her needs or wishes were not met, Paul recalls, she would accuse him of selfishness and even betrayal. These accusations were frequent and predictable. Paul learned to attune himself to his mother's moods and attitudes. He could sense when to keep a distance and when to approach her. In other words, they engaged in a form of "aesthetic dance" characterized by a fragile relation between attunement and disruption. Mostly (and most damaging to him) he learned to be preoccupied with any potential need of his mother, hoping to avoid or blunt the impact of her anger and blame. This obsessive focus on the needs of the other resulted in a disruption of Paul's self-experience, part of which involved a developmental failure in the elaboration of his aesthetic sense of self. Instead of being self-centered, he became increasingly mother-centered, until as an adult, he was no longer aware of it. Eventually his entire being and all his emotional energy became other-directed, extending his defenses beyond his mother, as he became increasingly concerned with trying to keep everyone in his life satisfied and happy

One habit that Paul had, often when he seemed frustrated and physically rigid, was to cough sharply, almost like a bark. I was always startled. He on the other hand didn't seem concerned – nor was there any sign of discharge. The air from his mouth seemed dry, harsh, and contentless. But this habit of his also felt as a piece with his entire body posture and gestural style. He would sit across from me, his shoulders high, his arms held in an angular fashion, stiff and awkward. But most importantly I felt there was no physical engagement between us. My motions did not seem to affect his – my nods went unrecognized, no response from him to my smiles or changes in my body posture. As noted earlier, often I was all aches and pains, shifting in my seat as I tried to get comfortable. My posture was obviously based more on my internal body experience, than a response to him. If this was a therapeutic dance, we were badly off beat, out of sync, stepping on each other's toes.

Not surprisingly, my ability to express my aesthetic sense, my way of feeling into his experience and my "being" with him was awkward, incomplete, and at times the best word would be "ugly." My normal physicality and firm touch became uncoordinated and uncertain, tentative as I repeatedly experienced disruption and a sensation of being off balance.

Clinically this aesthetic experience of myself with Paul was a crucial element in my effort to attune myself to his experience. I groped my way through our interactions. I did not fight the feelings of anxiety, the mismatched and awkward comments, and missed opportunities. These feelings, however awkward, were important guides to my own self-reflection and my growing "feel for" Paul's style and the evolving nature of his personal aesthetic of self, and of self-with-other. Certainly, the content of our dialogue was crucial as we explored the immediate experience of his relationship with his girlfriend and its link to his traumatic past. However, my participation in this dialogue was not determined by rational decision-making, linear logic, and/or conscious thought; perhaps more important were my developing aesthetic feel for our relationship, and the changing nature of that aesthetic over time.

Recently Paul entered my office, stood in front of my chair, and announced: "Hello" and took his seat. He smiled slightly (a bit sheepish I thought), yet he seemed more relaxed, his body more open and visible to me as if for the first time. I knew something had changed. I could feel my own body become more relaxed and less uncomfortable and achy. He said: "I think this is helping." He explained that although perhaps it was hard to see in any one session that he had begun to be more honest about his feelings and what he wanted, especially with his girlfriend. "I am much less concerned about making her or keeping her happy. I still worry about it, but I am much more willing to say what I feel and deal with the consequences."

He said that he felt that this would lead to some conflict but in the end, it would allow his girlfriend to both understand him better and to deal with him. He admitted that this increased the anxiety he felt about it not working out, but that if the relationship was going to change and grow, it was the only thing to do. As he spoke, he gestured with his hands in a way that was new (at least to me) as he talked about his relationship; he would throw his arms out, point with his fingers, and I imagined him manipulating the image of his relations with his girlfriend with his hands. He was clearly more willing to play with his language and include his body in the communication in a more flexible, expressive, and responsive way.

There had been no dramatic moments of meeting, or disruptions and repairs to point to as an explanation of the changes that occurred in our relationship. Most of our sessions seemed to be an awkward but stubborn effort to keep on going, on my part to find ways to be better fitted to Paul, on his part to feel less restricted and more expressive. Together we had to find a rhythm and style of attunement, so that rather than lurching awkwardly into his monologue, there might be some space for me and then for us as well. The improvisational aspect of our relationship became more attuned, trusting, and open, as we threw away "old scripts," and let our interaction unfold without restriction.

Apart from these very positive statements, it was the feeling of our being together that was most striking to me. Our dialogue became more animated and rhythmical. Our bodies felt more engaged and responsive. The aesthetic tone of the interaction was richer, more lively, and more brightly toned than the austere, grayish, and drab aesthetic of earlier sessions. These qualities were also accompanied by excitement, even a little joy, at our success but also, I think of the way our value affects augmented each other, as the clinical discussion became more animated and mutual, improvisational if you will. I became aware how each of us had a part in cultivating and elaborating these aesthetic feelings, as if we were cocreating a work of art.

For example, my personal aesthetic style is to be physically present; my motions are strong and emphatic. I can be verbally loud, and I gesture with various parts of my body as I talk. Aware that my style can be imposing, perhaps intimidating to some patients, I find the typical restraint of the psychotherapeutic stance helpful. In Paul's case, because I experienced our interactions as disruptive and coarse, I believed strongly that I had to restrain and monitor my aesthetic style in the sessions because of its potential negative impact on Paul – in other words I had to learn to follow his lead. I would begin the sessions sitting quietly, relaxing my body and mind, letting myself begin to response to him as he sat across from me. As if following my partner in a dance, I would allow him to lead, offering myself as a responsive other, willing to attune myself to his voice, body movements, and gestures – this was not easy for me, but I continually righted myself, monitoring the feel of my responses and his reactions to them. Our awkwardness and uncertainty were obvious, our steps uncertain and his lead rough and uncomfortable, but I adjusted, absorbed this ugliness and made the most out of our rough dance. But more than that, I also followed him as he shaped and structured the dialogue, creating a narrative of our session, coauthors of a short story.

Conclusion

The unfolding aesthetic of any psychotherapeutic relationship is co-constructed. This is at the heart of a creative psychotherapy (Hagman, 2015). Over time Paul and I engaged in constructing a structured exchange. He would act or talk, I would respond, he would take off from my remark, and we would gradually construct a form of being together – a form that had many facets, shapes, tones, lines, rhythms, colors, and sensations. In this way a subjective object crystalized, which was the externalization of our shared subjectivity (Winnicott, 1971). Earlier we spoke of this as the cotransference. Initially we were out of sync, awkward and out of tune with each other's bodies, moods, meanings, and gestures. However, we worked together on this structure, which became a living presence between us. However, I was not simply an equal partner in this creative process, I was also his psychotherapist/ instructor, reflecting to him my observation of his manner of relating, probing his sense of self, and facilitating the structuring of his self-experience through inter-pretations. In other words, I sought to articulate and attune the empathic link, to deepen formal organization of our being together, and of his sense of himself. On the other hand, Paul struggled to recognize the restrictive patterns which at first predominated. Gradually he changed the patterns of security and protection, risk-ing the expression of vulnerabilities and needs that had been long hidden. Like dancers, we played with the meaning, rhythm, and style of our engagement. When I say that this approach was like a dance, it was more like a dance lesson. I was not just a partner or instructor but a student as well. I needed to learn his style, but also offer my own style in a responsive fashion, which would eventually crystallize into an aesthetic of our own, a signature style for our relationship.

As illustrated by my psychotherapeutic work with Paul, our aesthetic sense of self and of self-in-relation to others, as well as our capacity for empathy are inti-mately intertwined.

Thus, the creative and aesthetic dimensions of therapy is not only a source of information but plays an important role in the therapeutic process. They also play a role in the experience of each partner, and by increasing our awareness of and sensitivity to the vicissitudes of our aesthetic engagement with our patients we, as therapists, can engage in the therapeutic interaction at a richer and more fundamen-tal level of communication.

I have argued in this article for a perspective on the psychotherapeutic process based on awareness of this "aesthetic responsiveness." I have traced this process back to the nonverbal emotional rapport and empathy of the earliest infant/parent interplay when empathic bonds and our sense of aesthetic were an inherent part of the early relational interactions between parent and baby. I hope the reader will have increased his or her awareness of and sensitivity to the aesthetic dimensions of the psychotherapeutic relationship, thereby opening a rich and complex realm of psychotherapeutic opportunity

Chapter 11

Festival

In this chapter, I will extend the ideas that we have discussed in the preceding pages and explore their implications for a general psychology of human aesthetic experience. To this end, I will integrate psychoanalytic thinking into a broader social framework, so that we can appreciate the full significance of aesthetic experience and creativity.

Some modern philosophers have stressed the pervasive influence of aesthetics throughout human history. Following that line of thought, I will reach beyond this book's earlier chapters and try to sketch a vision of the place of aesthetics in the evolution of human life. Therefore, I am offering these thoughts as preliminary and suggestive. The canvas is broad and deep, while the time is short; let me be the first to admit that this is just a beginning.

The celebration that Gadamer referred to is not any specific group of activities, but the continuing social dialogue of art and aesthetic experience. He refers to it as *festival* – the vast and timeless creation and appreciation of art that has endured throughout recorded history and across societies. In the end, Gadamer is uncertain about the ultimate purpose of the festival. In this chapter, I will argue that the festival of aesthetic life is celebrated at every level of our social and psychological lives, and that it comprises all the activities and psychic processes that articulate the formal experience of being and being with, and that its function and goals are the refinement and positive evolution of humanity.

In prior chapters, I have shown that aesthetic experience is fundamentally tied to the archaic infant/parent relationship; however, this most intimate and basic relationship is also influenced by the social and psychological dynamics of culture. This simple idea adds an entire dimension to the thesis of this book. Aesthetic life is not just the extension of childhood experience to mature relationships, since also the reverse is true: the aesthetic life of the mother and child is inseparably linked to the aesthetics of society. But I will add one more dimension – that individual subjective processes affect both the interpersonal and the social. Individual people are capable of creative acts that reverberate upward to affect the relationships and social structure out of which they emerged; in other words, we are not simply products of our culture, but also creators of it. The three levels – of the individual, relationships, and the social structure – interact and codetermine each

DOI: 10.4324/9781003532484-11

other's existence, dynamics, and character. Ultimately, those parts of the festival known as the arts have become the primary means by which society attempts to elaborate aesthetic experience (the basic forms of being and of being with) across the social landscape; in this way, the festival serves an important function in the establishment, maintenance, and regulation of individual psychological life and social relations.

Recently, much has been written about "the Art World" (Danto, 1964) and "institutional aesthetics" (Dickie, 1974; Townsend, 1997). Such authors argue that the aesthetic models that are based on universal principles – such as ideal forms, divine goodness, or even a priori formal ideas – are not provable, but crystallize out of the needs and priorities of culture, to ground aesthetics in some fixed and immutable set of beliefs. The very concept of the Art World conveys the impression that all that we include in our aesthetic belief systems (i.e., works of art, artists, art audiences) is ever changing and the product of social/historical forces. In the Art World, current economic, social priorities, and power relations are important to understand. Aesthetics and art are constantly evolving institutions that respond to the needs of communities over time.

In *An Introduction to Aesthetics* (1997), Dabney Townsend made the following comments regarding the institutional/postmodern viewpoint:

Instead of looking for characteristics of the object and its makers or of the experience itself (aesthetic attitude theories) one looks for the ways in which artists are being defined by the audience and the strategies that artists use to meet those expectations. Then, what one finds is a complex history of successful and unsuccessful attempts to satisfy a unique kind of relation – an aesthetic relation.

(p. 204)

In fact, the notion of the Art World is very similar to Gadamer's festival; both describe aesthetic life as a creative chaos that is constantly responding to the needs of communities, relationships, and individuals.

A major limitation of the model of the Art World is that it relies primarily on a social constructivist perspective. The forces of economics, politics, social and racial relations are the principal focuses of theorists, and it can seem like artists, art, and audiences are just by-products of these institutions, controlled by forces outside the psychological realm. However, Townsend also stresses the mutually constructive influences among artist, audience, and society. Through the production and promotion of works of art, artists create their audience, and through the expression of group needs, audiences create artists, and both audiences and artists influence and create the aesthetic life of their culture. Culture then creates new generations of artists and audiences, but these then return the influence on culture, and all this continues over time in a churning, marvelous, creative wave of aesthetic life.

Another useful way to understand this process is through the notion of multiple levels of subjectivity. This approach allows us to apply the relational/developmental aesthetics to the larger social canvas conjured by the Art World and institutional aesthetics theorists. Let me explain.

Human life involves multiple fields of subjectivity. These subjective realms are invariably both conscious and unconscious in nature, and they are characterized by transference and countertransference, projection and internalization, organization and disorganization. Most important, the aesthetics of human life at each level is motivated by the desire to establish, maintain, and nurture human connection, to idealize relationships, to seek beauty, to avoid (or transform) ugliness, and to cultivate the sublime; and it is these primary aesthetic forms that we co-construct in relationships with our parents in early childhood, forming templates for our experience of and engagement with the world, with others, and with ourselves.

This idea is supported by the anthropologist Ellen Dissanayake in *Art and Intimacy* (2000), where she describes the connection between the early developmental sources of aesthetic experience and the larger cultural activities of a community:

> The arts evolved as physical correlates of psychological concern. The inborn rhythmic-modal sensitivities of mutuality, through cultural elaborations, became adaptive means for arousing interest, riveting joint attention, synchronizing bodily rhythms and activities, conveying messages with conviction and memorability, and ultimately indoctrinating and reinforcing the right attitudes and behaviors. As rhythmic-modal sensitivities and capacities evolved to enable emotional dispositions by which mothers and infants engage in mutuality, so could elaborations of these sensitivities and capacities become vehicles for social coordination and concord, instilling belonging, meaning, and competence, which are feelings that comprise psychological well-being.
>
> (p. 139)

Consistent with Gadamer's and Dissanayake's theses, D. W. Winnicott argued that aesthetic culture is the social elaboration of play. Over historical and developmental time, play is extended and spread out across social relations and is engaged in by groups beyond the parent/child dyad. Larger communal activities are established that have roots in the archaic interpersonal environment and in transitional experience, which become established and necessary components of shared social life. Winnicott (1971) noted: "There is a direct development from transitional phenomena to playing, and from playing to shared playing, and from this to cultural experiences" (p. 51). In this short statement, he described the developmental elaboration of aesthetic experience from the earliest psychological processes through advanced forms of cultural communication and social ritual.

Aesthetic experience is the medium by which the formal aspects of relatedness and fantasy are articulated and expanded beyond the immediacy of dyadic interaction, into the individual's relationship to the environment as well as the people and institutions that make up social life. Most important, it is the extension of experiences of attunement, fittedness, and satisfaction – originally either experienced or wished for in the infant/parent interaction – that provides the phenomenological template for our relationship to the whole of reality.

Thus, aesthetic experience influences every level of human life, from the general psychological glue that binds society, to the forms of communication between two people, to the substance of our most private thoughts and fantasies. It is often hard to see this, given that most of our aesthetic life is prereflective and unconscious. However, from the color of our clothing and the cut of the cloth, to the shape and organization of our dashboards, to the expressions on our faces in greeting friends, to the rhythm of our handshakes upon meeting strangers, to the postures and gestures that we share when we have sex – the very deepest forms and textures of our lives are determined by an infinitely complex set of aesthetic principles and processes. In addition, our unconscious fantasy lives are also structured aesthetically; this is evident in dreams as well as in associations during psychoanalytic treatment, and there is a dynamic relationship between these very personal aesthetic structures and larger, communal aesthetic sensibilities.

There are three levels of subjectivity, and each level has a special function in adaptation and survival (I would like to acknowledge my indebtedness to Charles Tolman's 1994 discussion of the work of the critical psychologist Klaus Holzkamp in the development of my thinking about multiple levels of subjectivity). For people to respond effectively to the environment, they must do so at several levels: (1) *metasubjectively*, through group response, so that societies can provide the support, protection, and resources necessary for individuals to live in a particular environment (this level does not include, however, the flexibility and specificity necessary to ensure survival and/or efficiency); (2) *intersubjectively*, through cooperative responses, in which several people communicate, interact, and agree upon certain shared reactions to social and environmental demands (this level increases specificity and responsiveness); and (3) *subjectively*, through the specific capability of the individual to make highly discriminating responses to conditions and events within the immediate social and physical environment, and to develop internal regulatory capacities to adjust psychological states and processes to ever-changing demands, needs, and opportunities (this level is highly responsive and thus permits focused and prompt adaptations, but is not capable of ensuring the welfare of larger groups; it is dependent on the other subjective levels).

Human life is composed of the processes within these levels and the continual exchange among them. For example, the metasubjective provides knowledge to the individual, who then adapts this knowledge to individual circumstances, and thus, through feedback, that individual enhances the knowledge pool of the community, making it available to other individuals and small groups.

A central area of subjective life is the aesthetic. Our general tendency to focus on any one level of aesthetic elaboration, such as the individual creative process of the solitary artist or the communal development of rituals, is to miss the rich, essential interplay between multiple levels of human subjectivity.

Metasubjectivity

The metasubjective level is the interconnection of subjective life (both conscious and unconscious) that occurs continually between and within large social groups. Part of this exchange is the way in which experience and fantasy become organized and are given form. It is an infinitely complex system of transference and counter-transference that is chaotic, unpredictable, and protean. However, these systems are also self-organizing and seek attractor states in which common assumptions, values, and formal principles are shared, and to an extent are sustained as beliefs about "the way things are."

The primary function of the metasubjective level is to increase the probability of the survival of the social group. But survival depends on more than just the group acquisition of food and/or shared efforts at ensuring protection from exposure; it also depends on the refinement of community life. Specifically, this means the enhancement of basic units of relationship (the family, the mother/child dyad, mentorship), the good mental health of individuals, and the identification of certain aspects of the world as valuable (e.g., food, a peaceful landscape). As a community, we elaborate ourselves and our world in ways that enhance our tendency to be near good things, to use them and benefit from them. Thus, we establish special ways of structuring possessions, gestures, and important events; we idealize them and even make them beautiful. We seek out what is valuable, refine what is meaningful, and work together to create or find beauty.

These forms of aesthetic experience become the basis for customs, ritual, and other art forms, such as dance, theater, music, and the plastic arts. The goal is extension of internalized aesthetic imagoes into the relations of the larger social group, thereby providing a shared sense of meaning and value to help organize and regulate both personal and interpersonal levels of experience.

As we have seen, aesthetic sensibility is elaborated within the maternal/infant dyad and extended into (and changed by) the child's relationship with the father, and later with the environment and culture of which the child is a part. This results in an enduring sense of goodness and of beauty. Since all members of a community have had their own developmental experience and have elaborated an aesthetic sensibility that is similarly (but far from uniformly) grounded in the intimacy of the maternal/infant dyad, as a group, they engage in higher-level cultural pursuits that reflect the desire to enhance and maintain the original experiences of relatedness.

Thus, the glue of culture, the "dark matter," so to speak, which holds everything together and powers relational ties between people, is the prereflective, procedural knowledge that we call aesthetic experience. However, most of the time, what we think of as *aesthetics* and *culture* are only the most external manifestations of largely unconscious processes. We talk, think, and write about movies, paintings, musical compositions, and/or dances, but these are just the most visible and refined products of a pervasive and deep sensibility that determines the formal structure of human intrapsychic and interpersonal life.

More significantly and more obscurely, we seek out ways to restore idealizations, to repair self-injuries, to defend against inner conflict, and/or to protect against the terrors of mortality and vulnerability. We accomplish these goals by surrounding ourselves with things that we value, things that are formally refined and beautiful; for example, we might travel thousands of miles to stand on the edge of the Grand Canyon so that we can be awestruck and astonished at the world's grandeur. At the other extreme, the cultivation and enjoyment of fine art is the most exquisite and powerful way in which we seek out aesthetic experience.

Interestingly, as the adult members of a community create culture through multiple and complex dialogues, one of the important areas that they elaborate is the institution of parenting itself. Here I am referring not only to the types of relationships that make up families, but also to the ways in which parents interact with, think about, and feel about their children. Consistent with other forms of aesthetic effort, we value the parent/child bond and elevate the image and activities of the maternal dyad to beautiful, and even sublime, levels of idealization.

Thus, there is an endless feedback loop in which a culture – one purpose of which is the extension of childhood aesthetics into adult relationships – becomes itself the institution that promulgates the aesthetics of parenting. Given this, we would expect that culture would become reductive and static over time, but the additional levels of subjectivity assure that the unpredictable has an important role in the process.

Intersubjectivity

All societies depend on the effective cooperation of small groups, whether these are families, hunting bands, fruit gatherers, or artists. The most important function of these groups is dialogue, in which the communal aesthetic and personal aesthetic interpenetrate and change in response to shared experience. As Carol Press (2002) noted: "Through the inherent reciprocity between individuals and society, the arts ultimately reveal the heart and soul of a culture" (p. 157).

At this level of intersubjectivity, a shared (inter)subjectivity continually emerges, an area of meaning that is composed by but separate from the dialogue of individuals. New understandings, new feelings, and new activities crystallize and become factors effecting change. Most important, it is the dialogue between parent and child that has the biggest impact on the health and welfare of the larger society. One crucial function of the intersubjective is the development of the capacity to participate in relationships with other people. As we have seen, it is from the matrix of the parent/child relationship that the child learns the basic elements of dependency, cooperation, and love, as well as the aesthetics of texture, tone, color, shape, and rhythm that scaffold the child's psychological world and experience of external reality. It is also out of this matrix that the child's first experiences of power, beauty, and injury occur.

All mothers and children live in a particular culture. The average mother shares her community's idealization of her parental role. Her baby is beautiful, and she loves caring for him or her. The special way that a mother holds her child, her posture and grip, the way she talks or coos to the baby, the way she creates and maintains his or her environment – all these components of the maternal aesthetic are articulated out of and within a culture in which the dyad exists as a small but important part. In fact, every aspect of that relationship is socially grounded: the pink or blue sleeper, the crib and its bedding, the mobiles that float over the crib, the high-pitched nonsense phrases that we all use to entertain the baby. However, the way in which the cultural aesthetic of care gets elaborated is determined by the unique nature of this idealized dyad – the dialogue that develops between this mother and her baby (see next section).

In addition, each mother and child dyad has a biological and social background that is irreproducible. Therefore, the cultural aesthetic base from which they start and within which their dialogue develops is elaborated and re-created between them in unique, unpredictable ways. It becomes the form of their specific relationship and the source of the infant's aesthetic sensibility. The mother's touch, the child's touching her back, her rocking and singing, the child's pleasurable cooing and gurgling, the arch of the mother's back and neck, the colors of her skin, the sweep of her hand as she adjusts the blanket – all these experiences make up the idealized aesthetics of being and being with for the child and mother.

This dialogue forms the essential underpinning of aesthetic appreciation and creativity. The creativity of artists (individually and together) is part of the being and being with that finds its clearest and most basic manifestation in the mother/child dyad. The dyadic crystallization of aesthetic experience and the creative impulse is elaborated over developmental time and can be seen in the highly refined activity of the teaching of art (Press, 2002, pp. 157–205).

Subjectivity

> Individuals must engage their worlds with the exploration, assertion and vitality necessary to give shape and form to the subjective meaning of their existence. The reciprocity with culture is invaluable. I believe this is paramount to understanding the subjective necessity and significance of culture, for the individual's cohesion as well as the group's.
>
> (Press, 2002, p. 128)

Aesthetic experience is part of the self-organizing tendency of psychical systems, in which the drive to give form and the desire to perfect (even idealize) interact and become endlessly elaborated. There is a third level of human self-organization, the individual person (even a baby) who organizes him- or herself; this is the level of the subjective. What occurs at this level is the elaboration of personal aesthetic sensibility by an individual as he or she encounters and engages with psychological and environmental realities (including objects and people).

In fact, the relative independence of the subjective level is essential to the renewal (and perhaps survival) of any culture. It is here that rapid and responsive adjustments and accommodations are made to the immediate demands, dangers, and – most important – the opportunities of reality. Aesthetic developments that arise at the level of individual subjectivity occur in response to "events on the ground." Children, as they move away from their mothers and encounter new relationships, must be able to preserve and adapt the aesthetic sensibility that was originally tied to the relationship with the parents. The child must be able to use what was learned with the parents and to cultivate new relationships with what is good and beautiful.

In chapter five, we examined the dynamics of the subjective level as the artist seeks to externalize and refine self-experience – the goal being the ideal expression of the artist's self-experience. We saw that a dialectical process occurs as the artist creates experiences that confirm and enhance the self. Obviously, the forms and contents of the artist's creations are derived from the social surround as it has been internalized, both consciously and consciously. For the artist to sustain motivation in the face of inevitable anxieties associated with the creative process, he or she often relies on relationships with others, such as friends, lovers, or mentors. However, although the metasubjective and intersubjective can provide such support, resources, and stimulation, it is on the subjective level that the specific problems and opportunities of creativity are confronted and resolved. The success or failure of the artist will affect relations with friends, colleagues, and the larger social art community – in short, even the highly subjective creative process has a reverberating effect through every level of society.

Culture

Culture is the communal elaboration of subjectivity. It is an emergent phenomenon of the dynamic interaction between the three levels we have discussed. We usually think of culture as static and unchanging, but this is far from the truth. The forms and contents of culture reverberate and mutate continually. Cultural change is constant. When we speak of a culture, we are usually referring to part of a larger system, and then only one facet of that part, which is changing even as we consider it (in fact, we change it through the act of looking at it).

Nonetheless, despite constant flux and renewal, culture is also the consequence of our overarching desire for security, organization, and meaning in psychological and social life. We need to feel that we know what is true, what to expect, and what is expected of us (Dissanayake, 2000). The meaning and organization of cultural life is grounded in our belief that we know what is important, special, and beautiful. These values are continually being negotiated and explored at all levels of subjectivity. In this regard, culture is the ultimate social creation and has a relation to society like that of artwork to an artist. It is the external embodiment of the community's subjective life, and, like art, culture reflects to us who we are as a people; we continually act upon (and within) our culture to refine and perfect it – and in so doing, we perfect ourselves.

Even though culture is our creation, it ultimately takes on a life of its own. Culture must create and maintain institutions, develop the knowledge and technologies that foster aesthetic institutions (established rituals and other cultural forms), support the creative and nurturing dialogue between parent and child, and provide opportunities for individuals to elaborate and communicate their personal aesthetic vision. Through culture, we strive to create the perfect, beautiful image – made up of half fantasy, half reality – that represents who we are as a people.

The creative arts depend on the processes found in the three levels of subjectivity. Societies squabble about what constitutes "good" or "great" art (and even what *is* art); couples discuss the pros and cons of a particular new art form; and individual artists struggle to integrate disparate visions of an artwork, striving for a new synthesis. This new synthesis may come about only after a visit to an art museum by the artist, or because of a discussion with a friend over dinner. The new work begins to influence other artists and is discussed in journals or art magazines. The creation of the individual artist (the subjective) begins to influence society's idea of art (the metasubjective) as well as the discussion between artists (the intersubjective). In other words, there is a complex and ongoing exchange among the three levels of subjectivity that forms the life of the artistic culture of any society.

The factors that make art different from other forms of aesthetic experience are refinement and idealization. As we saw in chapter three, we idealize those people and things that are important to us. Awe and veneration are evoked for an object considered to be of high aesthetic value – we feel drawn to it; we are enthralled. The experience of the artwork vitalizes us, and through our appreciation of it, our self-experience is raised to a new level of refinement.

Art is the subjectification of reality. It is the most complete and specific way in which we realize our human nature, our essence. In the creation of art, we act upon the world not to use it as a tool or to extract resources, but to transmute our own subjectivity and make it objective and real to us. In chapter five, I referred to this as *transmuting externalization,* a process by which we create an encounter with ourselves (sometimes as strangers to ourselves), and we seek to refine what we see – to both articulate ourselves more clearly and to idealize our own subjectivity, making it (and thus ourselves) more valuable, better organized, more aesthetically pleasing. This is why the search for beauty and the sublime is so crucial to art (and the avoidance or transformation of ugliness is equally essential).

The process of dialectic between a society and its art, between artists and their work, in which the perfection of our subjectivity is the goal, is essential to the evolution of the human spirit. As we engage on all levels of subjectivity to refine our culture, we become better, more beautiful, and more sublime. This is not just because art is therapeutic or morally uplifting (though it can be), but because, in the creation and appreciation of art, there is a vast, complex dialectic, creative encounter with our own subjectivity by which we are renewed. It is a renewal through aesthetics and is thus grounded in our most intimate and important experiences of being and being with. In other words, beautiful art embodies the highest form of human being and human love.

In summary, art is a cultural construct by which the community extends these archaic processes to shared experiences of self, relationship, community, and world. Aesthetic standards are the formal configurations that the group establishes as the optimal and expectable embodiment of metasubjective attunement and mutual regulation. It is a social ideal in which communal subjectivity is concretized and elaborated. Art allows for a sense of shared creation and social recognition. It is intersubjective; there is always a sense of interaction, of mutual gazing between subject and object. The festival of art is the occasion for the shared experience of attunement, vital engagement, and mutual regulation. In this sense, aesthetic experience is conservative as well as transformative. It sustains the communal spirit and provides opportunities for new experience and for the facilitation, even promotion, of human development.

Chapter 12

The Musician and the Creative Process

Music, musical ability, and the psychology of musical performance have been of interest to psychoanalysts for some time even though Freud himself disliked the subject (Cheshire, 1996). Despite (Heinz Kohut's, 1950) early interest in music, his self psychological writings never took up the issue in any depth. This paper explores the psychology of music using a self psychological perspective. Specifically, I will be focusing on the dynamics of the creative process in musical performance.

After a brief review of the psychology of music and the self psychological theory of creativity, I will examine the creative processes as exhibited in musical performance. I will be discussing the classical performer whose art is an interpretation of another's (the composer's) text. I will then consider the psychoanalytic treatment of a musician in which the development of creative capacity was a primary therapeutic focus. The paper will close with a discussion and some general comments.

The Psychological Experience of Music

What is the relationship between the musician and his performance? To answer this question, I will start with the work of Suzanne Langer. A philosopher and aesthetician, Langer developed an approach to symbolization and art that emphasized the nondiscursive nature of artistic symbols whereby the essence of lived experience (what she calls "forms of feeling") is embodied in art. (See also the work of Carroll C. Pratt [1952].) Langer wrote:

> Music is a purely created form not of space, but of time; its materials are tones of varying pitch, loudness, and quality, but its elements are tonal forms, moving, mingling, resolving, having direction and energy, violently active or abating toward complete rest. Its time, as well as all the great and small tonal forms (melodies, progressions) that make it up, are appearances made of sound; music is time made audible and articulated as a perceptible dynamic form.
>
> (Langer, p. 144)

Langer believed that music embodies the temporal vicissitudes of subjective experience, of self-experience over time. Great music creates drama, not discursively as

DOI: 10.4324/9781003532484-12

verbalizable narrative, but a drama of tension and release, of the twists and turns of an evolving theme, of surprise and resolution. Playing or listening to music, we are engulfed or taken up by a vivid experience in which sound holds us in a self-state which progresses and unfolds within a landscape indescribable in other terms. Langer notes:

> The assignment of meaning is a shifting, kaleidoscopic play, probably below the threshold of consciousness, certainly outside the pale of discursive thinking. The imagination that responds to music is personal and associative and logical, tinged with affect, tinged with bodily rhythm, tinged with dream, but concerned with a wealth of formulations for its wealth of wordless knowledge, its whole knowledge of emotional and organic experience, of vital impulse, balance, conflicts, the ways of living and dying and feeling.
>
> (Langer, 1957, p. 244)

The meaning of music is altogether different from that of science. "Music articulates forms which language cannot set forth" (Langer, p. 233). Rather than approaching the world in terms of logic and verbal discourse (the realm of consciousness only), music is a lived experience captured in depth. Conscious and unconscious modes of subjectivity are woven together in a tapestry of tone and sound, which is less about the world and more the symbolic equivalent of human subjectivity itself.

> The import of artistic expression is broadly the same in all arts as in music – the verbally ineffable, yet not inexpressible law of vital experience, the pattern of affective and sentient being. This is the "content" of what we perceive as "beautiful form"; and this formal element is the artist's "idea" which is conveyed by every great work.
>
> (Langer, 1957, p. 257)

From this point of view music is the form of symbolism, which of all the arts is the closest to the representation of pure feeling. While one is involved in music (either playing it or listening to it), human subjectivity defines the world which one inhabits (for at least that brief time). The landscape reflects one's own heart, and self-experience intertwined with the externalized subjectivity of the music. The forms of feeling that music conveys are not limited to the realm of emotion or affect; rather it is the depth and breadth of human experience itself. In playing and/or listening to music, a person experiences the self as both passionately alive and whole. The sense of self-engaged with the world may be stirring, and even troubling (perhaps frightening) but always self-affirming. A great piece of music is a journey in which the crises of living are evoked in a form both beautiful and transcendent.

It is this aesthetic resonance that characterizes the artistic creation. Musicians experience their own subjectivity as vibrantly mirrored in the ideal form of the music. In fact, the experience of performing can in some cases take on the qualities found in the state of *archaic* merger. For example, Storr noted that:

> Musicians sometimes describe feelings of "being taken over," or "possessed" during a performance, a type of ecstasy. There may be an experience of being so much at one with the music that it seems to be playing itself. This is certainly being "taken out of oneself", and thus has something in common with the oceanic experience; but it is qualitatively different, because it lacks the sense of utter tranquility which is so characteristic of the latter.
>
> (Storr, 1992, p. 96)

Even when there is no loss of personal boundaries, performing a musical piece can entail the experience of a special state of being in which there is a sense of heightened self-cohesion, continuity, and vitality. Storr again noted that:

> Music makes us aware of important aspects of ourselves which may not ordinarily perceive; and that, by putting us into touch with these aspects, music makes us whole again.
>
> (Storr, 1992, p. 147)

The musician feels vitalized as self-experience becomes intertwined with rhythm and melody. Even when traditional musical conventions are challenged, the performer can be surprised or drawn into new forms of action and experience, of subjectivity and being. When the overall response is shock, sadness or fear, the experience of having been part of a brilliant, elegant, or beautiful experience results in a sense of living intensely, of being fully alive, or of being a part of greatness.

Music and the Creative Process

The musician's creative process involves two phases. The first, the *practice phase*, is the most psychologically dynamic and involves specific challenges to the musician's self-experience. It is during the practice stage that the musician is most creative (one exception to this might be the improvisations of jazz musicians). The second phase is that of the *public performance* at which time the results of the creative effort are displayed. Each phase possesses a different complex psychology that we will discuss. It is important to note that the creative process is not linear and typically does not unfold in a neat progression. In fact, the musician in preparation for a performance engages in these processes many times over. Nonetheless, I do believe that it is heuristically useful to delineate the components of the creative process in the following way.

The Practice Phase: Becoming aware that she is to perform a particular work, the musician responds with heightened anticipation. Often, she has already idealized the composer and the composition. During practice, she confronts the piece and begins the process of inspiration. Her first task is to accurately read the composer's musical text the tones, rhythms, phrases, accents, and the larger episodes of the music's design. But unlike the reading of a literary text, the performer must try to grasp the nondiscursive aspects of the composer's meaning – "the quality and character of the musical gesture." Reading also requires that the performer engage the composition with imagination and feeling. Paradoxically the musician seeks to externalize internal, subjective fantasy to truly know the composer's intention and thus bring the music into actual, physical being. As Roger Sessions (1950) noted:

> The agent of re-creation is the imagination of the performer, or, if you will, his "personality." It is his task to apply his imagination to discovering the musical gestures inherent in the composer's text, and then to reproducing them according to his own lights; that is the fullest participation on his own part.
>
> (p. 78)

The composer may create the composition, but the performer gives it life. The gradual refinement of the performance results in a unique interpretation. What will eventually interest the audience and that which is truly "new" is the way in which the musician's unique subjectivity gives form, substance, and spirit to the piece.

The most intense period of creativity occurs during the practice phase. Initially the musician's relation to the composition is fragmentary and incomplete. The musician is in what Kris referred to as the *inspirational phase* in which unconscious fantasy and primary process thinking predominate. During this phase the musician tries to access every aspect of conscious and unconscious subjectivity. As Nass noted: "The musical experience allows precise and more ambiguous states of consciousness to emerge together" (Nass, 1971, p. 308). Doubt, uncertainty, and confusion may trouble the musician, alternating with joy and exhilaration. A sense of perfection can be quickly followed by feelings of failure. Deflation and subjective turmoil can follow a heightened sense of self. This sense of failure and self-crisis may accompany experiences of aesthetic dissonance in which the anticipatory fantasy is not matched by external beauty. The truly creative musician can respond to failure by refinement of technique, or more careful analysis of the composition. The creative process is driven by the search to re-create the elusive state of unity, continuity and perfection, which characterizes the best performances. By searching for clearer expression, greater authenticity, improved timing and physical balance, the musician seeks to achieve increasingly refined levels of perfection and beauty.

Eventually, the performance is in sync, and there is a sense of resonance in which it seems to become the perfect reflection of the musician's inner fantasy life. I use the term *aesthetic resonance* to describe this intensification of feeling that the musician experiences both internally and externally due to the conjunction between self and music. This is the most affectively charged moment of the creative experience in which the musician feels both in the presence of the sublime and feels confirmed in his grandiosity. It is important to note that this resonance does not involve the imposition of personal preference onto the composition. It is not the simple acting-out of fantasy or the actualization of projective identification.

Aesthetic resonance implies the deepest respect for the musical text, as the performer's subjectivity becomes the medium through which the potential beauty of the composition (both profoundly human and ideal) is brought into being. Thus, musical creativity is not simply transcription, but interpretation. At the same time, what is new is *not* what performers *add* to the work but what they *reveal* to their audience through their performance of the work.

From the first moment of creation, the musician engages in a dialectic with the music. This dialectic is the engine of creativity. Musicians extend their subjectivity outward and engage the medium. In the case of music, the work of another is re-created considering the performer's imagination and feeling. From this point on, there is something new, which has been created out of a merger between the self-experience of the musician and the external world. The important thing is that the dialectic occurs between two realms of self-experience: that which is internal/subjective and that which is external/objective. However, during this process self-experience has become thoroughly intertwined with the musical text. Each influences the other (the imaginary and the manifest) and the result is further creation. But it is the drive towards idealization that fuels the process. As previously noted, the performer does not simply want to transcribe the composition from paper to sound. Her intention is to create beauty, truth, and perfection. Thus, by means of this dialectic there is an increasing elaboration of the musician's performance towards a level of refinement – in other words the musician finds in creativity an opportunity to give form to subjective experience in an increasingly articulate and formally refined manner. There is output, feedback, response/output, dialectic within the realm of the musician's subjectivity. The musician's measure and guide for this process is the delicate sense of resonance that he or she experiences during the performance of the music. It is the central paradox of musical creativity that the most exquisite experience of aesthetic resonance results from empathy *with* and judgment *of* another's subjectivity.

The experience of aesthetic resonance, while essential to the elaborative phase of musical creativity just discussed, is not the only factor in successful creativity. Inevitably there is an experience of failure in resonance. In most cases, this begins when the musician's feeling of certainty gives way to sober reflection and reassessment. Musicians may come to doubt their ability and talent, as they come to feel they may no longer to perform the work in the manner they intended. This phase is characterized by failures in which the resonance breaks down, and musicians must use all their skill and resourcefulness to reassess their technique and refine it to restore the selfobject tie. The selfobject experience is restored when the performance is felt to once again capture the ideal and grandiose components of fantasy. The process that occurs at this point I refer to as *transmuting externalization* in which the musician attempts to restore the selfobject tie not through the accrual of self-structure, but through refinement of her technique and performance. This may also require further study of the musical text, to discover and bring to light new facets of the composer's subjectivity. During this phase preconscious and conscious processes play a part in organizing and clarifying the elements of their technique as the musician attempts to bring his performance into harmony with self-experience. This is like Kris's notion of the elaboration phase. However, while Kris stressed the use of secondary process thinking during this phase, I believe that the musician must continue to respond to the work on multiple psychical levels. Like *transmuting internalization*, the response to a break in the selfobject tie is the development of structure; in this case the musician refines and strengthens her performance to be more resonant with an ideal. At the same time the musician's inner experience changes in response to the performance as well. The result of *transmuting externalization* is the restoration of the experience of resonance between musicians and their performance.

It is this complex dialectic between musician and performance, between selfobject experience and selfobject failure, followed by restoration, which drives musicians to seek increasingly refined and sophisticated formal means to express their subjectivity. The musician who engages in this process is driven to repeatedly seek out the wonder of the aesthetic selfobject experience; therefore, he or she must continually work to articulate and perfect a formally organized and ideal representation of lived experience. The skillful and talented musician can feel the potential for this experience in musical activity; this is perhaps the source of the feeling of joy quote. In a sense, the successful musician is possessed, even driven to seek to restore this experience until he or she reaches a point at which there is a conjunction between inner experience and performance. At this point comes the most critical moment of the musician's psychological life, the performance proper.

The Public Performance: In the public performance, the musician displays the results of the creative effort. Typically, the way in which society elevates the performing musician (often physically on a dais or stage) and brackets the performance as a special, even exalted event, amplifies its significance. Most musicians are not just satisfied with competence; he or she longs to fly as close to the sun as possible without falling (See Paul's fantasy in the upcoming case report). He or she *becomes* Brahm's *Second Symphony* or Beethoven's *Ninth*. In performance, the musician creates something beautiful and perfect, the externalization of an ideal level of self-experience through the most authentic interpretation of the musical text. The musician experiences him- or herself as transcendent, perfect, powerful, and whole. In self psychological terms, the performance is an occasion for selfobject experience.

The triumphant performer may feel that he or she transcends vulnerability and perhaps even mortality itself. The musician who knows that he or she is performing well may feel powerful, whole, and without flaw. If the audience responds enthusiastically, the performer's grandiosity is confirmed and mirrored, enhancing the artist's self-experience. Positive critical response from peers can be a compelling validation of fantasized greatness. This is the moment that the musician has been preparing for. In self psychological terms, the acclaimed performance is a form of selfobject experience in which for a time the artist experiences him- or herself as free of physical restraints and psychological vulnerabilities. Perhaps the musician's primary drive is for this experience of complete transcendence in which the recognition of mortality itself is eclipsed by a state of merger with the good and the beautiful.

Repeated experiences of dissonance and selfobject failure inevitably characterize this process, and it is the musician's search for more perfect and authentic forms of musical expression, which leads to the creation of something sublime. Through performance, the musician seeks to achieve a state of vitality and self-affirmation, and paradoxically of self-transcendence in which mortality and vulnerability are felt to be overcome. The presence and responsiveness of an admiring audience only heightens the opportunity for selfobject experience, but it can also accentuate the sense of risk. In fact, in the process of creation the musician is continually confronted by the need to surmount selfobject failure.

Case Illustration: Alan

Alan, a fifty-year-old married musician who works for a music publisher, was referred for psychoanalytic psychotherapy due to feelings of depression and a chronic sense of personal failure accompanied by very low self-esteem. His treatment, which is still ongoing, has addressed many areas of his psychological and social life, but for purposes of this paper I will be focusing on the specific issues that relate to the place of music in his life.

Alan has been a cello player since childhood. As a young man it was discovered that he had a substantial talent, and he remembers that his first and most central ambition was to be a musician. On the other hand, his father, a plumber with a successful repair business, discouraged Alan's ambition and countered the boy's dreams with exhortations to keep one's feet on the ground and be realistic. In fact, Alan recalls that music always played an important part in his childhood. His parents would fight frequently, and Alan was often frightened and alone. He would retreat to his bedroom and play his cello. Alan describes his playing as comforting and like having a "friend" with him.

Alan pursued his career and quickly proved to be a master of his instrument. Under the direction of his mentor an older successful conductor, Alan eventually began to acquire recognition, which led him to believe that his dreams were attainable. He remembered recently that "I felt I could do anything. I was that good." Unfortunately, two factors conspired to derail his career: one was the experience of betrayal that he experienced at the hands of his mentor, and the second was his growing addiction to cocaine. In his late twenties his performance began to suffer as he lost his focus on his work. He recognized that he was failing, and this led to panic and a worsening of his addiction.

Eventually Alan's musical career fell apart, and in search of a means to support himself and his young family, he joined his father in the plumbing business. He grew to loathe himself and to view himself as a despicable failure. His addiction continued, and he eventually lost the store and his father's investment. He almost lost his marriage. Over time, Alan was able to recover from his collapse, and he eventually got a well-paying job at a music publisher and stopped abusing drugs.

Recently, he joined several amateur orchestras and began playing his cello again. This is when he came to see me.

"It feels good being back playing the cello," He said during our first session, "But there is something wrong. I'm not happy with my performance. I get anxious, and I make mistakes. I'm just so tense about it. I wasn't like that before, no . . . I was fearless."

We discussed his experience of performing in front of the audience. I suspected that his anxiety may be a form of stage fright, that his inhibition may be related to the anxiety, but this did not appear to be the case. After several sessions, Alan revealed a fantasy that captured his self-experience.

"It's like I want to fly, to soar. That's what it used to feel like when I was playing. I felt like I was soaring. It felt great. I felt great. That's what I want to feel now, but I'm not sure I can do it. It's like if I try to soar . . . I'll fall. That's what I feel anxious about, not the audience, but my own fear that I'll fail."

Alan was a modern Icarus who, heedless of his father's warnings, had risen too close to the sun on wings of wax and had tumbled back to the earth.

In fact, my own experience of Alan also seemed to reflect this conflict. I remember the first day he came into my office. He was squat and overweight with an extremely depressed manner edged with hostility. I also felt loathing for him and at first felt regret about accepting the referral. However, as we discussed his music and especially his early experience of his talent, my perceptions changed, as he acquired more and more confidence in his music, he appeared noble to me. I began to recognize his specialness. I began to envy him.

Over time, it became clear that Alan's self-experience as a musician was a major source of sustenance to him. It had helped him survive a childhood filled with rage and at times violence between his parents. He had felt frightened and rejected and retreated psychologically to what he called a "dark place," which was his depression but also a place of protection. His music was a means of escape and liberation. He had built wings out of his talent with which he soared in fantasy, away from the darkness of home. Of course, it was this combined motivation of escape and transcendence that frightened him and had been forbidden by his father. He found performing music invigorating, but in the end, he would feel alone, without support, lacking the means to sustain himself. He had come to believe that he was doomed to failure.

Alan's initial reluctance to trust me and his persistent view of himself as a pathetic failure, who deserved his fate, resulted in many weeks of negativity and disbelief in the benefits of therapy. However, I grew increasingly interested in him and found his desire to recover his lost talents compelling. When he talked about music his affect was transformed, and he conveyed passion and deep interest. My sense was that music had functioned to vitalize and strengthen both his self-experience and relationship to the world. Despite his pervasive depression, music seemed to have been invested with his core selfobject longings. When his career collapsed, he lost his most important source of psychological nurturance. Eventually, a selfobject transference began to be mobilized in response to my interest in his music and ambitions. For several months, the selfobject experience in treatment became organized around the remobilization of his skills and ambitions related to his self-experience as a talented musician.

However, about a year into the treatment a crisis occurred in our relationship. Alan had given me a recording of one of his favorite composers as a Christmas present. I accepted it, expressing a sincere interest in the piece. Due to its length and the difficulty I found listening to it (lack of time and my meager musical background), I put the disc aside, planning to take it up at a later point. Of course, as time went by, I failed to listen to it. Occasionally and with mounting frustration, Alan would ask me about it. I repeated several excuses. Eventually, he came to a session furious with me.

"This was an opportunity," he said. "And you blew it. That piece of music is something that could have helped you understand me. Something we could have shared. I don't buy your excuses. In a way that's beside the point. It is just that this is something we could have shared, and it could have helped you understand me."

We explored the way in which Alan's experience of my failure evoked many of the feelings that he associated with his father's lack of interest and support for his career. He had hoped for a reparative experience with me, and instead he was once again disappointed. On my part I recognized how I felt intimidated by Alan's talent and competitive with his abilities and success. I was protecting my own self-esteem by avoiding listening to the recording and talking with him about it. In the end I felt much worse, that I had failed him as a therapist as well.

All this was of course grist for the mill. Alan continued in treatment, and we explored both his longing for mirroring and his sense of disappointment and loneliness. His experience of my continued responsiveness and support allowed him to verbalize his reaction, and gradually a sense of security was restored. In fact, over the next several months Alan's confidence in his musical abilities increased. He was able to view his performance more critically without having to reference other people's responses. His sense of self-experience was more stable, and he began to attempt to address certain technical problems that had been undermining his performance. For example, he remarked one day: "You know I've been able lately to focus more on exactly where the problems are in my playing. Music really has to do with your body. For example, I realized that I had been tightening my fingers in a certain way, that effected my playing, and when I made a slight change, I noticed a big difference." Several months later, he was able to work on relaxing his posture, which had been tight and constrained.

Eventually, Alan described his experience of his performance:

It's really all about taking risks. You play music through your body. You must relax and give yourself over to it. You sort of go out into the music. You can't think about yourself. It's almost like you are gone, or you get very small [he cups his hands] so that is not very safe. The risk is if you fail or if something goes wrong, it can be horrible for you, devastating. But you can't really play without taking these risks. I feel that lately, that's what I have been able to do again, and my performance, my playing just feels great. I am really, really enjoying playing again.

At this point in the treatment, we had begun to work on difficulties in Alan's marriage and work but the presence of music in his life was never far away. In fact, during a recent financial crisis, Alan became more aware of the function that music plays in his psychological life. He had lost a large amount of money in the stock market and was feeling like a failure once again. Alan brought his horn to one of our sessions during that time since he had to go to a rehearsal immediately after leaving me. He expressed concern that his sense of despair would affect his playing: "I need to feel more confident, I need to feel that I am up for it. I am worried that I will begin to feel that it isn't worth it." He recalled how he had stopped playing music when he joined his father's plumbing business. "I hated myself. I had lost everything. I felt so alone." Alan described how the language of a composition would become something he shared with the composer: "I could be playing Mozart, and it would no longer be just Mozart's language but mine too, sort of the Mozart–Alan language. That what I would be speaking would be both mine and Mozart's." He talked about how during performances he would feel like the audience were his friends, but more importantly he described how invigorated and wonderful he himself would feel as he was playing. His face became filled with pleasure: "That's the most incredible feeling without a doubt." Alan put his hand down on the black leather instrument case: "This is it. This is what saved me. The music was like a place where I could go, anytime that I wanted to escape. It was a place filled with beauty, where this beautiful stuff would just lift me up, and you couldn't not feel happy. I would feel perfect and protected. In that world nothing could be bad. I would take the beauty and happiness in, and then give it out. No one in that world could be bad or cruel. Everything is perfect."

Discussion

Alan's involvement in music compensated for both the empathic failure of his parents and the resulting damage to his self-experience. Like Icarus he wished to rise above the world and achieve a state of transcendence that would shore up or heal his sense of being damaged. In fact, it is probable that Alan, like other musicians, has an innate, perhaps physiologic, inclination towards the auditory realm of experience. Perhaps the frequent arguments in the childhood home, motivated Alan to seek out experiences that would structure sound and soothe his emotions. Apparently, for Alan, fantasy and music are closely related, and performance allows Alan to have his core self-organizing fantasies mirrored by the admiring audience. In other words, music offered Alan an opportunity for selfobject experiences that was sorely absent in his family life. Unfortunately, due to their intensity and associated feelings of vulnerability, these selfobject fantasies also lead to defense and inhibition. At the beginning of treatment, Alan complained of defuse tension and anxiety during performances, which impacted on the quality of his art and his ability to enjoy himself while playing. Similar anxieties were evident in the transference as Alan longed for a positive selfobject tie. He anxiously expected disappointment.

When disappointment came in the form of the experience of selfobject failure in response to my not listening to the recording, he was able to retain his confidence in me despite frustration and anger. Alan's self-experience remained comparatively cohesive despite the failure. This was also the case with Alan's experience of his music, and his capacity to sustain self-experience in the face of creative challenges improved over time. Any creative endeavor requires that we willingly put ourselves at psychological risk. If we do not, out of fear or cautiousness, the necessary inspiration of artwork with subjectivity does not happen. The world remains unchanged, or our fantasies hover before our eyes like dreams, the transformative dialectic is missing. When a musician's self-experience is fragile or precarious, the creative engagement between internal and external aspects of self-experience combined with the activation and externalization of idealized or grandiose fantasies is just too hard to sustain. The desire may be there, but confidence in the integrity and resilience of self-experience is absent.

For years, Alan had been unable to creatively engage his music. He harbored grandiose fantasies of being a powerful musician; however, the normal difficulties that accompany practice and performance stimulated equally powerful fantasies of failure and humiliation. Thus, he became anxious and unable to approach his creative problems as a challenge. Eventually, with the development of the selfobject transference, he was able to sustain a cohesive sense of self and explore ways to address the problems in his technique. Eventually he was able to sustain his core fantasy during performances without anxiety. No longer plagued with fears of humiliation, he could perform successfully and enjoy himself at the same time. In other words, the mobilization of creative drive in the context of a secure selfobject tie facilitated the full expression of his self-experience. Willingness to tolerate selfobject failure and transitory negative self-images without defense liberated his capacity for inspiration and willingness to risk failure.

Chapter 13

Cruising Beauty

Obsession and Self-Crisis in Thomas Mann's *Death in Venice*

Death in Venice concerns the last days of a middle-aged writer named Gustave Von Aschenbach who is both popular and revered in his home country, as well as fatefully discontent with himself and his career. At the beginning of the narrative, Gustave von Aschenbach has grown troubled. His creative work provides him with little solace; it is "hard, nerve taxing work that has not ceased to exact his uttermost in the way of sustained concentration, conscientiousness and tact" (Mann, 1911, p. 378). He is described as "powerless" and in need of "relaxation in sleep" (p. 378).

As the tale begins, Von Aschenbach's goes wandering through Munich seeking relief and restoration. He is alone. The streets are empty. Eventually, he lingers beside a graveyard and a stone masonry, beguiling some minutes with reading the holy platitudes that decorate the mortuary chapel. He is thinking about death. Then, apparently out of the very doors of the literal death house (the chapel) "above the two apocalyptic beasts that guard the staircase," Von Aschenbach sees a man standing. The stranger's appearance is described in stark detail, and the overall description conveys a sense of menace, ruthlessness, and physicality. As Von Aschenbach contemplates the man, their eyes meet. He feels "an unpleasant twinge" and hurries away. However, Von Achenbach cannot shake the memory of that ominous figure, he is gripped by a fantasy of a compelling nature:

> Yet whether the pilgrim air that the stranger wore kindled his fantasy or whether some other physical or psychical influence came in play, he could not tell, but he felt the most surprising consciousness of a widening of inward barriers, a kind of vaulting unrest, a youthful ardent thirst for distant scenes – a feeling so lively and so new, or at least so long outgrown and forgot, that he stood there rooted to the spot, his eye on the ground and his hands clasped behind him, exploring these sentiments of his, their bearing and scope.
>
> (p. 380)

He detects within himself a longing to travel; but in no ordinary sense; rather, he is overcome by a quasi-hallucination of a primordial swamp populated by wild, misshapen birds and a lurking tiger. "And he felt his heart throb with terror, yet

DOI: 10.4324/9781003532484-13

with a longing inexplicable." Gustave Aschenbach's self-crisis has begun. He realizes he longs to escape from the art that has sustained him and given him joy but had become a prison.

> This yearning for new and distant scenes, this craving for freedom, release, forgetfulness – they were, he admitted to himself, an impulse towards flight, flight from the spot which was the daily theatre of a rigid, cold, passionate service (his art) . . . what sapped his strength was distaste for the task, betrayed by a fastidiousness he could no longer satisfy . . . he got no joy from it – not though a nation paid him homage. To him it seemed his work had ceased to be marked by the fiery play of fancy which is the product of joy.
>
> (p. 381)

Aschenbach, feeling "dread" at the thought of remaining in Munich, plans a vacation journey to the Mediterranean. After an unsatisfying visit to the Adriatic coast Aschenbach finally realizes that Venice is the destination he longs for. During the voyage he has a disquieting experience. He observes a group of young men, one of whom the loudest and most gaily dressed, catches his eye.

> He was shocked to see that the apparent youth was no youth at all. He was an old man, beyond a doubt, with wrinkles and crow's-feet around eye and mouth; the neck was shrunken and sinewy, his turned-up moustaches and small imperial were dyed, and the unbroken double row of yellow teeth showed when he laughed were but too obviously a cheapish false set. Aschenbach was moved to shudder as he watched the creature and his association with the rest of the group. Could they not see he was old, that he had no right to wear the clothes they wore or pretend to be one of them? Aschenbach put his hand to his brow, covered his eyes. He felt quite canny, as though the world were suffering a dreamlike distortion of perspective which he might arrest by shutting it out for a few minutes.
>
> (p. 390)

It is as if some horrible distorting mirror has been held up to Aschenbach. In the figure of the old dandy, he experiences the impending deterioration that will throw his entire self-experience into doubt and crisis. The old man can also be understood as "anti-beauty," an ugliness that attempts to clothe itself in youthful perfection and fails miserably. In fact, this is the very embodiment of ugliness according to Bernard Bosanquet: "If there is a truly ugly which is aesthetically judged, and which is not merely a failure of imagination, it must be an appearance which is both expressive and inexpressive at once, aesthetically judged, yet unaesthetic. That is to say, the appearance must suggest an adequate embodiment of a feeling and frustrate it" (p. 420). Rather than binding the anxiety associated with age and mortality, the finery and gaiety of the old man intensifies the sense of terror and fragmentation. Aschenbach is disoriented and unexpectedly alarmed by the experience in which his sense of reality is threatened (see Hagman [2003], for an extended discussion of ugliness and its disruptive impact on self-organization). Aschenbach's moment of confrontation with ugliness represents the objectification of his self-crisis – he flees to Venice, the aged but still beautiful city on the lagoon.

After his arrival in Venice, Aschenbach settles down in the lounge of the hotel before dinner. He casually scans the well-dressed crowd of vacationers, and a particular group catches his eye.

> Around a wicker table next him was gathered a group of young folks in charge of a governess or companion – three young girls, perhaps fifteen to seventeen years old, and a long-haired boy of about fourteen. Aschenbach noticed with astonishment the lad's perfect beauty. His face recalled the noblest moment of Greek sculpture – pale with a sweet reserve with clustering honey-colored ringlets, the brow and nose descending in one line, the winning mouth, the expression of pure and godlike serenity.
>
> (p. 396)

Soon Aschenbach finds himself enthralled, his escalating passion for the boy disrupting his obsessive, almost ritualistic self-structure. Eventually a return to the older obsessive self-organization is no longer possible. Tadzio beckons with a promise for a renewed self-experience. Aschenbach experiences Tadzio's beauty as a profoundly vitalizing and transformative relationship; ultimately the boy becomes his only hope.

> Was not the same force at work within himself when he strove in cold fury to liberate from the marble mass of language the slender forms of his art which he saw with the eye of his mind and would body forth to men as the mirror and image of spiritual beauty?
>
> Mirror and image! His eye took in the proud bearing of the figure there at the blue water's edge; with an outburst of rapture, he told himself that what he saw was beauty's very essence; form as divine thought, the single perfection which resides in the mind, of which image and likeness, rare and hold, was here raised up for adoration. This was very frenzy – and without a scruple, nay eagerly, the aging artist bade it come. His mind was in travail, his whole mental background in a state of flux.
>
> (p. 412)

Accompanying the intensification of Aschenbach's obsession with Tadzio is his growing awareness that a plague has entered the city. Despite the attempt to deny the escalating fatalities, Aschenbach realizes that the entire city is effected and the vacationers are leaving because of fear of infection. Nonetheless, he remains.

The infatuation with Tadzio does not halt Aschenbach's deterioration and perhaps hastens it. The sense of beauty that holds Aschenbach in bondage beckons but gives nothing back; rather, it drains him. Yet Aschenbach begins to believe that he can only survive in the boy's presence. Separation leads to panic. Internally,

Aschenbach becomes increasingly fragmented and overwhelmed by the passionate affective and fantasy products of his disintegration. Only within sight of the boy does he find any peace. As Aschenbach slides into psychosis, he relies more and more on the boy's presence to shore him up. But when alone, separated from the protective presence of the boy, Aschenbach's psychological destruction proceeds. This is vividly conveyed by a horrifying dream:

> That night he had a fearful dream. Its theatre seemed to be his own soul, and the events burst in from outside, violently overcoming the profound resistance of his spirit; passed through him and left him, left the cultural structure of a life-time trampled on, ravaged, and destroyed.
>   The beginning was fear, fear and desire, with a shuddering curiosity.
>
> (Mann, 1911, p. 430)

The dream is one of a fantastic bacchanal with wild beasts, half-naked women, and satyrs, with wild strange music and dancing. There is "flute-notes of the cru-elest sweetness, deep and cooing, keeping shamelessly on until the listener felt his very entrails bewitched. He heard a voice naming, though darkly, that that was to come: "The stranger god!" He observes a mountain scene in which the revelers gather and engage in violent and sexual behaviors that reek of stench. Fantastic hypnotic music is playing, and Aschenbach feels himself succumbing: "His heart throbbed to the drums, his brain reeled, a blind rage seized him, a whirling lust, he craved with all his soul to join the ring that formed around the obscene symbol of the godhead." Aschenbach finally throws himself into the scene, biting, tearing and swallowing "smoking goblets of flesh. In his soul he tasted the bestial degradation of his fall" (p. 431).

When Aschenbach wakes, his self-deterioration is complete. This is conveyed dramatically by the open panic of the people in the town and the full recognition by his fellow vacationers of the danger of plague. There is also a pathetic and comical scene where he tries to restore his youthful appearance by means of makeup. (He becomes the old fop whom he was revolted by on the boat.) He continues to follow the boy about the city, but he has become a stalker following Tadzio through "the city's narrow streets where horrid death stalked too, and it seemed to him as though the moral law were fallen into ruin and only the monstrous and perverse held out any hope" (p. 434). At one point he loses track of the boy, and Aschenbach, alone, sits down in a small-town square talking deliriously to himself as if musing to his young lover on beauty and desire:

> For mark you, Phaedrus, beauty alone is both divine and visible; and so, it is the sense way, the artist's way, little Phaedrus, to the spirit. We poets cannot walk the way of beauty without Eros as our companion and guide. We exult in pas-sion, and love is still our desire – our craving and our shame. And from this you will perceive that we poets can be neither wise nor worthy citizens. We need be wonton, must needs rove and pretense, our honorable repute a farce, the crowd's

belief in us merely laughable. Our concern shall be with beauty only. And by beauty we mean simplicity, largeness, and renewed severity of discipline. But detachment, Phaedrus, and preoccupation with form lead to intoxication and desire, they too lead to the bottomless pit.

(p. 435)

At this point it becomes clear that Aschenbach has fully accepted the collapse of his old self. Evidence of worsening epidemic concretizes the sense of Aschenbach's full deterioration, and it also becomes evident that Aschenbach himself is ill. The next morning, he finds that Tadzio and his family are leaving. He walks down to the beach to find the boy playing with several friends on an otherwise deserted and desolate beach. He sits down and watches the boy one final time. The old writer is barely able to lift his head from fever. After a scuffle with a friend, Tadzio wanders out onto the sandbar to be alone. He stands silhouetted against the sea, seeming to flaunt the power of his beauty.

Once more he [Tadzio] paused to look: with a sudden recollection, or by an impulse, he turned from the waist up, in an exquisite movement, one hand resting on his hip, and looked over his shoulder at the shore. It seemed to him [Aschenbach] the pale and lovely Summoner out there smiled at him and beckoned; as though, with the hand he lifted from his hip, he pointed outward as he hovered on before into an immensity of richest expectations.

Some minutes passed before anyone hastened to the aid of the elderly man sitting there collapsed in his chair. They bore him to his room. And before nightfall a shocked and respectful world received the news of his decease.

(p. 437)

Discussion

Death in Venice is a work of exceptional complexity – that is part of its beauty. In this section I will not offer a complete analysis. I will limit myself to the study of Von Aschenbach's process of self-disintegration and the function of the sense of Tadzio's beauty on his attempt at self-repair or at least self-maintenance. *Death in Venice* is a story of self-crisis; an aging man faced with the loss of the self-sustaining function of his work and character, experiences the deterioration of psychological compensations and defenses accompanied by the emergence of archaic needs and desires. At the heart of the story is the writer's obsession with the boy Tadzio that becomes the sole sustaining experience in the old man's collapsing psychological life. But more specifically it is not only the physical boy that Aschenbach craves – it is his beauty.

Heinz Kohut (1957) viewed *Death in Venice* as a story of an artist who, due to age or just failing talents, has lost the ability to sublimate through the creation of art the narcissistic cathexis that thus provided him with the "needed experience of psychological perfection and wholeness – i.e., the experience of basic self-esteem"

(p. 821). The resulting fragmentation of Aschenbach's self results in his obsession with "the sexualized precursors of the artistic product: the beautiful boy" (p. 822).

Aschenbach's self-crisis predated his encounter with Tadzio. It was already well advanced when he arrived on the Lido where he undergoes the final phase of a deteriorating course of some year's duration. I suspect that the initial phase of this crisis occurred long before, perhaps in response to his wife's death – but we really do not know, the source of Aschenbach's crisis not being the point of the story. Be that as it may, at some point years before, he had transformed his youthful rebelliousness using a set of characterological defenses of an obsessive-compulsive nature to manage himself and his life. He grew isolative, regimented, and masochistic. His fantasy of the man "holding fast" despite great suffering, is the perfect metaphor for the self of the writer holding himself together through self-denial and deprivation. For years this method was successful in creating a public persona and a private psychological prison to maintain self-experience. In fact, Mann points out the dreadful burden and stresses that Aschenbach must endure to create and sustain the persona of the great artist.

> Aschenbach was the poet of all those who labor at the edge of exhaustion; of the overburdened, of those who are already worn out but still hold themselves upright; of all the modern moralizers or accomplishment, with stunted growth and scanty resources, who yet contrive by skillful husbanding and prodigious spasms of will to produce, at least for a while, the effect of greatness.
>
> (p. 385)

I think what Kohut missed was the terrible toll which the pursuit of artistic perfection and fame can take on the artist. If Aschenbach sought sublimation through his art, it seems to have rarely brought him happiness, and the search for the experience of perfection through art remained precarious and at times a crushing burden. From this perspective the self-crisis that Aschenbach experiences at the opening of the story is not due to the failure of sublimation but the consequence of a lifetime of sustained creative effort in the face of cumulative exhaustion. Sublimation, though a goal of art is hard sought, and often not successful. And the joy of success and perfection is often fleeting, elusive, and insubstantial. The fear of failure and strain of sustained creative performance can take its toll on the artist, as it does on Aschenbach.

At the start of the narrative Aschenbach's resilience and capacity for self-sacrifice to his artistic project is breaking down. He feels no joy in his work. Having lost his taste for the "task," he now dreads his solitary labors at his summer cottage. His isolative, ascetic disciplined, and obsessive-compulsive life can no longer provide the gratifications that sustained his self-experience as a youth. His disciplined artistic efforts can no longer compensate for his failing self-structure, nor can they contain the surging eruption of fantasy and desire which begins to confuse, frighten, and arouse him. The function of work to bind, organize and channel his subjective life is failing, and he begins to experience dissociate states, which are essentially projected or split off products of his disintegrating self.

Aschenbach is literally adrift (physically and emotionally) as we meet him. He wanders aimlessly, we soon observe that he has begun to experience intense, disso- ciative states characterized by almost hallucinatory fantasies and archaic affective states. He attempts to rationalize these experiences as the desire for travel, but he is in fact fleeing. He is driven by desperation to find someplace or something that may offer him solace. By the time he reaches the Lido and sits down in the lobby to await dinner with the other guests, he is in a highly vulnerable state. Strange impulses, fantasies, uncertain desires, humiliating experiences, and altered states of consciousness have buffeted his internal life. Arriving at the beach, he attempts to revert to his normal obsessive rituals, but we already know that things are not right, the very atmosphere seems to take on a noxious disintegrative effect. It is at this point that he encounters Tadzio and he begins to center his affective life and self-organization on the beautiful boy.

Aschenbach is aware that his fascination with Tadzio's beauty is in large part an illusion. It is certainly true that the boy would be considered beautiful by con- ventional standards, but the real issue is Aschenbach's fantasies of ideal perfec- tion and his powerful emotional response. The gradual elaboration of idealized and erotically charged fantasies involving the boy's beauty speak to the largely subjec- tive nature of the experience. Psychologically in need of a compelling restorative experience, Aschenbach selects Tadzio to become the object of idealization (see Hagman [2002] for a discussion of the psychological desire for idealization under- lying the sense of beauty, and the obsessions to which it often leads). However, as Aschenbach quickly learns, this form of obsession with beauty can result in an excruciating experience of vulnerability. Regarding his own obsession, the psycho- analyst Allen Wheelis writes (Wheelis, 1999):

> Great beauty inflicts a wound. Private and somehow shameful. It can neither acknowledged nor complained about. A burning pain. It will not go away. The pain is longing; the wound is knowing that the longing can never be fulfilled that, like Hell, it will go on forever, always there inside. Beauty calls it forth from a dark cavern, from some hidden forlorn place in me, and I know then that this longing is my essence.
>
> (p. 16)

Similarly, to Wheelis, Aschenbach's emotional response to the boy combines experiences of elation and torture. His aesthetic emotions involve fascination, joy, awe, even rapture. At times he experiences peacefulness and fulfillment. On the other hand, the erotic quality of his obsession fills him with intense sexual long- ing and even sadism. He is terrified by the boy's beauty and at least once he runs from him. What we see is how beautiful form evokes entirely different emotions as compared to the content. This accounts for the strange way that Aschenbach's feelings of fear and horror mingle with exultation and joy. Overall, the experience of beauty is an intensely reassuring thing to Aschenbach, this I believe makes the erotic impulses and negative affects endurable.

Regarding the archaic sources of Aschenbach's sense of Tadzio's beauty, there are clues in his fantasies about the boy's place in the Polish family to which he belongs. The other children, all girls, are dressed plainly and are of drab appearance, and this reflected the lack of concern by the parent. But the boy, Aschenbach speculates and comes to believe, is a "pampered darling the object of a self-willed and partial love." It is the worshipful doting of his mother, who makes a "fabulous" appearance with her looping strands of pearls the size of cherries – the grande dame of narcissism – who Aschenbach believes is the source of the boy's "spoilt, exquisite air." This should remind us of Kligerman's claim that the artist in childhood is treated as the special one, and when this state is lost, he attempts to recreate the lost beauty and perfection (Kligerman, 1980). If Kligerman accepts the idea that Tadzio is Aschenbach's creation, it is also conceivable that part of the fantasy of the boy is that he enjoys the state of narcissistic bliss of which the artist is deprived and for which he longs. Thus, the beauty that Aschenbach senses in the boy has its source in fantasies of an archaic self-state, which the old writer can share through his linking of his psychological life with Tadzio's beauty.

Heinz Kohut (1957) argues that Aschenbach's erotic fixation with Tadzio is the cause of his deterioration. To the contrary, I would argue that Tadzio is not the cause of Von Aschenbach's breakdown, nor is the obsession with the boy simply a symptom of disintegration and loss of sublimatory capacity. The obsession with the boy's beauty is an attempt at restoration, a strategy by which Aschenbach seeks to organize his failing self according to a newly emerged set of fantasies and needs. His deteriorating self-state, which necessitates increasingly desperate efforts to shore himself up, causes the intensification and disruptive effect of his obsession. Sexualization and malignant dependency are symptoms of his self-crisis, not the cause. Beauty also functions to protect Aschenbach from the recognition of his own mortality. I don't just mean this regarding his fear of death – although death is clearly a major theme of the story. But I would include in the concept of mortality, the general vulnerability of a person to abandonment, self-crisis, and loss. In the presence of beauty Aschenbach knows no fear. Even after he has direct confirmation of the extent of the plague, and the danger he is in, he does not move and takes no action to protect himself. He fantasizes that he and Tadzio will be the only survivors, alone together at last. Even during his last moments his concern is with beauty, not with the seriousness of his illness.

One of the extraordinary tensions in the work is the subtle co-conspiracy between the old man and the boy. Aschenbach is not simply a passive, distant voyeur. Even though the two never "meet," Aschenbach is convinced that there is a powerful relationship between him and his lover. We have no way to know whether he imagines the boy's responsiveness or his belief in the reciprocal engagement is real. Whatever, his sense of beauty is powerfully determined by what he experiences as secret communications and purposeful gestures from the boy toward him. But even apart from the question of the boy's complicity, Aschenbach's relation to the boy's beauty is dynamic and interactive. He always observes (and desires) Tadzio from a distance, while at the same time experiencing an intensifying relationship with the boy, suffused with a feverish erotic resonance, which he increasingly believes is shared.

Regarding what Lee (1948) refers as "love worthiness," this is certainly the case with Aschenbach. Through most of the story he fantasies that the boy shares his infatuation and Aschenbach experiences himself in the boy's presence as a formidable lover and, in fantasy, equates himself with Socrates. However, after the bacchanalian dream, Aschenbach is unable to sustain this grandiosity. He experiences himself as old and repulsive. He is continuing to deteriorate, and the boy's beauty is no longer able to sustain him. This becomes dramatically clear when he has the barber apply hair color and makeup to bring back a youthful look. His appearance transformed; he now feels ready to offer himself as a love object himself. But he is too far gone; complete annihilation follows the collapse of Tadzio's sustaining function.

Lastly, Aschenbach's obsession with Tadzio's beauty functions as a defense. During his self-crisis, in flight from the geographic and professional epicenter of that crisis (after all it was in Munich that his real deterioration began, and it was in the continuance of that life that his real fears lay), he comes upon a consuming, vitalizing experience. In a very real sense, the boy is his creation, and the story is about how Aschenbach elaborates and makes use of this fantasy as his self-state declines. But Tadzio's beauty cannot save Aschenbach – beauty by itself never can. What the sense of beauty does in the narrative of *Death in Venice* is to provide a transcendent organizing experience in which, for a time, Aschenbach seeks respite from his suffering and his inevitable, tragic collapse. In this regard it is important to note that Aschenbach's experience of Tadzio's beauty is never in itself disorganizing or disruptive, rather it binds Aschenbach's psychic wounds and sooths him. But the solace of Tadzio's beauty ultimately fails the old man, and Aschenbach's self-disintegration continues unabated. A remarkable passage describes how he leaves the Lido to visit the City of Venice where he experiences the very air as threatening and diseased. He endures another attack of disorientation and panic and decides to leave. But when he attempts to flee Venice, the problem is he has nowhere to go. By this point his self-collapse has progressed to the point where his life in Munich would be unsustainable. His self-disorder has progressed too far. He has begun to feel that the only sustaining experience and hence the focus of his life have become the beauty of the boy –he even comes to believe that he cannot exist without him. It is one of the tragic elements of the tale that Aschenbach's worsening self-deterioration disrupts even the perfection of the boy's beauty. However, even at the point of death, Aschenbach's sense of Tadzio's beauty never succumbs fully to his collapsing sensibility. In the final death scene, Tadzio is playing roughly with his companions on the beach and at one point has his lovely face thrust fully into the sand. But he recovers and wanders away disconsolately through the shallow still water to the sandbar. Aschenbach watches, his consciousness failing, yet his vision of the boy is renewed; once again Tadzio is unsullied consummate beauty, beckoning to him. We are struck by the power of beauty to lift Aschenbach out of the experience of mortality and offer the fantasy of transcendence. The story ends with his death, but the ending can also be interpreted as Aschenbach's final, complete giving over of himself to beauty, surrendering himself (in Ghent's [1990] meaning of the word) to the ideal. Thus, his old false self dies as new forms of being become manifest in "an immensity of richest expectation" (p. 437).

Conclusion: Triumphant Beauty

Death in Venice is about the frightening experience of annihilation anxiety and the desperate psychological measures to which a man resorts in the effort to defend against the disintegration of self-experience. Aschenbach's submersion in the experience of beauty ultimately fails to save him. But as a work of literature *Death in Venice* is what Bernard Bosanquet called *triumphant beauty* (1915), a phrase he defined as: "Beauty that, although of the most distinguished quality, is universal in appeal" (p. 417). In the end, it is the transcendent, perfect beauty of the work that is the best example of my thesis. Von Aschenbach's decent into obsession and death is, from an everyday point of view, a frightening and ultimately despairing process. For the author of the work, it must have represented a personal nightmare (as much as it is a fantasy of erotic fulfillment). But it is the sheer beauty of *Death in Venice* that permits the full expression of such terrors in a form that is sublime and ultimately transcendent. *Death in Venice* does not claim that we can be saved through beauty – that would cheapen and trivialize the message. No, the fantasy of salvation is a defense. The sense of beauty is not some type of therapy; it is better than that. Beauty transcends both health and disease, but also contains them both in a single compelling experience of perfection.

Chapter 14

Hitler's Aesthetics

A Psychoanalytic Perspective on Art and Fascism

Beauty, the formal aspect of idealization, can embody the finest and most trans-cendent values in human aesthetic experience (Hagman, 2002), but beauty can also be perverse and in some instances, it can serve the needs of evil. This chapter will examine the dark side of beauty. We will see how beauty can become grotesque and ultimately be destroyed when it is forced to fulfill the needs of the most terrible of self-disorders.

> Mankind has a natural drive to discover beauty. How rich the world will be for him who uses his senses. Furthermore, nature has instilled in everyone the desire to share with others everything beautiful that one encounters. The beauti-ful should reign over humans; the beautiful itself wants to retain its power.
>
> (Adolf Hitler, 1941 as quoted in Spotts, 2003, p. 119)

In his book *Hitler and the Power of Aesthetics*, Frederic Spotts argued that our image of Hitler as a monster is incomplete. He asserted that historians have failed to appreciate the place of Hitler's aesthetics in our understanding of his motives and aims. Spotts pointed out that the young Hitler was an ambitious bohemian artist who pursued a career as an artist for several years, until professional failure and the opportunity for political success offered him the narcissistic gratification through demagoguery that he so longed for from the arts. Once in power, it was Hitler's obsession with aesthetic matters that dominated his passion for culture and disguised his hatred of people. Monomaniacal, he pursued the destruction of west-ern culture in his quest to remake and mold the aesthetic landscape according to his own idealized and grandiose self-image. In the face of his own self-disintegration, this passion for a depersonalized and inhuman beauty became fanatically driven; enthrallment in the beautiful was his last refuge, yet even those ideals finally and fatefully become lost in his lust for death and destruction.

In the following paragraphs I will elaborate on Spott's historical approach to Hitler's aesthetic from the perspective of psychoanalysis. This approach is not meant to minimize other aspects of Hitler's psychology (e.g., his obsession with power, malignant narcissism, psychosis). I also do not mean that aesthetics was a principal motivation for Hitler, but as we will see it was important to him to manage

DOI: 10.4324/9781003532484-14

and resolve psychological deficits and conflicts. In response to a combination of early deprivation and flawed mirroring by a depressed and desperate mother, Hitler constructed a compensatory self-structure known as an "artistic self." The function of his art was to actualize fantasies of grandiosity and the creation of a relationship to reality that would make up for developmental failures and the psychological damage resulting from years of childhood physical and emotional abuse by his father (Dorpat, 2003). Hitler's failure to have this grandiose artistic self-confirmed, led to severe states of self-crisis and fragmentation. In response to the failure of his artistic self, Hitler turned to political ends to seek self-restoration through the self-aggrandizement he longed for. Thus, his failure as an artist became transformed into a monomaniacal fantasy of social transformation, in which the entire universe would be forced to comply with his archaic wishes for protection, mirroring, and control. All dictators crave power, using it to bring reality into conformity with their needs. One symptom of Hitler's psychopathology was his need for the aesthetic transformation of the entire cultural landscape of Germany and, ultimately, the world. He would attempt to accomplish this thorough conspiracy, despotism, and terror.

The Role of Aesthetics in Hitler's Life

Art, aesthetics, and culture played an important role in Hitler's psychological life and social policy (Spotts, 2003). As a boy and a young man, Hitler devoted much time to sketching, painting, and preliminary attempts at architectural design. He studied art and was a voracious student of opera and music in general. His first and primary ambition was to be an artist, and he attempted to actualize this dream through academic training (although eventually this failed). In his young manhood he worked as an artist and for a time was able to make a meager living from painting. Although his talent was limited and his work habits spotty at best, he took his artistry seriously, and throughout his life, even when politics, power, and war dominated his life, he maintained an active interest in broad areas of cultural life. In fact, the extent of his interest in art was at time disconcerting to his associates, especially in the final, desperate months of the Third Reich.

Heretofore little attention has been paid to the extent of Hitler's, the Dictator's, obsession with art. Upon seizing power, one of the first activities that he and his new Reich engaged in was the purging of all non-Germanic and anti-Nazi elements from positions of cultural leadership, Museum directors, opera conductors, and art exhibitors were all reviewed and many replaced by Nazi sympathizers. Those who did not support Hitler's cultural agenda were fired or pressured to comply. Jews and socialists among many other groups were blacklisted or forced to flee the country. This became part of Hitler's racist policies in which he accused these outsider groups of conspiring to undermine the cultural purity of Germany through corrupt art and music. Eventually all major cultural leaderships positions were filled with Nazi sympathizers, and most art exhibitions and concerts reflected Hitler's values. Only Germanic art and the classical arts of Greece and Rome were designated as worthy of promotion. Modern art and the art of other cultures were repudiated and considered inferior or dangerous. Exhibitions were held that criticized modernist art and alternative museums, and shows were held promoting "Aryan" values. In fact, Hitler throughout his Reich pursued a program of cultural institution development on a national scale. Vast new museums, grand opera houses, enormous new holdings of art, and entire cities were redesigned to embody the Fuhrer's aesthetic principles. Spotts pointed out that Hitler's means of achieving and holding onto political power was aesthetically based. The creation of amphitheaters, flags, uniforms, the use of lighting and music at party rallies all played a part in the creation and propagation of the cult of personality and the emotional power of the Reich in the minds of the people (the contribution of the talents of Director Leni Riefenstahl should be noted here).

As a national leader Hitler was one of history's greatest art promoters and sponsors, albeit only those arts that he approved of and that reflected his personal ambition. He created government stipends for composers and artists. He devoted monies to the purchase of art and the creation of institutions to house these collections. Hitler believed that music was a comfort and inspiration to all people, so he constructed opera houses and sponsored performances in small towns, factories, and for his army. He befriended artists and took a great interest in their work, often privately compromising some of his public statements in the face of real talent. All this also must be considered considering the vicious attacks and even murder of artists who opposed the Reich or happened to be Jews. Most of the real talent, which had been active in Germany before 1930, was gone, either dead or become refugees, by 1939.

Given all this, I would like to ask several questions: (1) Why was art and culture so important to Hitler? Many of his fellow dictators, such as Mussolini or Stalin, were indifferent or openly hostile to the arts, yet Hitler loved art more than anything in life. (2) If Hitler loved art, why did so much go wrong? And how did his aesthetic values become so corrupted and forced to serve such evil ends? To begin to answer these questions we will now turn to a discussion of Hitler's developmental history and the role art played in Hitler's struggle with the aftereffects of trauma.

The Longings and Failures of a Young Artist

In 1889 Adolf Hitler was born in Austria to Alois Hitler, a successful civil servant, and his wife Klara, the mother of six children, four of whom would die in childhood. Alois, a distant and avoidant father, was also an alcoholic. Most nights he would return home to vent his rage on his son, whom he beat viciously behind closed doors as Klara listened helplessly to the suffering of her beloved boy. As much as Alois criticized and punished Adolf for his many mistakes and disobediences, Klara doted on her son, who could do no wrong in her eyes. Adolf's mother was depressed and ineffectual; she had no authority in the household and acceded to her husband's angry dictatorship with pathetic resolution. No doubt she was depressed over the losses of her four children and was terrorized by her husband's violence. One way she sustained herself was by entering into close attachments to her two surviving children. Many people remarked at Adolf's extreme affection for her, and the attachment endured; he hung her picture over his bed as an adult, and it was the same picture that he brought with him into the bunker at the end of his life.

Eventually as Adolf entered adolescence the question of career became inevitable. An ineffectual and discontent student, Hitler rejected his father's instructions to pursue a secure path (his path) as a career civil servant. Hitler, increasingly committed to art, insisted that his goal was to be one of the greatest artists of his time, and he intended to study at the Academy of Fine Arts in Vienna. This was not simply a career choice; the assertion of his desire to cultivate his artistic self was a repudiation not only of his father's line of work, but who the father was as a person; on the positive side it was Hitler's way of cultivating and actualizing a form of self-aggrandizement that was a continuation of the mirroring by his mother that sustained him throughout the long years of abuse.

Recently several analysts (Mitchell, 1993; Bromberg, 1996) have asserted that the concept of a normal unitary self has given way to a more complex model. They argued that people tend to organize themselves around multiple selves, which are structured according to differing needs and contexts. In his book *Dreams and Drama* psychoanalyst Alan Roland argued that one type of self-organization, the artistic self, is a frequent occurrence, "that may exist in a fair number of persons but is only developed in a relatively few" (Roland, 2002, p. 30). Roland explained that the successful development of an artistic self depends on several factors: parental encouragement, identifications, and counter-identifications with a parent who is an artist, inborn aesthetic sensibilities and resonance, as well as talent. These factors draw the person towards the arts, but the full potential of the artistic self is only realized within an artistic tradition and culture. Much of the ongoing encouragement and support, according to Roland, comes from idealized figures, mentors, or fellow artists – feeling confirmed and validated as an artist and having heroes to model oneself on is important to the elaboration of an artistic self. "When artists have teachers or others who are not attuned to the sensibility of their artistic self, it can be very painful" (Roland, 2002, p. 31). Roland adds that in Western societies the artistic self is highly individualized, often alienated from the social group and oriented towards self-promotion.

For Hitler his artistic self had multiple functions. His only source of self-sustenance during childhood, as well as psychological protection for his daily traumas, was the mirroring of his adoring mother. In her eyes Adolf could do no wrong, and throughout his life he looked to her gaze to confirm his greatness. The fact that the creative process in art involved the externalization and perfection of self-experience, and success as an artist would involve praise and admiration from others, even fame, Hitler saw in the ambition of his artistic self a means to extend his mother's love into his adult life. In addition, the creation of beautiful and compelling images and structures out of his own talent and imagination would function to mirror back to him his greatness and the self-perfection he longed for as an antidote to the shattered self-esteem, fear, and helplessness he experienced under his

father's blows. Lastly, Adolf's pursuit of his artistic self was a means to differentiate himself from his father by asserting his identify as an artist he expressed his full
repudiation of everything that his father was and stood for. It was an act of defiance
that asserted his self-integrity and self-esteem, while utterly devaluing his father.

As a boy Hitler clung to and nurtured the fantasy that he would one day be considered a great artist. However, his nascent artistic self lacked many of the essential
components that Roland stressed were so important to success. First, he did not
appear to have any real talent, and as he pursued his art, any facility may have been
restricted by his emotional conflicts (Victor, 1998, p. 42). Second, neither of his
parents were artists, nor were there any members of his family in the arts. In fact,
neither of his parents supported his choice of vocation. Even outside the family he
did not have any adult support for his aesthetic ambitions. Eventually in adolescence he did find some young artist friends, but he generally kept his ambitions
secret from them, especially his failures. Third, he never engaged himself with any
mentors in the field. When he had a referral to an influential artist in Vienna who
might have helped with Adolf's application to the Academy – he never followed
up. In fact, Hitler did have idealized figures that he used as guides, but they were
more fantasy than reality. Adolf modeled his artistic self on Wagner and the myth
of the Germanic hero. The unrealistic and childish nature of these professional
models was a fourth factor acting against the realization of his artistic ambitions.
Eventually the discrepancy between the grandiose fantasies and his abilities and
opportunities created a self-crisis. Applying to the Academy of Fine Arts he was
rejected. This was an unexpected and devastating blow. George Victor wrote in this
regard: "Rejection by the Academy was the hardest blow that Hitler had suffered.
He had burned his bridges to become an artist, and continued support from his
mother was contingent on studying at the Academy. Humiliated by the rejection,
at a loss about what to do, he requested an interview with the academy Director.
The result was a crushing pronouncement: Adolf had no future as an artist" (Victor,
1998, p. 39). Some months later, after a half-hearted attempt to prepare himself,
Hitler reapplied to the Academy, and his application was once again rejected. Soon
after he dropped out of view, ceasing communication with his family, and began a
long decline into poverty and despair.

From 1909 until 1913 Adolf Hitler endured the complete and humiliating
collapse of his life and self. Forced to live for some months in a shelter, at
times without housing or money for food, his life became abject and pathetic.
Eventually he began to scrounge out a living painting postcard-sized paintings
of Vienna sights, mostly for the tourist trade. In other words, Hitler suffered a
total failure in his selfobject surround; his mother had died, he had rejected his
family, and his few acquaintances were derelicts and petty thieves. However,
rather than turn away from art, he harbored a private fantasy that his greatness as
an artist had been thwarted by the malevolence and jealousy of others. Regarding his second rejection by the Academy, Adolf raged to his friend Gustl: "The
academy, a lot of old-fashioned, fossilized civil servants, bureaucrats devoid
of understanding, stupid lumps of officials, The whole Academy ought to be

blown up!" (Victor, 1998, p. 41). Thus, in the end, the same type of person had thwarted the realization of his boyhood dreams of greatness, the civil servant, and the bureaucrat – his father.

The ultimate structuralization of Hitler's mature aesthetics occurred because of his most devastating humiliation – the defeat of the German army during World War One. Adolf was a patriotic and enthusiastic soldier. Most of his earlier humiliation was split off as he identified himself with the German army whom he believed would ultimately triumph. In fact, he never considered the possibility of loss. Theo. Dorpat (2003) argued that given Hitler's long exposure to battle (he was mobilized for four years and was in fifty battles) he must have subsequently suffered from some degree of post traumatic stress disorder. In addition, he was injured twice; the second time he was gassed and for a time lost his sight. While he was recovering, he heard of the defeat, and he became consumed by rage and, according to his own account, psychosis. He claimed to have had a revelation that he would lead a resurgent and triumphant Germany to glory. This delusion became the core of his claim to ultimate political power. An important component of his political and personal agenda was the forceful transformation of the cultural and aesthetic life of the nation – and world. His artistic self, the repository of all his hopes and dreams, became transformed from utter devastation to a delusional obsession with the aesthetic groundwork of social life. He realized that as he was, nameless and penniless, the only way to ensure the enactment of his fantasies was to control the cultural apparatus (the German cultural establishment) by political means. He began his relentless pursuit of power.

The path to power was opened to Hitler through the aesthetics of political performance (Spotts, 2003) – this is what allowed an ineffectual and uncertain failed artist to gradually transform himself into the fire breathing performance artist of the Nuremberg rallies. With his slowly accumulating political authority, the possibility of realizing his creative dreams became possible without the risks of engaging in the creative process. The risky self-disorganization that accompanies true creativity was bypassed as he systematically bent German cultural life to his will. For example, as a young man Hitler saw himself as a talented architect, fascinated by opera and devoted to the fantasy that he would one day design and build immense new opera houses for the people. He completed some serviceable sketches but did not have the knowledge or skills to design a building. As Fuhrer he bypassed any creative risk. He would sketch an opera house and hand over the sketch to a true architect to complete the work, to solve all the technical problems, Hitler would then review the plans, criticize them and then either demand that the same architect revise then, or fire the architect and assign someone else to complete the work. Typically, these buildings were derivative of classical designs (Roman and Greek) yet simplified and expanded to immense size. This was a pseudo-creative process in which fantasy could be converted to reality by bypassing the heart of the creative process, the state of self-disorganization that accompanies the effort to achieve something honest and new.

But Hitler's aesthetic ambitions far exceeded the personal creative needs of most artists. In his search for confirmation of his archaic grandiosity, Adolf identified with an elaborate fantasy that he was the savior of the German community and "Aryan" civilization. He believed that he had not been the only victim of the Armistice, the nation itself had been shamed and betrayed, and the social devastation and humiliation that followed the war proved this. An important part of his program of rebirth would be aesthetic; Hitler saw art as a means for spiritual regeneration, cultural triumph, and revenge:

> Art is the clearest and most immediate reflection of the spiritual life of the people. It exercises the greatest conscious and unconscious influence on the masses of the people. . . . [I]n its thousand-fold manifestations and influences it benefits the nation as a whole.
>
> (Spotts, 2003, p. 27)

Once Hitler's dominance of the German state had been accomplished, the full elaboration and realization of the great artist hero was possible. However, as we shall see later the promotion and maintenance of this "heroic" work required a vigilance to the point of paranoia, a dictatorial level of social control, and ultimately a great deal of violence. Nonetheless Hitler saw this ruthless barbarity as serving a higher purpose. In his biography *Hitler*, Ian Kershaw summarized the extreme distortion that became Hitler's pathological artistic self:

> Hitler, the nonentity, the mediocrity, the failure, wanted to live like a Wagnerian hero. He wanted to become himself a new Wagner – the philosopher king, the genius, the supreme artist. In Hitler's mounting identity crisis following his rejection at the Academy of Arts, Wagner was for Hitler the artistic giant he had dreamed of becoming but knew he could never emulate, the incarnation of the triumph of aesthetics and the supremacy of art,
>
> (Kershaw, 1999, p. 43)

The Psychological Function of Hitler's Aesthetic

In his work *The Cult of the Avant Garde*, Donald Kuspit (1993) described the psychological function of aesthetic experience. This is relevant given Hitler's vulnerabilities and defenses. Kuspit wrote:

> The aesthetic state is one of hallucination or hallucinatory exaggeration brought about by self-intoxication. That is, it is a narcissistic state of self-affirmation, a state in which the wish to be an integral self with a strong will is realized in fantasy. In this state the will is magically restored, as though reborn, and the disintegrated self magically integrated. The vitality whose loss signaled the loss of the will to live, the sense that life has no value – the ultimate morbidity – is renewed. There is in effect a transfer of vitality and willpower from artist to

audience. The artist is a natural therapist, as it were, and the work of art a natural medium of healing.

(Kuspit, 1993, p. 11)

For Hitler aesthetic experience compensated for the unrelenting sense of disorder within himself. But far more than just covering over his distress it offered him a means to transcend the clear limitations of his aesthetic life through the realization of a fantasy of the fusion of artist and audience in a single person, Adolf, who would bring about and control a universe structured by and infused with an idealized aesthetic that would continually mirror the Fuhrer's grandiosity.

Hitler's aesthetics managed his psychological suffering that resulted from the intense experience of shame. Symptoms of shame were rampant in his personality: narcissism, vulnerability to slights to self-esteem, obsession with control, and powerful episodes of rage and destructiveness. Hitler's avoidance of intimacy and need to project an image of power and invulnerability increased in severity with time. The sources of this enduring shame were several. Most importantly the ongoing subjection to his father's scorn and rage must have resulted in a severe distortion of both internal self-structure as well as the elaboration of a primitive and severe superego. Later in life the extreme stress of combat combined with his rage at the German defeat after the First World War, strengthened and solidified both his internal shame and the powerful defenses which he elaborated and then enacted to manage the resulting self-damage (Dorpat, 2003). Over time he seemed to struggle with both internal states of self-loathing and a tendency to project the most damaging aspects of his superego outward in the form of paranoia and blame that he expressed towards Jews, homosexuals and non-Germans. In addition, the combination of his father's scorn and his mother's doting idealization resulted in a split between grandiose and degraded self-structures. This led to the strange discrepancy between the lover of culture and the scourge of civilization that he became. The idealization of aesthetics became the repository of idealized aspects of the self. This was his primary means of sustaining himself in the face of a vulnerability to crippling shame states that in his young manhood led to depression, inhibition, and perhaps psychosis. As the guardian of what he believed to be the finest forms of culture and creative expression, Hitler became aggrandized and purified himself; his failure as an artist, his oppression by his father, his self-hatred was surmounted (dissociated) as he identified himself with what he considered to be the most elevated values of human cultural life.

It is no surprise that he promoted a form of classical art and conservative standards of beauty. (Hitler described Greek art as "a beauty which exceeds anything that is evident today.") Unlike the modernists (which we will be discussing next) the classical artist (in fantasy at least) was in harmony with his society and culture. The use of the medium followed traditional techniques and methods. The subjects of art were variations on traditional, acceptable themes. The psychological goal of the classical artist was to offer to the audience a chance to escape into a world in which beauty, nobility, and grandeur mirrored back the viewers' desire to feel whole, comfortable, and inspired. Hitler's youthful paintings were traditional, non-experimental, and depicted an idealized world of idyllic German countryside and street scenes. Many of his paintings are more like architectural renderings, very carefully drawn, with mundane and uninteresting compositional structure. Where he depicted people, they appear stiff and lacked liveliness. Although some of this style can be explained as inexperience and lack of talent, that is not enough. Given our knowledge of his later mature aesthetic, these images represent the young Hitler's idealization of classical aesthetic forms and values, and the identification of himself with a premodern world in which traditional aesthetic forms structure and organize life. In other words, classicism functioned to sooth, organize, and restore self-experience when Hitler was undergoing external and internal stressors. Spotts summed this up in the following quote:

> Hitler was wont to describe the arts as "a truly stable pole in the flux of all other phenomena", "an escape from confusion and distress", a source of "the eternal magic strength . . . to master confusion and restore a new order out of chaos". At all times in other words, they provided a refuge from harsh reality.
>
> (Spotts, 2003, p. 15)

For Hitler, "the arts" were a variety of classical art forms and premodern aesthetic values, which reflected his nostalgia for what he saw as more noble and morally pure times, given that his aesthetics and his violent promotion of cultural change put him at odds with the primary mission of twentieth-century art.

Hitler's Hatred of Modernism

Hitler possessed an enduring and influential hatred of modernism. Along with Jews, Freemasons, and homosexuals, Hitler blamed modernist artists for the erosion of German cultural life and the promotion of perverse value. Soon after his ascension to the position of Chancellor, the Nazi party began a systematic and relentless purging of all cultural institutions, forcing modernist artists from their jobs and blackballing them from competitions and exhibitions.

In *Hitler and the Power of Aesthetics*, Frederic Spotts admits that rather than a distortion of modernism, Hitler's understanding was correct. Modernism was "guilty as charged" in its promotion of a new aesthetic that challenged and attacked traditional culture-bound notions of art and aesthetic experience. The idiosyncrasies of perception, the authenticity of primitive forms of expression, the power of ugliness, the importance of social critique, even radical political action were all essential elements of the modernist aesthetic that Hitler recognized and hated.

Why such intense and enduring hatred for the modernist movement? Most authors have stressed the political motives behind the Dictator's control of cultural life. Modernism purposely threatened the status quo and was rightly viewed by Hitler as a threat to his political agenda; but I also believe that

198 The Psychoanalysis of Aesthetic Experience

modernism posed a powerful psychological threat to Hitler whose vulnerable self-organization could not tolerate the disorganizing and disruptive functions of modernist aesthetics.

Donald Kuspit (1993), in his book *The Cult of the Avant-Garde*, noted that for many people modernism represented a significant threat to psychological equilibrium and sense-of-self; however, that is the initiation of a process that is ultimately therapeutic. He wrote:

> The provocatively distorted work of art forces recognition of primordial contradiction upon the viewer. Such recognition is inevitably traumatizing for it implies intuition of one's own incompleteness, "unwholesomeness" self-contradictoriness – intuition of the deep, permanent split within oneself. Recognition of one's inner distortion evokes disintegration anxiety. This threatens the complete collapse of the self. At the same time, the intense awareness of internal contradictoriness catalyzed by the explicitly distorted work of art, has an abreactive effect, ultimately emancipating and maturing. One spontaneously coheres again and acquires fresh self-possession, greater ego-strength. One has a sense, however short-lived, of being whole.
>
> (Kuspit, 1993, p. 32)

Kuspit is describing the therapeutic project of modernist art where aesthetic disruption (which is initially experienced as ugly) results in renewal and healing. However, Hitler never got beyond the experience of disruption. His self-vulnerability was such that the state of anxiety before the distortions of medium, form, and subject that characterized modernist art was intolerable to him. But rather than simply critiquing and avoiding modernist art, he sought to wipe it from the face of the earth. Such was his dread of the disintegrating effects of modernism that he used all his power and money to make it not exist. Only then could he rest, surrounded by a world that mirrored his ideals and sense of beauty.

Spotts described how Hitler's imperative resulted in a distortion of the aesthetic values that he claimed to hold in such esteem. For example, Spotts wrote concerning Hitler's plans for a new architecture to embody the restored glory of Germany:

> "In our plans we shall strive for an architecture that is stronger and more austere, a classicism more in keeping with the simpler forms of our way of thinking." Hitler stated. Every design had to strictly conform to Hitler's stylistic imperative. In their coldness, uniformity of size, the results were destructive of any sense of humanity or individualism. With their massiveness, solidity, deep-set windows and spare decoration, the buildings gave the impression of fortresses exuding the raw power of the National Socialist state. The overall effect – and indeed, intent – was to aggrandize himself and to debase human beings into tiny objects, automatons as insensate as the stone of the buildings.
>
> (Spotts, pp. 335–3336)

Hitler's aesthetic reflected the psychological struggle to defend against the anticipation of self-annihilation; an experience that we know he in fact had as a young artist unable to obtain the conformation of his artistic self. His mature aesthetic resulted in the distortion of many "classical" styles traditionally viewed as beautiful. To maintain control and avoid stimulation, Hitler eliminated decoration, ornamentation, and humanness from the beautiful forms that he used to construct his new aesthetic universe. The playfulness and joy that characterize the best forms of creativity and the enjoyment of beauty (especially in classical art) needed to be eliminated and replaced by a grim sense of order and awe. Hitler abused many of our culture's beauties, enslaving them, perverting them into monstrous reflections of his desperate grandiosity.

As I argued in chapter 5, "The Creative Process," the artist attempts to externalize his subjectivity in a form that he or she then subjects to a process of perfecting. Thus, a dialectic is established as the artist works to alter the work and is simultaneously altered by it in a process of refinement and idealization. Gradually the external work becomes both beautiful and authentic – representing, embodying the feelings of the creator in an ideal form. Hitler sought to externalize not his human subjectivity but a defensively organized fantasy, which reflected his desperate attempt to protect his self-vulnerability though extreme forms of aesthetic self-aggrandizement. Honesty was besides the point, tolerance of the experience of failure (so crucial to real creativity) was unbearable to him, and recognition of the artworks own necessities and independence was anathema; his sole interest was in the forceful and complete propagation of archaic fantasies of grandiosity. In the end the intent was to stimulate in the audience not admiration and positive mirroring of the self but fear and primitive states of awe; Hitler wanted, through the creation of a new aesthetic universe, to be God – thus he was repelled by the normal human creative process, he needed to feel that creativity arose directly and unambiguously from his own omnipotent power.

The Abuse of Beauty: A Fascist Aesthetic

For Hitler the intoxication of the aesthetic experience was a drug. Beauty's function to heighten and clarify our relationship to the world, and to reconcile discrepancies within the self and especially in our tie to other persons, was perverted by fascism and made to function as a stimulant to self-vitality, a distorting lens in which reality was both idealized and forced to comply with the Fuhrer's archaic needs.

Returning to the quote that started this paper Hitler stated: "The beautiful should reign over humans; the beautiful itself wants to retain its power." I can imagine no better statement of the fascist aesthetic. The universal and compelling hunger of people for beauty and perfection was transformed into a means to exert and retain power. But what was "the beautiful" that he was referring to? Hitler's beauty was based on formal order, simplicity, grandiosity, and power. Rather than eliciting contemplation and disinterested enthrallment, beauty was fascistic, intended to be compelling and awesome, closer to the sublime – the beauty encountered in the child's astonishment at the father's power. But unlike the sublime, Hitler's Beauty was clear, nonambiguous, confining, ordered, and most importantly controlled. Rather than capturing the wild power and disorder of nature, Hitler's beauty embodied the control and power of the State, and its leader the Fuhrer himself. Thus, beauty was not only valued for the regression and stimulation it produced, but it was forced to function for the purpose of control, repression, and ultimately to rationalize and cope with the destructive impact of war and genocide.

Bollas (1978) has explored how aesthetic experience involves a fantasized restoration of the tie to the available and resonant mother of early childhood. As we enjoy art or create art, we are once again playing joyfully in the secure arms of the mother, who, still vital deep in our minds, allows us to engage the world with the joy and spontaneity of a self unconstrained and untainted by life. But mature aesthetic experience also requires several things: (1) a continued capacity and willingness to recognize, acknowledge, and value reality (without this aesthetic experience would just be psychotic fantasy or dream), and (2) the ability and willingness to view the experience critically and to reflect on the experience. Hitler was driven by the need to override the constraints of reality to realize his longed-for aesthetic experience in which the entire world would be reconstructed and compelled to embody his aesthetic ideals. And it follows that he was completely unwilling to step out of and reflect on his aesthetic values as this would mean risking the disintegration and collapse of self that he increasingly feared.

In the End

> Heroism, blood death, fire – in both literal and mythic forms – added up to the supreme paradox of Hitler's rule: the conscious pursuit of antithetical ideals – culture and vandalism, creativity and destruction, beauty and horror, life and death. Everything and everyone was drawn into Hitler's grand dream. Art, creativity, beauty and life were indissolubly linked to their opposites not just by party officials but by conductors, singers, instrumentalists, and actors who performed in support of the regime and its war effort, by art connoisseurs and museum curators who plundered and destroyed artworks, by impresarios who disbanded orchestras and opera companies in occupied countries, by the heads of concentration camps who savored chamber music played by Jewish inmates before executing them. The combining of culture and barbarism was the essence of Hitler's Reich. It is the conundrum that Hitler himself epitomized.
>
> (Spotts, 2003, p. 117)

In the end self-hatred, rage, paranoia, and annihilation overwhelmed the capacity for aesthetic experience to provide solace and support to Adolf Hitler and the nation he led for 15 years. The normal defenses that allow governments (and societies) to function and flourish were absent from the Third Reich from the start. Most importantly the failure to adequately dissociate aggression and hatred from patriotism and love resulted in the paradox just described. Perhaps the rapid reconstruction of German civilization from a state of humiliating degradation to a manic, militaristic dictatorship was just a massive compensation for enduring psychological deficits and damage; hence the brittleness and vulnerability to regression. As the Thousand-Year Reich confronted the probability of annihilation, the intensification of rage and aggressive action was the by-product of psychological disintegration. Death and murder became increasingly eroticized as the climactic death of the hero approached.

In the years after his father's death, the Hitler family lived in the city of Linz near the Austrian border. This city was where Klara Hitler lived when her son went off to Vienna to find fame and fortune as an artist. Kershaw in his biography of Hitler wrote that Linz would always be associated in Adolf's mind with his beloved mother. From the time he was a boy until the very end of his life, Hitler nurtured the fantasy that he would design and reconstruct the city of Linz, which would become the cultural center of the new civilization that he was destined to create. Sketches and plans constructed in private during the years of his boyhood became grand schemes funded by massive government budgets sanctioned by the adult Hitler, now the Fuhrer. Adolf always claimed that the people needed illusion to tolerate the shocks of reality. Hitler's last illusion involved the splendid scale model of his boyhood plan, realized at last. The broad and regal avenues, the monumental cultural buildings, spread out along the gleaming river embodied the essence of his attachment to the beautiful maternal ideal, reconstructed, reborn out of his own imagination and will. With grim reality approaching, Hitler took solace in aesthetics. In the end the failure of these illusions to provide refuge would be made clear with his suicide.

References

Ashfield, A., & De Bolla, P. (1996). *The sublime: A reader in British eighteenth-century aesthetic theory.* Cambridge, England: Cambridge University Press.

Barr, A. (1951). *Matisse: His art and his public.* New York: The Museum of Modern Art.

Beckley, B. (2001). *Sticky sublime.* New York: Allworth Press.

Beebe, B., & Lachmann, F. (2002). *Infant research and adult treatment: Co-constructing interactions.* Hillsdale, NJ: The Analytic Press.

Bollas, C. (1978). The aesthetic moment and the search for transformation. *Annual of Psychoanalysis*, 6, 385–394.

Bosanquet, B. (1915). Three lectures on aesthetic. In K. Aschenbrenner & A. Isenberg (Eds.), *Aesthetic theories: Studies in the philosophy of art* (pp. 415–424). Englewood Cliffs, NJ: Prentice Hall.

Bromberg, P. (1996). Standing in the spaces: The multiplicity of self and the psychoanalytic situation. *Contemporary Psychoanalysis*, 32, 509–536.

Chasseguet-Smirgel, J. (1984). *Creativity and perversion.* New York: Norton.

Cheshire, N. (1996). The empire of the ear: Freud's problem with music. *International Journal of Psychoanalysis*, 77, 1127–1168.

Daniels, L. (2002). *With a woman's voice: A writer's struggle for emotional freedom.* Latham, MD: Madison Books.

Danto, A. (1964). The art world. *Journal of Philosophy*, 61, 571–584.

Dewey, J. (1934). *Art as experience.* New York: Capricorn Books.

Dickie, G. (1974). *Art and the aesthetic: An institutional analysis.* Ithaca, NY: Cornell University Press.

Dissanayake, E. (1992). *Homo aestheticus: Where art comes from and why.* New York: The Free Press.

Dissanayake, E. (2000). *Art and intimacy.* Seattle, WA: University of Washington Press.

Dorpat, T. (2003). *Wounded monster: Hitler's path from trauma to malevolence.* Lanham, MD: University Press of America.

Ehrenzweig, A. (1967a). *The psychoanalysis of artistic vision and hearing.* New York: Julian Press.

Ehrenzweig, A. (1967b). *The hidden order of art.* Berkeley, CA: University of California Press.

Emde, R. (1992). Positive emotions for psychoanalytic theory: Surprises from infancy research and new directions. In T. Shapiro & R. Emde (Eds.), *Affect: Psychoanalytic perspectives* (pp. 5–44). Madison, CT: International Universities Press.

Emde, R., Johnson, W., & Easterbrooks, M. A. (1987). The dos and don'ts of early moral development: Psychoanalytic tradition and current research. In J. Kagan & S. Lamb (Eds.), *The emergence of morality in young children* (pp. 245–276). Chicago: University of Chicago Press.

Esman, A. (1973). Primal scene: A review and reconsideration. *Psychoanalytic Study of the Child, 28*, 49–82.

Ferenczi, S. (1952). The ontogenesis of the interest in money. In *First contributions to psychoanalysis* (pp. 319–331). New York: Brunner/Mazel.

Fleiss, R. (1961). *Ego and body ego: Contributions to their psychoanalytic psychology.* Madison, CT: International Universities Press.

Freiberg, L. (1965). New views of art and the creative process in psychoanalytical ego psychology. In H. Ruitenbeek (Ed.), *The creative imagination* (pp. 223–244). Chicago: Quadrangle Books.

Freud, S. (1905). Three essays on the theory of sexuality. In J. Strachey (Ed. & Trans.), *The standard edition of the complete psychological works of Sigmund Freud* (Vol. 7, pp. 125–245). London: Hogarth Press.

Freud, S. (1908). Creative artists and daydreaming. In J. Strachey (Ed. & Trans.), *The standard edition of the complete psychological works of Sigmund Freud* (Vol. 9, pp. 142–153). London: Hogarth Press.

Freud, S. (1910). Leonardo da Vinci and a memory of childhood. In J. Strachey (Ed. & Trans.), *The standard edition of the complete psychological works of Sigmund Freud* (Vol. 11, pp. 59–137). London: Hogarth Press.

Freud, S. (1914a). On narcissism. In J. Strachey (Ed. & Trans.), *The standard edition of the complete psychological works of Sigmund Freud* (Vol. 14, pp. 69–102). London: Hogarth Press.

Freud, S. (1914b). The Moses of Michelangelo. In J. Strachey (Ed. & Trans.), *The standard edition of the complete psychological works of Sigmund Freud* (Vol. 13, pp. 210–238). London: Hogarth Press.

Freud, S. (1915). On transience. In J. Strachey (Ed. & Trans.), *The standard edition of the complete psychological works of Sigmund Freud* (Vol. 14, pp. 303–308). London: Hogarth Press.

Freud, S. (1923). The ego and the id. In J. Strachey (Ed. & Trans.), *The standard edition of the complete psychological works of Sigmund Freud* (Vol. 19, pp. 3–68). London: Hogarth Press.

Freud, S. (1925a). Note upon a "mystic writing-pad". In J. Strachey (Ed. & Trans.), *The standard edition of the complete psychological works of Sigmund Freud* (Vol. 20, pp. 227–232). London: Hogarth Press.

Freud, S. (1925b). An autobiographical study. In J. Strachey (Ed. & Trans.), *The standard edition of the complete psychological works of Sigmund Freud* (Vol. 20, pp. 7–74). London: Hogarth Press.

Freud, S. (1930). Civilization and its discontents. In J. Strachey (Ed. & Trans.), *The standard edition of the complete psychological works of Sigmund Freud* (Vol. 21, pp. 64–145). London: Hogarth Press.

Fuller, P. (1988). *Art and psychoanalysis.* London: Hogarth Press.

Gadamer, H. G. (1986). *The relevance of the beautiful and other essays.* Cambridge: Cambridge University Press. Author Query: Please indicate where the in-text callout for this Reference should appear in the text.

Ghent, E. (1990). Masochism, submission, surrender: Masochism as a perversion of surrender. *Contemporary Psychoanalysis, 26*, 108–136.

Greenacre, P. (1953). Penis awe and its relation to penis envy. In *Emotional growth: Psychoanalytic studies of the gifted and a great variety of other individuals* (pp. 31–49). Madison, CT: International Universities Press.

Greenacre, P. (1956). Experiences of awe in childhood. In *Emotional growth: Psychoanalytic studies of the gifted and a great variety of other individuals* (pp. 67–92). Madison, CT: International Universities Press.

Hagman, G. (2001). The sense of beauty. *International Journal of Psychoanalysis, 82*, 1011–1025.

Hagman, G. (2003). On ugliness. *Psychoanalytic Quarterly*, 72, 959–985.

Hagman, G. (2010). *The artist's mind: A psychoanalytic perspective on creativity, modern art and modern artists*. London: Routledge.

Hagman, G. (2015). *Creative analysis: Art, creativity and clinical process*. London: Routledge.

Hagman, G. (2016). *Art, creativity and psychoanalysis: Perspectives from analyst-artists*. London: Routledge.

Hartmann, H. (1955). Notes on the theory of sublimation. *Psychoanalytic Study of the Child*, 10, 9–29.

Hartmann, H. (1958). *Ego psychology and the problem of adaptation*. Madison, CT: International Universities Press.

Hickey, D. (1995). *The invisible dragon*. Los Angeles: Art Issues Press.

Hume, D. (1775). On standards of taste. In K. Aschenbrenner & A. Isenberg (Eds.), *Aesthetic theories: Studies in the philosophy of art* (pp. 107–119). Englewood Cliffs, NJ: Prentice Hall.

Jacques, E. (1965). Death and the mid-life crisis. *International Journal of Psychoanalysis*, 46, 502–514.

Jeffrey, F. (1816). Essay on beauty. In K. Aschenbrenner & A. Isenberg (Eds.), *Aesthetic theories: Studies in the philosophy of art* (pp. 277–294). Englewood Cliffs, NJ: Prentice Hall.

Kainer, R. (1999). *The collapse of the self*. Hillsdale, NJ: The Analytic Press.

Kant, I. (1790). The critique of aesthetic judgment. In K. Aschenbrenner & A. Isenberg (Eds.), *Aesthetic theories: Studies in the philosophy of art* (pp. 171–224). Englewood Cliffs, NJ: Prentice Hall.

Kershaw, I. (1999). *Hitler: 1889–1936 hubris*. New York: Norton.

Kirwan, J. (1999). *Beauty*. Manchester: Manchester University Press.

Klein, M. (1929). Infantile anxiety situations in a work of art and the creative impulse. *International Journal of Psychoanalysis*, 10, 436–443.

Klein, M. (1930). The importance of symbol formation in the development of the ego. *International Journal of Psychoanalysis*, 11, 24–39.

Kligerman, C. (1980). Art and the self of the artist. In A. Goldberg (Ed.), *Advances in self psychology* (pp. 383–391). Madison, CT: International Universities Press.

Kohut, H. (1950). On the enjoyment of listening to music. *Psychoanalytic Quarterly*, 19, 64–87.

Kohut, H. (1957). Death in Venice by Thomas Mann: A story about disintegration of artistic sublimation. In P. Ornstein (Ed.), *The search for the self: Selected writings of Heinz Kohut 1950–1978* (Vol. 1, pp. 107–130). New York: International Universities Press.

Kohut, H. (1957). Observations on the psychological functions of music. *Journal of the American Psychoanalytic Association*, 5, 389–407.

Kohut, H. (1966). Forms and transformations of narcissism. In C. Strozier (Ed.), *Self psychology and the humanities* (pp. 97–123). New York: Norton. (Original work published 1966)

Kohut, H. (1971). *The analysis of the self*. Madison, CT: International Universities Press.

Kohut, H. (1976). Creativeness, charisma, and group psychology. In C. Strozier (Ed.), *Self psychology and the humanities* (pp. 793–843). New York: Norton. (Original work published 1976)

Kohut, H. (1977). *The restoration of the self*. Madison, CT: International Universities Press.

Kohut, H. (1985). *Self psychology and the humanities* (C. Strozier, Ed.). New York: Norton.

Kris, E. (1952). *Psychoanalytic explorations in art*. Madison, CT: International Universities Press.

Kuspit, D. (1993). *The cult of the avant-garde artist*. Cambridge: Cambridge University Press.

Kuspit, D. (2006). The emotional gain of aesthetic shock. In C. Rotenberg & G. Hagman (Eds.), *Art, creativity, and psychoanalysis: Current psychoanalytic perspectives* (pp. 23–45). Hillsdale, NJ: The Analytic Press.

Langer, S. (1953). *Feeling and form*. New York: Charles Scribner's Sons.

Langer, S. (1957a). *Philosophy in a new key* (3rd ed.). Cambridge, MA: Harvard University Press.

Langer, S. (1957b). *Problems of art*. New York: Charles Scribner's Sons.

Lee, H. B. (1947). On the esthetic states of mind. *Psychiatry*, 10, 281–306.

Lee, H. B. (1948). Spirituality and beauty in artistic experience. *The Psychoanalytic Quarterly*, 17, 507–523.

Lee, H. B. (1950). The values of order and vitality in art. In G. Roheim (Ed.), *Psychoanalysis and the social sciences* (Vol. 2, pp. 231–274). Madison, CT: International Universities Press.

Lichtenberg, J. (1989). *Psychoanalysis and motivation*. Hillsdale, NJ: The Analytic Press.

Lipscomb, P. A. (1997). Aesthetic pleasure and the rhythms of infancy. *Psychoanalytic Study of the Child*, 52, 140–158.

Loewald, H. (1960). On the therapeutic action of psychoanalysis. *International Journal of Psychoanalysis*, 41, 16–33.

Loewald, H. (1988). *Sublimation*. New Haven, CT: Yale University Press.

Longinus. (1991). *On great writing: On the sublime* (G. M. A. Grube, Trans.). Indianapolis, IN: Hackett Publishing.

Mann, T. (1911). *Death in Venice and other stories*. New York: Random House.

Mitchell, S. (2002). *Can love last?* New York: Norton.

Mondrian, P. (1937). Plastic art and pure plastic art. In S. D. Ross (Ed.), *Art and its significance: An anthology of aesthetic theory* (pp. 554–567). Albany, NY: State University of New York Press.

Nass, M. L. (1971). Some considerations of a psychoanalytic interpretation of music. *Psychoanalytic Quarterly*, 40, 303–316.

Newman, B. (1948). The sublime is now. In *Selected writings and interviews* (pp. 170–174). Berkeley, CA: University of California Press.

Noy, P. (1979). Form creation in art: An ego psychological approach to creativity. *Psychoanalytic Quarterly*, 48, 229–256.

Orange, D. (1993). Countertransference, empathy and the hermeneutical circle. In A. Goldberg (Ed.), *Progress in self psychology* (Vol. 9, pp. 247–256). Hillsdale, NJ: The Analytic Press.

Oremland, J. (1997). *The origins and dynamics of creativity*. Madison, CT: International Universities Press.

Pacteau, F. (1994). *The symptom of beauty*. Cambridge, MA: Harvard University Press.

Person, E. S. (1992). Romantic love. In T. Shapiro & R. Emde (Eds.), *Affect: Psychoanalytic perspectives* (pp. 383–412). Madison, CT: International Universities Press.

Phillips, A. (1998). *The beast in the nursery*. New York: Pantheon.

Pratt, C. (1952). *Music as the language of emotion*. Washington, DC: The Library of Congress.

Press, C. (2002). *The dancing self: Creativity, modern dance, self psychology and transformative education*. Cresskill, NJ: Hampton Press.

Protter, E. (1997). *Painters on painting*. Mineola, NY: Dover Publications.

Rank, O. (1934). *Art and artist*. New York: Knopf.

Rickman, J. (1940). On the nature of ugliness and the creative impulse. In H. M. Ruitenbeek (Ed.), *The creative imagination: Psychoanalysis and the genius of inspiration* (pp. 97–122). Chicago: Quadrangle Books.

Rittenberg, S. (1987). On charm. *International Journal of Psychoanalysis*, 68, 389–396.

Roland, A. (2002). *Drama and delusions*. Middletown, CT: Wesleyan University Press.

Rose, G. (1980). *The power of form*. New York: International Universities Press.

Rose, G. (1992). *The power of form* (Expanded ed.). New York: International Universities Press.

Rotenberg, C. (1988). Selfobject theory and the artistic process. In A. Goldberg (Ed.), *Learning from Kohut: Progress in self psychology* (Vol. 4, pp. 193–213). Hillsdale, NJ: The Analytic Press.

Rotenberg, C. (1992). Optimal operative perversity: A contribution to the theory of creativity. In A. Goldberg (Ed.), *New therapeutic visions: Progress in self psychology* (Vol. 8, pp. 167–188). Hillsdale, NJ: The Analytic Press.

Rothenberg, A. (1979). *The emerging goddess: The creative process in art, science, and other fields*. Chicago: University of Chicago Press.

Sachs, H. (1942). *The creative unconscious*. Cambridge, MA: Sci-Art Publishers.

Sandler, J. (1987). Ego ideal and ideal self. In *From safety to superego* (pp. 127–144). New York: Guilford Press.

Santayana, G. (1896). *The sense of beauty*. New York: Dover Publications.

Scarry, E. (1999). *On beauty*. Princeton, NJ: Princeton University Press.

Schafer, R. (1960). The loving and beloved superego in Freud's structural theory. *Psychoanalytic Study of the Child*, 15, 163–188.

Schiller, F. (1793). On the sublime. In W. Hinderer & D. Dahlstrom (Eds.), *Friedrich Schiller essays* (pp. 22–43). New York: Continuum.

Schiller, F. (1801). Concerning the sublime. In W. Hinderer & D. Dahlstrom (Eds.), *Friedrich Schiller essays* (pp. 70–85). New York: Continuum.

Schjeldahl, P. (1999). Notes on beauty. In B. Beckley & D. Shapiro (Eds.), *Uncontrollable beauty: Toward a new aesthetics* (pp. 53–59). New York: Allworth Press.

Segal, H. (1952). A psychoanalytic approach to aesthetics. *International Journal of Psychoanalysis*, 33, 196–207.

Segal, H. (1957). A psychoanalytical approach to aesthetics. In M. Klein, P. Heimann & R. E. Money-Kyrle (Eds.), *New directions in psychoanalysis* (pp. 384–405). New York: Basic Books.

Segal, H. (1991). *Dream, phantasy and art*. London: Routledge.

Sessions, R. (1950). *The musical experience*. Princeton, NJ: Princeton University Press.

Spitz, E. H. (1985). *Art and psyche*. New Haven, CT: Yale University Press.

Spotts, F. (2003). *Hitler and the power of aesthetics*. Woodstock, NY: Overlook Press.

Stern, D. (1985). *The interpersonal world of the infant*. New York: Basic Books.

Stern, D. (2010). *Forms of vitality: Exploring dynamic experience in psychology, the arts, psychotherapy, and development*. New York: Oxford University Press.

Stokes, A. (1957). Form in art. In M. Klein, P. Heimann & R. E. Money-Kyrle (Eds.), *New directions in psychoanalysis* (pp. 406–420). New York: Basic Books.

Stokes, A. (1963). *Painting and the inner world*. London: Tavistock Publications.

Stolorow, R., & Atwood, G. (1993). *Faces in a cloud: Intersubjectivity in personality theory*. Northvale, NJ: Jason Aronson.

Storr, A. (1992). *Music and the mind*. New York: Free Press.

Tolman, C. W. (1994). *Psychology, society, and subjectivity: An introduction to German critical psychology*. London: Routledge.

Townsend, D. (1997). *An introduction to aesthetics*. Oxford: Blackwell.

Tyson, P., & Tyson, R. (1990). *Psychoanalytic theories of development: An integration*. New Haven, CT: Yale University Press.

Ulman, R., & Brothers, D. (1988). *The shattered self: A psychoanalytic study of trauma*. Hillsdale, NJ: The Analytic Press.

Victor, G. (1998). *Hitler: The pathology of evil*. Washington, DC: Brassey's.

Wheelis, A. (1999). *The listener: A psychoanalyst examines his life*. New York: Norton.

Winnicott, D. W. (1971). *Playing and reality*. New York: Basic Books.

Index

addiction 154; creativity compared to 59–60, 70, 72, 136; drug 174
Addison, J. 120
aesthetic emotions 88
aesthetic experience: affect and 19, 30; case example (Paul) 152–156; creativity and 150–151; development of 27–36; idealization and 37–54; idealization in creativity and 52–54 in life and therapy 146–148; new psychoanalytic model of 24–26; philosophy of 13–24; sense of quality of 148–150; understanding 13–26
aesthetic processes in infancy and the young child 22, 30–31
aesthetic relating 36
aesthetic resonance 5, 11, 35, 68–69, 71–72, 171
aesthetic responsiveness 157
affect(s) 38, 151; aesthetic experience and 19, 30; aggressive 127; music and 169; mutual 150; negative 43, 94, 105; positive 43–44; rawness of 128; ugliness and 105–106; value 42, 44–45, 53–54, 118–119, 148; vitality 44
affective flooding 98
affective states 95, 111, 121
affect sharing 43–44
affect states 79
aggression 10, 47, 79, 120, 145
alcoholics 142, 191
anorexic, the 93, 106
anti-aesthetic 94
anti-beauty ugliness 180
area of cultural experience 85, 102
area of yearning 88
Aristotle 94
art: creativity and 146–157; as cultural construct 167; as festival 167; gesture and 136–139; healing and 140–143; self and 129–145; where art is 139–140
Art World, the 159
Ashfield, A. 112–113, 120, 127
Atwood, G. 70
awe 7, 13, 15, 38, 52, 54, 79, 88; in *Death in Venice* (Mann) 185; the sublime and 111–113, 115–117, 119–120, 122, 125–127; universal 23; veneration and 166
awestruck 163

Barr, A. 71
beauty: abuse of (on Hitler's fascist aesthetic) 199–200; *Beauty* (Kirwan) 78; contribution of psychoanalysis to our understanding of 79–85; cruising (on *Death in Venice*) 179–188; as a defense 90–92; idealization and 86–87; as interactive process 87–88; Kant on 24, 77; matrix of 118; mortality and 92; psychoanalytic understanding of sense of 85–92; restorative function of 90; self-integrative function of 90; sense of 6–7, 77–92; "Sense of Beauty" (Santayana) 78; as sublimation 85–86; surrendering to 89–90; transcendental and/or reparative function of 80, 82, 84; triumphant 188; *Uncontrollable Beauty: Toward a New Aesthetic* (Beckley and Shapiro); wild 89
Beckley, B. *Sticky sublime* 114; *Uncontrollable Beauty: Toward a New Aesthetic* 78
Beebe, B., & Lachmann, F. 32–33, 44, 118
Beethoven, L. von: *Ninth Symphony* 173
Benzara, N. *Regarding Beauty* 78
Bierstadt, A. 122
Bollas, C. 17, 29–30; on the aesthetic experience 17, 200
Bosanquet, B. 52, 180; on triumphant beauty 188

Freudian theory of the comic 115
Freud, S.: aesthetic experience as
understood by 15–19, 25, 52; on
castration anxiety 96; *Civilization
and its Discontents* 79, 92, 145;
dream interpretation of 56; reverence
for beauty of 6, 79–80, 85, 145; on
idealization 37–39, 43; on *Moses*
(Michelangelo) 16; music as a subject
disliked by 168; *On Narcissism* 39;
second theory of narcissism of 85, 101;
sublimation as understood by 27–28;
sublime not referred to by 111; *On
Transience* 92; ugliness never discussed
by 95; views on creativity and art 2–3,
26, 55, 129–130
Fuller, P. 33

Gadamer, H. G. 139, 158–160; on festival
158–159
genitals 79, 91, 95–98, 150
Ghent, E. 89, 188
"good enough" mothering 35
"good feed" by infants 34
Greenacre, P. 7, 115–116; theory of a
psychoanalytic sublime and 117

Hagman, G. 180, 185
healing 23, 61, 66, 132; art and 140–143;
self-healing 90
healing of the cleft 81
Hemingway, E. 142
Henri, R. 145
Hickey, D.: *The invisible dragon* 78
Hitler, Adolf: abuse of beauty and fascist
aesthetic of 199–200; aesthetics of 12,
189–201; artistic longings and ambitions
of 191–195; Aryan values promoted by
191, 195; early years of 191–192; the
end of 200–201; hatred of modernism
of 197–199; importance of art and
culture to 191; monstrosity of 189;
psychological function of aesthetic of
195–197; role of aesthetics in life of
190–191; Third Reich and 190, 200
Hitler, Alois 191
Hitler, K. 191, 201
Holzkamp, K. 161
Homer 111
homosexuality and homosexuals 99, 108,
116, 196–197
Hume, D. 13–15, 77

idealization 3–4; aesthetic experience and
21, 37–54; affective response to 88;
of art 141; authentic and inauthentic
forms of 66; beauty and 77, 86–87, 147;
clinical illustration (Dave) of 48–52;
collapse of idealization in 103–104;
creative process and 55, 65; enthrallment
and 38, 47, 52; experience(s) of 79,
84, 116; Freud on 37–39, 43; the
intersubjective and 41; Kohut on 40, 45,
65, 84; maternal 120; objects and 37–39,
43; paternal 119, 122; of self-experience
71; value affects and 118
imagination: creative 60, 131; failure of
180; music and 169, 171–172; the
sublime and 113, 120–121
imago(es) 83; idealized parent 40, 86,
116–117; internalized aesthetic 162;
paternal 117, 119, 120, 127
immensity: of the father and the real
world 119, 123, 124, 128; of "richest
expectations" 183, 188; the sublime
and 7, 111, 112, 114, 122–123; of the
sublime object 127
immortality 70, 81–82
incomprehensibility 147; the sublime and
7, 111, 123
infinite and the sublime 112
intersubjective, the: aesthetic experience
and 9; aesthetics of play and 31;
creativity and 3–5, 66; idealization and
41; internal beauty and 78; sense of
beauty and 87
intersubjectivity 163–164; art and 8;
relatedness and 2; Rotenberg on 135;
self-experience and 129; three levels of
subjectivity including 161
I–You barrier 134

Jacques, E. 25
Jeffrey, F. 24

Kainer, R. 52
Kant, I. 13–15; on aesthetic experience
13, 14; "Analytic of the Sublime" 113;
on beauty 24, 77; *Critique of Aesthetic
Judgment* 113; on the sublime 111, 113,
114, 123
Kershaw, I. 195, 201
Kirwan, J.; *Beauty* 78
Kleinians 21, 57
Klein, M. 18, 21, 53, 57–59, 82, 96–97, 107

ugliness 1, 7, 93–110; affect and 105–106; clinical illustration (Jim) of 107–108; collapse of idealization in 103–104; encountering 98–106; failure of sublimation of 101–103; interaction and 104–105; problem of 94–95; psychoanalytic theory and the problem of 95–98; psychopathology and 106–107
Ulman, R. 100
unthought unknown 17

value: affect sharing and 44
value affects *see* affects
Van Gogh, V. 142
Venice 180
Victor, G. 193; *Hitler: The Pathology of Evil* 194
Viso, O.: *Regarding Beauty* 78
vitality affects 44
Von Aschenbach, G. 105, 183, 186

Wagner, R. 111, 114, 193, 195
Wheelis, A. (1999). *The Listener* 87, 185
Winnicott, D. W.: on aesthetic processes in infancy and the young child 22, 30–31; on the area of cultural experience 85, 102; on the area of yearning 88; on creativity 21; on "good enough" mothering 35; on the "good feed" 34; on play and aesthetic culture 160; on play and the other 31; on the spontaneous gesture 138; on the subjective object 136; on transitional experience 134; on transitional objects 45, 58; on transitional space 121, 141; on the transitional zone of experience 29
writing: book, by patient's father 108; psychoanalytic 7, 10, 94–95; psychological 168; by Richman for her father 141–143; by Richman's patient Marni 142

For Product Safety Concerns and Information please contact our EU
representative GPSR@taylorandfrancis.com
Taylor & Francis Verlag GmbH, Kaufingerstraße 24, 80331 München, Germany

www.ingramcontent.com/pod-product-compliance
Lightning Source LLC
Chambersburg PA
CBHW070323270326
41926CB00017B/3739